TALKING

This book consists of protocols and notes describing actual events which took place in Hungary during the years 1943 and 1944.

TALKING
WITH
ANGELS

A document from Hungary
transcribed by Gitta Mallasz

English rendition
by Robert Hinshaw

assisted by Gitta Mallasz
and Lela Fischli

DAIMON
VERLAG

With heartfelt thanks to all those who have been so helpful and encouraging along the way.

Talking with Angels,
a document from Hungary transcribed by Gitta Mallasz,
English rendition by Robert Hinshaw,
assisted by Gitta Mallasz and Lela Fischli.

ISBN 3-85630-505-X

First Edition, 1988.

Cover design by Joel T. Miskin, assisted by James Kalin.

For a complete listing of other-language editions of *Talking with Angels*, see the last page of this book.

PREFACE

This publication of the 'angel dialogues' has been a long time in coming: the remarkable events documented here took place in Hungary during the late stages of the Second World War, in 1943 and 1944.

As their life situations, and gradually, their very chances for survival, grew ever darker, the close-knit group of 4 friends encountered a force which came to be known to them as angels. Their 'encounter at the threshold,' as it might be called, continued for 17 months and *Talking with Angels* is the first unabridged edition of the original Hungarian protocols to be published. Three of the friends perished in the aftermath of the war and the lone survivor, Gitta Mallasz, was obliged to remain underground with her precious documents and to concentrate solely on supporting her family of 7 (her parents, her brother, and his wife and children), who had gone from being relatively wealthy to utter poverty almost overnight. This phenomenon of radical change from one moment to the next has accompanied Gitta throughout her life. Her struggle for survival in postwar Hungary was to last for more than 15 years. When the opportunity finally came for a new start – her parents had died and her nephews and nieces reached adulthood – Gitta was able to make her way to France with the precious notes wrapped tightly in bed sheets in her one small suitcase.

In Paris, in 1960, life began anew at the age of 53: Gitta reestablished her considerable reputation as a theater set and graphic designer and she met and married a dear man, Laci. With his help and that of a few close friends, she began the difficult task of assembling and translating the protocols of the dialogues into French, her third language after Hungarian and German. Through one of these friends, the existence of the dialogues was brought to the attention of a prominent French radio journalist, Claude Mettra, who, after reading them, invited Gitta to be a guest on his weekly national program, "The Living and the Gods." That famous first 90-minute interview, broadcast live by *Radio France* on April 22, 1976, marked the beginning of the dialogues becoming publicly known.

Gitta had actually always been convinced that making the dialogues widely known was part of their reason for being, that is, she understood them to be important for more than just the four original participants, and at last this was beginning to happen.

Radio France was deluged with letters responding to the impressive interview: one day, Claude Mettra packed together a large bundle of them and marched over to show them at the small but renowned Parisian publishing house, Aubier Montaigne. There the manuscript was trimmed and quickly prepared for publication, appearing later in 1976 as *Dialogues avec l'ange*. Even without mentionable advertising, it became an immediate sensation and was reviewed and discussed on radio and in newspapers throughout the land.

It is remarkable that the dialogues had their first and greatest public success, that they were met with such a resounding echo, in France, of all places: a country known for its sharp intellect and skeptical rationalism. Perhaps this is because of the document's straightforward, down-to-earth character, in contrast to so many other publications dealing with esoteric matters.

Gitta herself chose to remain in the background. After her radio appearance, she declined all of the inevitable public-speaking invitations, and continued to live her normal daily life, in relative anonymity. It was not only her natural modesty that kept Gitta out of the limelight: she had a strong aversion to the tendency people often have of attributing their hopes, fears and admiration to her personally, to their making her into a kind of "guru." She was convinced that the real message is for each reader to find an own personal relationship to the words of the document, *to go through it themselves.* This is also the reason why photographs of Gitta and the other participants have never been published with the dialogues.

In 1973, Gitta and her husband had retired from Paris to a small farmhouse which they themselves restored in the southwest farming region of the French countryside. Laci built all of the furniture by hand from local materials. Far from the city at last and close to nature again, as in her childhood, Gitta continued to live a simple life, to respond to the many letters concerning *Dialogues avec l'ange* over the years and, to her greatest joy, to devote her energies to working on foreign language editions of the dialogues.

In 1983, her quiet life in retirement was to end when she received a speaking invitation she had never anticipated: the C.G. Jung Institute of Zürich asked her to address its students on the subject of her experience with the angels. Having been deeply impressed during the arduous years in Budapest after the war by Jung's writings, then comforted by the description of his dialogues with his inner guide, Philemon, in his biography,* Gitta felt that she could not

---

* *Memories, Dreams, Reflections* (C.G. Jung), recorded and edited by Aniela Jaffé. Pantheon, New York, 1961, pp. 182 ff.

say 'no' to this invitation. She made the long train journey to Zürich and spent 2 lively evenings, first describing and then discussing her experience of the dialogues with a full house of fascinated listeners.

The tremendous resonance in Zürich convinced Gitta that it was, indeed, appropriate for her to reveal more of her individual experiences in connection with the dialogues, along with the actual protocols, and in the years since, she has made extensive speaking tours and conducted workshops throughout France, Switzerland, Germany and Belgium.

Further, Gitta came to feel that it was right to put her full energies to work forming the often personal material of her correspondence, and later, of her speaking encounters, into book form, and the result was *Die Engel erlebt* (roughly: "the angels experienced"), which was published late in 1983 in German and French. A third book, *Weltenmorgen* (roughly: "dawning world"), published in 1986, continues Gitta's ever more personal response to the many questions that have been addressed to her in the time since the dialogues' first publication.

Work on this English-language edition began in 1984. A somewhat shortened English edition had been published in 1979[*] in a very small printing, but it became unavailable shortly thereafter and was never reprinted. After careful consideration, it was decided to go back to the beginning and work with Gitta word by word on the basis of the original handwritten Hungarian texts. This was to prove a laborious and time-consuming process, but a very rewarding one. Just as Hanna conveyed from her inner ear

---

[*] *Talking with Angels,* Watkins, London & Dulverton, 1979.

to the Hungarian language, this publication takes the dialogues one step further into English.

In numerous sessions in Willerzell, Einsiedeln and Gitta's Girardel, and with frequent correspondence between these meetings, the new English edition slowly took form. Along the way, several fragments came to light that had been neglected or edited out of previous editions, and as questions arose during the English-language formulation, extensive explanatory notes were added.

Gitta continues to reside in her simple stone house in the rolling hills of the Dordogne region within walking distance of the caves of Cro-Magnon man. She is alone, her beloved husband Laci having died in 1982. And when she can, she still makes her way to the lecture halls of various European cities – most recently the UPP-Sorbonne in Paris – to share the story of her experience with ever larger audiences.

What is it, besides the story itself, which makes *Talking with Angels* so gripping, so humanly appealing? For me, it is the *naturalness* with which these 4 'ordinary' young people – none of whom had ever had religious 'instruction' – accepted this sudden appearance of 'angels' (!) into their everyday lives. That 'the unexplainable,' this 'numinous event' came just at the darkest hour of their lives is surely significant: it shows that possibilities for new ways and for transformation *do* come to us when there seems to be no way out – if only we are open to them.

The angels taught Gitta and her friends – and continue to teach us – that earthly existence is only a part of a whole: and if we are aware of this, we no longer need fear and death. Eternal is not the eternally repetitive but the *eternally new*. We are encouraged to become aware of the ever moving, the undogmatic: *Light*. The angels teach that the more light we are able to bear, the more aware we become and the closer we can come to our 'peak,' the meeting point with our own angel. At the same time, our individual angel strives to descend and meet us at this same 'peak.' Thus, we are not alone in this endeavor, even if our way of going about it is very individual. *How* each of us goes through this experience is not important: only *that* we go through it, each in his or her own individual way. That is, for me, the essence and the inspiration of this book.

Gitta frequently and rightfully protests that she is not the 'author' of this text, but 'merely' the *scribe*. She considers it her task to make the dialogues known to others.

When asked how she feels about the dialogues today, Gitta answers:

"You know, those words are like seeds that were sown by the angels. They lay dormant in the earth for 32 years. They finally broke through the hard crust of the surface for the first time in 1976 with the publication of the French *Dialogues* in Paris and from there, they spread like wildfire – no, like *Lightfire*. Now the new, the Springtime of humanity, is here – and these words represent a very real possibility for all."

The angels said:

> WHAT COULD BE MORE NATURAL
> THAN OUR TALKING WITH EACH OTHER?

May this book help many new dialogues to be born ...

Willerzell, April 1988   R.H.

A TECHNICAL NOTE

The dialogues which make up this book have been transcribed from handwritten notes made in the Hungarian language by Gitta and Lili during the actual events, as dated. Many of the original dialogue notes (including all of Joseph's and the personal notes of Lili) were subsequently lost, and a few dialogues were incompletely recorded (as indicated). Some of the accompanying explanatory texts in italics were added immediately after a dialogue, others were added during the preparation of this text.

It is hoped that the rather unusual system of notation employed in this edition will help to convey at least an approximate impression of the *experiential* quality of these dialogues.

Certain words were pronounced with emphasis and subsequently underlined in the notes (indicated here by italics). Others had an almost palpable feeling, engraving themselves indelibly into the participants. They were designated in the notes by capitalization of the first letter, and this has been retained in the present edition. The most powerful words and sentences of all are indicated by the use of only capital letters.

There is one peculiarity in particular requiring explanation: The word, Ő (pronounced ü, as in *lu*te), is an all-encompassing Hungarian pronoun used by the angels for the Divine. This simple word has neither masculine nor feminine connotations: it is both and all. Because there is no equivalent in the English language, we have elected to retain use of the word Ő here. This may seem strange at first, but it is hoped that the reader will soon adjust to it. The advantages of being able to avoid using inappropriate pronouns seemed to outweigh all other considerations.

The specific intonation of Ő enabled the participants to immediately know whether *God* or *Jesus* was being referred to. As a means of differentiating in this edition, we refer to the Divine with Ő, and to Jesus with 'He,' 'Him,' 'His.'

INTRODUCTION

As a point of departure for the events which follow, I would like first to give a brief introductory sketch:

It is important to note the *ordinariness,* the normality of the life led by my three friends and me up until the dialogues began. Nevertheless, this life was a preparation for what was to follow.

I was sixteen years old in 1923 when I first met Hanna. We were both students at the School of Applied Arts in Budapest, where we sat at neighboring tables. From the first moment, Hanna was open and very friendly towards me. However, I was the product of a military family proud of its motto: 'Above all, be tough!' Thus I was quite surprised and puzzled by Hanna's affectionate nature. In my upbringing, any showing of feelings had been considered a sign of weakness and even a simple kiss of departure was cause for embarrassment.

Hanna, whose father was an elementary school principal, grew up in the more natural atmosphere of a modern Jewish family and she was accustomed to showing her feelings spontaneously. Despite these differences in temperament and upbringing, we became close friends in the course of the next three years.

After final exams, however, our ways parted and we seldom had contact. Hanna continued her studies in Munich, while I threw myself totally and blindly into sports: swimming championships, national records and the adulation which Hungary showered upon its sports heroes fed my pride and kept me indulging in a superficial lifestyle for the next four years. It was during this time that I made the acquaintance of Lili, who was giving courses in movement therapy. Her warm and natural manner attracted great numbers of pupils and I soon realized that the reason for her overcrowded classes was that her students were experiencing something going far beyond physical relaxation: their inner essence was being nourished.

I heard little from Hanna during my sports idol days. She had married Joseph, a quiet man, who was a furniture designer by profession. His very presence had a soothing influence on his surroundings. I often observed this later when we lived together in Budaliget: in the village inn, where the townspeople had the habit of engaging in heated political quarrels, the atmosphere would inevitably calm and all would become peaceful within moments of Joseph's arrival. This was a typical effect of his silent presence.

When I finally had had enough of sports, I decided to seek out Hanna once more. She and Joseph had settled into a work studio in the *Ilona-utca* on the hills of Buda, over-looking the Danube to a gorgeous view. With great patience and understanding, Hanna helped me to find my way back to artistic activity, something I had completely neglected since completing my studies. Without her accompaniment, I would never have been able to regain my joy in creative work. As it turned out, the three of us eventually founded what soon became a very successful graphic arts studio.

In the years 1934 and 1935, anti-Semitism was already widespread in Hungary. Thus, as the only non-Jew in the group, it was my role to obtain government commissions, primarily for touristic events and advertising, whereby my sports reputation and status as the daughter of a high-ranking military officer were beneficial assets. Unfortunately, I always had to hide the fact that my colleagues were Jewish.

The 'soul' of our professional group was undeniably Hanna. She possessed tremendous powers of concentration and intuition which enabled her to immediately grasp the essence of an artistic conception, as well as its practical realization. She had the knack of being able to solve problems with a wonderful blend of common sense, clear psychological insight and, above all, with humor.

By this time, Hanna already had some graphic pupils of her own and, many years later, one of these young artists, Vera, told me: "The intensity of Hanna's teaching touched not only our professional development, but our entire being. It demanded so much of us that some students simply could not bear it and chose to leave. Hanna never critiqued a design without our feeling personally touched, even if it involved only the most trivial advertising graphics. She considered every line of a drawing to be the manifestation of an inner event. During the actual lessons, our contact with her was quite different: she would intuitively tune in to another wavelength and read our drawings like a doctor reads an X-ray. This she did with affection, firmness and cheerfulness.

Before beginning to speak, she sometimes had no idea of what she was going to say and was then astonished at her own words. As a young student, I was very attached to her and she became a model for me. But Hanna completely rejected this dependency on my part. She would say to us, 'After two or three years of my teaching, you must find *your own inner teacher*.' For her, the most important thing was to awaken the new being in us: *'the creative individual, freed from fear.'*"

Our studio prospered. And yet, ever more, we had the feeling that we were living on the edge of a cliff. Collective blindness was on the rise, along with a flood of organized political lies. If something were promised by the Nazis, for instance, one could be sure that just the opposite would occur. A strong desire was welling in us to find the truth – *our truth* – beneath so much deception. This led Joseph and Hanna to seek and ultimately find a small house not far from Budapest in the little village of Budaliget, for the purpose of starting a new and simple way of life. I soon joined them there and we worked just enough to support our daily needs. Lili joined us on the weekends.

The quiet village life was beneficial to our inner development. However, this period began for me with a growing feeling of emptiness. An inexplicable expectation of a coming *something* deeply disturbed me and I often went for daylong walks in the forest in search of peace. Again and again, even at mealtimes, I would catch myself looking toward the garden gate in expectation of this 'something' or 'someone' that should come and change my life. In the evenings, we would often discuss our experiences and try to discover the sources of our problems.

Hanna's intuitive gifts were a great help, but still we all felt ourselves to be at a dead end. We were interested in the great religious currents of humanity and our bookshelves held the Bible, the Bhagavad Gita and Lao-Tse; yet none of us was practicing a religion.

We felt ourselves to be standing before a world of lies, brutality and all-pervading evil. At the same time, we were convinced that the meaning of our lives must be buried somewhere, and that the cause for our not finding it must be in ourselves.

With this in mind, we decided at one point that each of us should write down as clearly as possible our particular problems, so as to better be able to discuss them together. One day over black coffee, I read aloud what I had written to Hanna, who dryly remarked that this was nothing but the familiar old stories, warmed over yet again. It was all too true, and I was painfully aware of my blatant superficiality. I was asking Hanna questions that I could just as easily have answered myself, but it was less strenuous to have the answer simply 'served' to me.

> *At this point, the dialogues begin. They were to take place nearly every Friday afternoon at three o'clock for the following seventeen months.*

PART I

THE DIALOGUES IN BUDALIGET

"Go your *own* way!
Any other way is straying."

Friday June 25, 1943

1. DIALOGUE WITH GITTA

In the face of my superficial attitude, Hanna feels a tension arise which grows into indignation. And then, fully awake and with eyes open wide, she suddenly has the following vision: a strange force seizes my pages of notes, rips them to shreds and dashes them to the floor in complete disapproval of this inferior effort, so short of my capabilities. Hanna is about to say something but suddenly stops as she senses that it is no longer she herself who is about to speak. She just has time to warn me: "It is not I who will speak to you." And then I hear the following words:

— Enough of your shallow questions!
It is time for you to assume responsibility for yourself!

It is Hanna's voice that I hear, but I am absolutely certain that she is not herself speaking; her voice is serving as a kind of instrument. I have the feeling that I know whoever is addressing these stern words to me and so I am not totally overwhelmed; I rather feel that something quite natural, which had to occur, is finally taking place. I am filled with a bright light, but there is nothing joyous about it. On the contrary, it illuminates my darkest interior with merciless clarity and I am compelled to see myself without deception.

1

I am shown what I might well have written about myself, had I truly been self-searching and honest, and I feel deeply shaken – and guilty. In the wake of my sincere shame, Hanna senses the indignation ebbing in the one who is speaking through her.

— It is better now: repentance is also forgiving.
It is time for you to transform yourself.
BE INDEPENDENT!
You have too much and too little.
G. I do not understand …
— Too much inert matter – too little independence!

I feel that this refers to my lazy and dependent way of thinking.

— The seed is not sown on hard ground.
You will be tilled by endless searching.
What has been good will become bad.
What has been bad will become good.

A long silence ensues. It is finally broken by the following question:

— Do you know me?

These words touch me to the core. I feel with an inexplicable certainty that I do know the questioner, that it is my inner teacher and guide; but I have no memory-image to accompany this feeling. I perceive only thick layers of mist, which obscure and prevent recognition. I am unable to break through it, despite my best efforts.

— Do you know me?

2

This repetition penetrates me all the more. I am at the threshold of remembering and try with all my strength to illuminate the dark layers. But it is for naught. I cannot.

Hanna feels that the one who speaks through her watches me with empathy during my struggle.

— You are pagan, but that is *good.*

I sense that, by 'pagan,' my roots are meant.

— You will be baptized with the Water of Life.
You will receive a new Name.
The Name exists, but I cannot yet reveal it.
Prepare yourself for it!
You may ask a question!

I am incapable of asking even a single question. I am too filled with the growing awareness of what is happening to me.

— 'The one who speaks' is tired.
Give her strength!
We will meet again!

Immediately after this remarkable encounter, Hanna and I write down what we have heard. This is not difficult, for every word has engraved itself permanently into our memories. Hanna describes her experience of the event as follows: "During the entire dialogue, my perceptions were heightened. I could see the room, you, and all that was going on inside of you, with great clarity. At the same time, I was fully aware of our visitor, whose feelings were of an entirely different quality than ours. But I can describe them only in inadequate terms such as 'indignation,' 'love' or 'tenderness.' It was difficult to find words to express what was to be communicated through me. In one and the same moment, I was experiencing both intense anticipation and great joy."

A single question burns in me: "And the promise of return ... when – if ever – will it be fulfilled?"

Hanna answers: "Perhaps in seven days."

In the evening, we tell Lili and Joseph about our extraordinary experience. Joseph, who had been a materialist in his youth, reacts skeptically and adopts a cautious attitude. Lili, however, very much wants to be present the following week and offers to take notes of any subsequent dialogues.

Friday, July 2, 1943

2. DIALOGUE WITH GITTA

It is a difficult week: the uncertainty of my inner visitor's return makes me uneasy. In addition, the starkly accurate image of me which had been revealed is difficult to bear. At about three o'clock on Friday afternoon, we are sitting in waitful expectation and I am painfully aware of having made no progress during the week.

Suddenly, the silence is broken by these words:

— What have you achieved? Have you learned?

> *I think back on the past week and, at this moment, I would like nothing better than to sink beneath the floor. Nonetheless, I feel that I have changed in some small way, and I say timidly:*

G. Yes.

— For the time being, or forever?

> *Now I feel so worthless that I burst into tears.*

— No self-pity! Are you afraid of me?

G. No.

— I, too, serve.

> *These words console me, and I am filled with a joyous feeling of trust: my teacher* serves *and this is something we have in common.*

— Ask!

> *As a birthday present, Hanna had recently painted a portrait of me in which I sit on a mountain top holding a crystal sphere, whose facets shine in a rainbow of rich colors. The symbol of this sphere of light has great meaning for me, and I long to hear my teacher say something about it.*

G. How might it be possible for me not only to *understand,* but also to *live* the symbol of the sphere?

— I have the sphere of Light with me.

I DESCEND TO YOU – YOU ASCEND TO ME.

G. How?

— Believe it, and you shall grow with this belief.

> *In the word 'belief,' I feel a living force, in no way connected with the intellectual affirmation of a religious creed.*

— When the time is ripe, it will happen.
Can you bear the sphere of Light?

> *I answer superficially, without really understanding the question:*

G. Yes.

— Are you worthy? Are you *pure* enough?

> *I hesitate:*

G. *You* know it.

> *Hanna feels that the one who speaks through her is observing me as though I were a foolish child, ignorant of what she is saying.*

— Though the sphere is heavier than the earth,
the CHILD plays with it,
for it is formed of one and the same substance: LIGHT.

> *The word 'CHILD' is used in an entirely new way which I am unable to grasp. I listen as if through fog, and bluntly ask:*

G. Can one play with it?

— The CHILD plays – the adult creates.

> *The fog thickens. I am completely confused.*

G. Then am I too small for the sphere?

The piercing reply strikes me like lightning:

— Too *big* !

Hanna sees that my little 'I' is too big and dominating. But I do not understand, and ask stupidly:

G. Where am I too big?

Hanna feels indignation rise in my teacher at this lack of comprehension on my part. Although a powerful purifying gesture would have been called for, she fails to rally sufficient strength in herself to carry it out and is only able to transmit the following words:

— Be reborn!
What is big – collapses.
What is hard – disintegrates.

The gesture of burning force, which Hanna had been unable to make, would have set off this 'collapsing' and 'disintegration' inside of me, Hanna later tells me.
After a long silence, I hear the consoling words:

— You are never alone.

Friday, July 9, 1943

3. DIALOGUE WITH GITTA

This week has been less difficult than the previous one, but on Friday, the obscuring inner layers of fog return. It begins to dawn on me that I have been living carelessly in this fog for 36 years without even being aware of it. But now I do at last see it, and it is a real problem.
As we chat together after coffee, Hanna suddenly hears a single word, sternly spoken:

— Enough!

It is three o'clock and I had not been ready to receive my inner teacher.

— Have you prepared yourself for the feast?

I feel so worthless that I begin to cry.

— Do not cry in my presence. There is no time for that!

Hanna feels my visitor's indignance. Clearly it would have been more suitable to be joyful.

— Ask.
G. How might I hear your voice *always* ... ?
— ... and be a *puppet* !
G. I do not understand.
— THEN YOU WOULD NOT BE INDEPENDENT.
It is *your* task to approach *me*.
G. *(Timidly:)* May I ask a question?
— That is why I am here.

8

G. Should I fast on Friday?

> *I thought that fasting might be a means of spiritual purification.*

— No. Let the proper measure of each day
be your fasting.

> *Pointing to Hanna:*

— Give her something to drink!

> *Very surprised, I get Hanna a glass of water.*

G. Why is it so difficult to really love my family?
— The family is flesh …

> *Hanna sees that my family strengthens just what is already too strong in me: matter.*

— When you have rid yourself of the superfluous,
then you will be able to love.
G. Is that far off?

— THE FAR IS NEAR — THE NEAR IS FAR.

G. May I know your name?

> *This question comes from a desire to be able to call my teacher at any time, and thus feel secure.*

— The name is still matter. Seek what is *behind* it!

> *The dark layers of fog torment me. My question is actually a desperate cry for help:*

G. I am in the dark … what should I do?

— GO YOUR *OWN* WAY! ANY OTHER WAY IS STRAYING.

After a long silence:
— Sing for me in the forest!

> *I cannot believe my ears: me ... sing? Having hidden my feelings behind a thick coat of armor since childhood, this strikes me as absolutely absurd.*

G. I think I misheard ...

> *Each word is now uttered with emphasis:*

— SING - FOR - ME - IN - THE - FOREST !

> *Without being aware of it, I lean forward, and I am immediately held back by a gentle but firm gesture:*

— You are too near.

> *I ask myself if my density is unbearable ... ?*
> *Or is the radiance of my teacher too strong for me?*

G. I had a dream, but its meaning is not clear to me.
— You are a part of the way. I am a part of the way.
Ő* is the WAY.

> *The word Ő is pronounced with utter reverence. Hanna is now too tired to go on. Thus, the remainder of what she was to convey is related to me afterwards as a message:*

— To *will* is not a step forward; it is a hindering wall.

> *I feel this is a reference to my overzealous, willful striving.*

---

* See the Technical Note on p. vii for an explanation of Ő.

Friday, July 9, 1943

3. DIALOGUE WITH LILI

Lili would also like to ask some questions. She takes the place opposite Hanna, who is resting, as I move over and prepare to take notes. After a brief silence, we feel a presence of warmth and gentleness.

— I am here.
You called me – I called you.

The intonation of the voice has changed completely: now it is tender.

— You may ask!
L. When will I open myself to what is above?
— You are deceiving yourself. Deception is fear.
But you have no cause to fear.
L. What is my first task?
— Do you know your sign?
Here it is: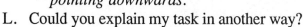
Gesture outlining a triangle pointing downwards.
L. Could you explain my task in another way?
— You are named: *'the one who helps.'*
The helper should not fear.
I bring good news: you are dear to me.
Do you *want* to see me again?
L. Yes.
— Then you will not see me.
Do you *wish* to see me?

11

L. Yes.

— Then you will not see me.

> *In light of the previous dialogue, I now realize that neither* will *nor* wish *can bring our teachers closer to us. Lili, rather confused, bursts out:*

L. I only want to see you better …

— WHEN THE TASK REQUIRES IT – YOU WILL SEE ME.
I obey.

L. I would also like to be able to obey.

> *Touching Lili's forehead:*

— There is too much here …
In the body, you are the last-born.

> *(Lili was the youngest child of a large family.)*

— In spirit, you are the first of the new-born.
I now take leave of you.

> *I am absolutely delighted that Lili has found her inner guide, whose tender, radiant presence allows even me to completely relax.*
> *In the days that follow, I am totally occupied with "not wanting" and "not wishing."*

Friday, July 16, 1943

4. DIALOGUE WITH GITTA

It is Friday. My life has gone through a fundamental change: possibilities hitherto undreamed of have appeared and I am aware of so much that is new. Joyfully, I prepare myself for today's dialogue. But then, after lunch, a cold fear suddenly seizes me, and I become haunted by the question: "What if my teacher does not come ... does not appear anymore?" I desperately try to cast this thought away, but it returns again and again, ever stronger, fed by a fear of falling into the void of my previous empty life. Then, all of a sudden, I realize that it is wrong for me to bind *myself, even to the very thing which means the most to me. This fearful clinging to my inner teacher will have to be sacrificed. It is an unavoidable challenge, and I know it is my task.*

Inner detachment is more difficult than anything I have ever before experienced. It is as though I cut myself off from my own life. At three o'clock, Hanna calls me. I soon sense the presence of my guide, who, however, remains silent and, after a while, I am nervously uncertain about whether the silence is going to be broken. With a sigh of surrender, I say to myself: "Thy Will be done." At this moment, I see [my eyes are open] a fire burning before me, its smoke rising straight up to heaven. Then I hear the following words:

13

— The time has come. *Now* you may ask!

G. What is my path?

— Listen well:

AT ONE END, LOVE. AT THE OTHER END, LIGHT.
YOU ARE SUSPENDED BETWEEN THE TWO.
THAT IS YOUR PATH.

A hundred deaths are between the two.
Love is bearer of Light.
Love without Light is nothing.
Do you understand me?

> *I do understand, but it strikes me as very difficult to let my 'little I' die a hundred times. I sink my eyes, discouraged.*

— Look at me!

> *The familiar face of Hanna, neither beautiful nor ugly, takes on another expression and reflects an almost frightening dignity.*

— At one end ... I.

> *Gesture from above to below:*

— At the other end ... it.
Between the two ... you.

G. What is 'it'?

— Your 'little I.'

> *Disdainfully, I think: "What a self-centered creature, this 'little I.' "*

G. I know my 'little I' well, all too well, but you I do not know well enough!

— Foolish child!

> *I later come to understand these two words as meaning: 'How could you possibly know your little I? You do not know even a single cell of your body! As little as you know me! How long will you continue to be so blind?'*

— *It* and *I* are united in the task.
Do not divide what is one!
Before the Divine, nothing is small!
Do not judge!

G. Teach me, for I know nothing!

— Have I not taught you?

> *With false modesty, I say:*

G. Oh, yes, I know that I ask silly questions.

> *Hanna perceives my teacher's thoughts:*
> *'What a childish game!' But she feels authorized only to say:*

— You are foolish!... Ask!

> *I know that I have been seen through like glass, and I stubbornly protest:*

G. Why should I even ask, when you always know beforehand what I want to say ... you see my thoughts!

— From the heart to the mouth is a handspan.
Make this your way! Do you wish to know much?

G. Only as much as my task requires.

— THOSE WHO ASK ARE MORE DEAR TO THE DIVINE THAN THOSE WHO KNOW.

Last night, I dreamed I saw a human figure in glowing colors, radiating harmony, strength and peace.

G. What does my dream mean?
— The new Individual formed from your image.
G. Will I become this individual when I shed what is superfluous?

— YOU ARE THE ONE WHO FORMS –
NOT THE FORMED.

G. What must I do to become *the one who forms?*

Now Hanna's body seems to lose its usual qualities and transform into an instrument serving totally, with nothing held back: her movements are simple, meaningful and dignified. Even her arm seems different to me. It radiates concentrated force, the muscles tense, and I am strongly reminded of Michelangelo's sculptures. An abrupt gesture strikes like lightning.

— BURN!

I am struck, jolted, filled with wonder. But all this vanishes instantly when I notice that Hanna is shivering. She bids me to bring her alcohol: just today, by 'coincidence,' I had bought a small bottle of pure alcohol. I drip some onto a sugar cube and give it to Hanna. Soon her strength returns and she reveals: "I had to concentrate all of my energy so that a burning force would ignite in you. Your detachment was the key. You had to sacrifice and to learn independence, even from your inner teacher."

Friday, July 16, 1943

4. DIALOGUE WITH LILI

After a short rest, Hanna feels ready for the dialogue with Lili, who is wearing a blue skirt and a red blouse.

— You have dressed yourself upside-down.
L. What do you mean?
— Blue belongs above – red, below!
Red carries the blue.
This is also relevant for your work.

Lili immediately understands that the bodily 'red' should support the spiritual, the 'blue.' Then she reflects on her teaching of the previous week and its results.

— Pay no attention to results!
What *'was'* … is no more.
What *'is now'* is already the *'it was.'*
There you can no longer help.
May 'the one who helps' direct her attention
to where the *'shall be'* is born.
It occupies little space, but from it,
everything can be formed.

Lili, who is physically fragile and often in poor health, has been ill.

— Are you tired?
L. No, I just don't feel well.

17

— This we know.
    If blue is above, it strengthens;
    if red is below, it softens, it weakens.
    In the same way,
    the weak body is a burden when it dominates.
    Red, Eros … is earthly love.
    Blue is heavenly love.
    Purple is *His* color.

> *The word 'His' vibrates with deep reverence. As a painter, I know that the combination of red and blue results in purple. I understand the word 'His' as referring to Jesus, who united earthly and heavenly love.*

— You may ask another question!
L. Will I receive *help* with my work …
    or will I have to do everything by myself?

— IF YOU BEGIN BY YOURSELF,
    THEN YOU WILL RECEIVE HELP.

> *In the ensuing silence, I begin to wonder just what sort of evolutionary possibilities are open to us as humans, and immediately I receive a response to my silent question:*

— I am speaking to you:
    This is the direction of human evolution:

> *These words are accompanied by an upward gesture at a 45° angle to the right.*

18

I am astonished to learn that human evolution is not only a matter of spiritual (vertical), nor only of material (horizontal) development, but of equal parts of both.

Friday, July 23, 1943

5. DIALOGUE WITH GITTA

All week long, I have been thinking about 'burning.' On Friday morning, I decorate the little room that opens to the garden with flowers. As we sit waiting for the dialogue, Hanna feels luminous forces assembling in a semi-circle behind her.

— Speak!
G. Last week, you spoke of the 'hundred deaths.'
    I would like to 'die' now, to *surpass* my 'little I' …
— It is not a matter of *surpassing,*
    but of *becoming a bridge.*

I am so overjoyed at the presence of my inner teacher that tears well up in my eyes.

— Do not flood the seed with water!

I understand that all my emotions have to be transformed into burning.

— THE DIVINE SPARK SPRINGS BETWEEN ACT AND MATTER.

I am aware that something extremely important has been revealed to me, but I have no idea what it means. In the silence that follows, Hanna continues to feel the presence of luminous beings. All eyes are focused on me.

— We are many and we expect much of you.

A sense of responsibility arises in me, and I offer all of my strength joyfully.

G. I would so much like to know my *task* now!
— *Task* is just a word to you.
G. Can you reveal the task to me?
— The one who speaks finds no words.
  These words have not yet been born.
G. What could bring them to birth?
— Your deepest desire.
G. My desire to serve?
— Mighty and wondrous is your task.

The vibration of these words conveys to me a foretaste of a completely new life-intensity.

G. You said, "we are many." Who are you all?

— THE CHORUS.

Behind the spoken words, I sense an infinite multitude in perfect harmony. I wonder: could my teacher be what we humans call an 'angel'?
With lowered eyes and upward turned hands, the following words are gently spoken:

— We sing praise, we praise the Divine.

For the first time in my life, I feel what genuine adoration is, and I softly ask:

G. Do you always see Ő?

A swift motion stops me, as though I had touched something forbidden.

— You know not what you say. Ask another question!
G. How could I always hear the voice of my heart
without having my head interfere?
— Do you not feel the difference?
G. Yes, but everything moves so slowly,
and I want to serve now!
— You often lose your way.

Hanna senses a hesitation: before me lies a long and difficult path which gradually leads to awareness, to more consciousness. My angel sees a storm approaching, and sees that the heavy weight of my family and my lack of self-confidence might overwhelm me before my goal is reached. Time is short. Hanna pleads in her heart: "Please show her the short way! I will vouch for her!"

— Listen well! Your path is not difficult!
Be cheerful! Be light!
The one who speaks cannot express it clearly!

A vertical flamelike motion of remarkable lightness, and then a heavy, downward motion like flowing water.

21

— FIRE IS LIGHT – WATER IS HEAVY.
  IF YOU FEEL HEAVINESS,
  THEN YOU HAVE STRAYED FROM THE PATH.

> *After the dialogue, Hanna explains in detail what
> she had not been able to verbalize at the moment: "It
> is important for you to find a happiness you have
> never known before, a new smile: Lightness! If you
> feel weighed down, you are off the path. If you
> carry your burden lightly, then you are on the path.
> It all depends on you. You will be able to find this
> new smile only by living life to the fullest!"*

— Ask!
G. Where are my limits?
— Limits are only here:

> *The hands form a cylinder, closed on the sides,
> open at the top. It seems to express that limits are
> necessary in matter, but that the way up is free.*

G. Then I am you?
— *(smile)* Not yet. Enough for today!

> *By this time, Hanna is so tired that she immediately
> falls asleep. Lili was unable to be here today.*

Friday, July 30, 1943

6. DIALOGUE WITH GITTA

*I have carefully prepared a long list of questions
for today's session:*

— I cannot stay for long today.

*This opening of course disappoints me,
and I say very hesitatingly:*

G. May I ask a question?

There is a silent nod.

G. Why were there so many of you last time?
— Because your task has grown.
G. What do you expect of me?
— When the seed sprouts, you will know.

*I have worked hard on myself all week
and am hungry to hear some praise.*

G. Do I water the seed enough?
— You know that perfectly well yourself.

*This dry reply makes the falsity of my attempt
to draw praise all the more obvious.*

G. The dead of my family came to me in a dream.
   Can I do something for them?
   Am I neglecting them somehow?
— Many of the dead are weaklings ...
G. How could I help them?
— By harvesting.

23

G. How can I harvest?

— Ő CREATED YOU AFTER MY IMAGE.

> *These words touch me deeply: I exist in the image of my angel!*

G. Why do you have so little time today?
— So as to teach you measure.
   I will answer one last question.

> *I hurriedly search through my papers for the most important question.*

— I have time …

> *I relax, and now my question comes from the heart:*

G. In what way do I least resemble your image?
   Once I know, I will tear it out of myself!
— Uncertainty.
G. I do not understand.
— Do not waver.

> *I lower my eyes.*

— Look at me!

> *Hanna's facial expression transforms, seeming to take on the austere solemnity of an other-worldly dimension.*

— I depart …

> *I continue to feel the silent presence of the angel for a few minutes more, and in this stillness, the deep longing awakens in me to become identical with my inner teacher's image.*

Friday, July 30, 1943

6. DIALOGUE WITH LILI

L. Thank you for coming again!
— Thank Ő, who sent me!
L. Why is it so difficult for me to free myself
from my 'little I'?

— WHEN YOU TASTE THE BETTER –
YOU LEAVE WHAT IS LESS GOOD.

With unquenchable thirst,
you will search for the better.
L. Why am I so unsure of myself that I don't even know
what I need?
— Freshen up your palate, for you have spoiled it
with so much worthless food.

> *This appears to refer to Lili's having studied a wide
> variety of educational methods of body movement
> in past years at foreign schools.*

L. Why do I progress so pitifully slowly,
and why do I so often lose my head?
— They are directly related:
one is the consequence of the other. Do not rush!
I am protecting you.

> *Gentle, protective gesture around Lili.*

L. I don't even know what to call my work,
what kind of a name to give it.
— A name is already a conclusion.
But at this point, you are still at the beginning!

25

The numbers of young students who participate in Lili's courses are swelling by the day. As political uncertainty and mistrust spread and decimate morale everywhere, the task of teaching relaxation becomes ever more vital – and more difficult!

L. My work seems to be lacking something basic ...
    What is it?

—   BELIEF IN Ő ... IN ME ... AND IN YOURSELF.

Listen carefully! In preparation for our next meeting, try to formulate the essence of your work.

L. Thank you!

Friday, August 6, 1943

7. DIALOGUE WITH GITTA

As a result of last week's lesson in 'measure,' I decide to ask very few questions today.

—   Ask!

G. I don't see things clearly, my heart is weak and hesitant. How could I see you more clearly, how could I better feel your presence? I would like to form myself after your image.

—   The creature perceives the lack;
    yet the Divine, the only Reality, can be but intuited.
    May your intuition guide you!

G. How could I carve your words into myself?
I am always afraid that they will fade ...

— FEAR IS THE REFUGE OF THE WEAK.

> *There is no question of my wanting to belong to the weak! Thus, I am quick to protest:*

G. I am not *that* afraid!
— *(with severity:)* You *are that* afraid.
G. Then I will work to free myself from it.
— Do not work – believe!
Believe, and then there is nothing to be afraid of.

> *I feel this belief to be not religious confession, but a living,* transforming *force.*

— Listen well!
The measure of suffering is unknown to you.

> *Ever since childhood, I have avoided suffering whenever possible by lying. But when I do suffer, then I torture myself mercilessly with self-reproaches.*

— WELCOME SUFFERING AS A MESSENGER
FROM HEAVEN.
BUT LET IT DEPART WHEN IT IS READY TO LEAVE.

G. How can I welcome suffering and still be joyful?
— *(smiling)* By following the good path: your *own* path.

> *I have more questions, but, recalling the lesson of measure, I remain silent.*

— I speak: We are not disappointed in you.

27

In the word, 'we,' echoes once more the perfect harmony of a multitude: the Chorus. Hanna later tells me: "Your teacher was pleased that you exercised measure. And your unanswered questions will be answered: Imagine a white sheet of paper. The answers will appear on it. They will be ignited by the intensity of your questions."

Friday, August 6, 1943

7. DIALOGUE WITH LILI

L. I thank God that you were allowed to come again...

An atmosphere of deep reverence follows the word, 'God.'

... and I am grateful for all that I received this week in Bupapest.

Lili had felt unexpected help.

L. I have not thanked with prayer for all this ...

— YOUR WORK IS YOUR PRAYER.
PRAYER IS WINGS FOR THE WINGLESS.

Your wings are already growing.

L. Will you tell me what my weakest part is?
I would like to improve it.

— No. For the time being, simply *rejoice!*

*Lili has suffered from an extremely unhappy
childhood and joy has been her greatest lack.*

L.   I was happier this week than ever before in my life.
—   I was happy, too, my little servant.

Lili has been trying to define her professional work.

L.   I was unable to complete my task …
—   It will never be *completed* …
L.   I wanted so much to bring something whole,
     something well-rounded.
—   Roundness belongs to the infinite:

Gesture forming a spiral.

L.   I feel that I have so *much* to do!
—   *Much* is illusion. If you feel it to be *much,*
     then you are in error. There is not *much,*
     but just *one* thing to be done.

Gesture of offering upwards.

—   May heaven bless you.

*There are moments during the dialogues when I am
afraid that I will not be able to write down
everything that is said. But then Lili's teacher waits
until I have caught up before proceeding to the next
topic. This occurs several times, which seems to
indicate that our note-taking is desired.*

Friday, August 13, 1943

8. DIALOGUE WITH GITTA

Before the dialogues began, we all occasionally had impressive dreams, and to distinguish these from 'ordinary' ones, we referred to them as 'teaching dreams.' Each of them had a powerful effect on all of us. We would often discuss them at the breakfast table and try to unveil their hidden meaning together. Hanna's dreams, in particular, were often concerned with universal themes, as I became more and more aware with the passage of time.

— It is time to ask!

G. Last night, I know that I dreamed of a new Host,
but I do not understand the meaning of the dream.

— The Host is an image of creation.

G. Matter appeared to be very important in the dream,
but that, too, is unclear to me.

— Listen carefully! Human sin – Adam's sin –
caused matter to be cursed.
When the curse ends, matter will again be sacred.

MATTER IS THE CHILD OF GOD.

G. How might I strengthen my belief in such a way that it
would lift me above duality?

— It is not your belief that is weak, but your vision.

G. I do not understand.

— You look – but you do not *shine*.
Your eyes are not made for looking.

G. Do I look to the outside too much?

30

— No. Look in a completely different way: transform!

> *There is lightning – fast flick of the hand,*
> *conveying a sense of immediate and total change.*

G. My love often fails ... and it is so difficult with my family.

> *Raising the left hand:*

— THE CREATURE YEARNS FOR LOVE.

> *Raising the right hand:*

THE CREATOR LOVES.

The two are not balanced in you.
And this will continue to be so for a long time to come.

G. Last week, I expected your answer to appear on a white sheet, as you had said. But it came in another form.

— *(smiling)* Your mistake was that you paid attention only to the form.

G. That is true, but you answered me just the same.

— THE TRUE QUESTION
BRINGS FORTH ITS OWN ANSWER.

> *Hanna later warns me: "Don't ever – even for a*
> *moment! – depend on the strength of your angel!*
> *Only your fire calls forth the answer."*
> *After a silence:*

G. Even now, I have tears of emotion in my eyes, though I am well aware that you do not like sentimental feelings ...

— Such feelings separate you from me.

I cannot descend to that level.
True feeling is different, as I will soon show you …
Let us pray …

> *We all remain in silent prayer.*
> *My heart lifts, and I am filled with a deep peace.*

— *This* is true feeling.
May you be blessed!

Friday, August 13, 1943

8. DIALOGUE WITH LILI

L. I thank God that you have come again!
— I am listening to you.
L. Is it all right to completely let myself go when I am alone?
— Only upward.
L. Why am I so often in despair, and torn in half?
— You are not always united with your other half.
But you are not far from being ONE.
You are making progress.
L. Would it be right for me to teach small children?
— You are a child yourself. What is the problem?
L. I do not have enough contact with children.
— The separating veil is: what is known.
Believe me,
there is *no difference* between adults and children.
L. Why is it that I am so seldom able to be a child?

32

— KNOW THE DIVINE
  AND YOU WILL AGAIN BECOME A SMALL CHILD!

L. I still try too hard to find the Divine.

— IT IS Ő WHO SEEKS YOU.
  LET YOURSELF BE FOUND!

L. That is very difficult.
— That is your task. Help others to learn it too!
L. I would like to always feel as happy and fulfilled as I
  do now, but often, I just feel 'flat.'
  Why does this happen to me?
— Because the sprout is still small.
  Speak!
L. I am afraid to go back into the city ...

> *Lili spends only the weekends in Budaliget. The
> dark political atmosphere in Budapest creates an
> unsettling pall that affects all of its inhabitants.*

— What are you afraid of?
L. That the city will drag me down, because I am not yet
  strong enough.
— Fear not – I am helping you. We will be together.
  The city has become an empty sea-shell ...
  inside, it no longer exists.
  It is a petrified curse.
  Even its dust is cursed, for nothing grows in it.
  But in you, the sprout grows.
  Take good care of it!
  Raise your heart!

> *For the first time in her life, Lili feels the force of
> true prayer. She bursts into tears.*

33

— See how near Ő is! If you raise yourself up
  into the infinite, we can always be together.

Friday, August 20, 1943

9. DIALOGUE WITH GITTA

Last night, I had a dream: I am standing on a
seemingly endless plain. Suddenly, a white horse
of tremendous strength and beauty appears. At the
same time, a spiral-shaped pathway winds up into
the heights. I feel that the white horse would be able
to carry me into these heights.

— I am ready.
G. What does the white horse mean?
— Become able to ride it!
G. How ?
— By becoming lighter than the horse.
G. What is it in me that is so heavy?

During the dialogues, Hanna's language is of
exceptional beauty and simplicity, close to the very
roots of Hungarian. However, in this case, she
finds only a trivial slang expression for what is to
be communicated, and my angel is reluctant to
accept this:

— Don't let yourself '*be done in*' by the deceiver!

I recall that I was very judgmental the day before.

34

G. Oh, do you mean yesterday? Yes, I fell right into the
   trap. How could I avoid that in the future?
— Be more *aware!*
   Ask!
G. How might my pictures radiate the new Light and
   awaken desire for it in everyone who sees them?
— The Light shines through you.
   I will tell you something.
   LIGHT is the same as light.
   They sound the same, but the weight of the sound
   – the resonance – is different.
G. Should I take up painting?
— You will surely succeed at it.
   Each of your pictures is a step upward.
   Begin at the bottom. Don't fly!
   You have wings, but many others do not.
   Do you understand now?
G. Oh, yes – now I do!

   I am happy, and Hanna feels my angel rejoice.

— We can already talk together. Ask!
G. How can everything I do become an offering?
— Every act that is not for yourself is an offering.
G. How might I free myself from my '*little I*' ?
   I *despise* it!
— By *not* despising it!
G. I do not mean my body ...
— I know perfectly well what you mean.
   It is clear:
   you despise it because you are afraid of it.
   It teaches you in the same way as I do.

LEARN TO LOVE THE CURSED,
AND YOU WILL FIND YOUR RIGHTFUL PLACE.

G. What is the quickest way to find my place?

— BY NOT HURRYING …
The one who hurries, hurries only towards death.

> *Pointing in the direction of the garden, where Joseph is reading.*

— He tarries …
G. Who?
— The *son*. I cannot name names.

> *I realize that our 'given' name is not the true one – that which expresses our deepest, inner nature.*

— IN HASTE, YOU APPROACH DEATH FROM THE FORE.
IN LINGERING,
YOU APPROACH DEATH FROM THE REAR.
IN ACTING AT THE RIGHT INSTANT,
YOU KNOW NO DEATH.

> *Hanna sees an image of what has been said: life itself as a vertically vibrating line, fine as the finest edge of a sharpened sword blade.*
> *By acting in the right instant, we are this line – in the 'here and now' – and alive.*
> *If we rush, we are in the future: death from the fore. If we linger, we are in the past: death from the rear. Acting at the right instant is being in touch with eternity.*

— Enough for today.
You will be able to create.

The hands hover over mine,
and I feel a force pass through them.

Friday, August 20, 1943

9. DIALOGUE WITH LILI

L. May I ask?

Affirmative gesture.

L. I don't understand the lesson I received last week in Budapest.

Lili had tried to sense in which of her students the new seed might sprout.

— DO NOT JUDGE!

Ő is the driving force.
If a seed is there, it will sprout.
Do not try to find where it is …
Your judgment is not necessary.

L. Thank you! And thank you for last night's dream.

— Being awake is more important
than dreaming dreams.

L. I would like so much to be awake …

— YOU ARE DREAMED.

L. What does that mean?

— DREAMS ARE IMAGES – YOU, TOO, ARE AN IMAGE.
BUT SOON THE DIVINE WILL AWAKEN IN YOU.

L. How can I help the members of my family?
— You have a big family. Ő helps through you.
Have faith!
L. Why do I have pains in my back and neck every
morning?

> An undesired, youngest child, Lili has been
> oppressed by her family since birth.

— You were obliged to bow before the *unworthy*.
If you bow before Ő – Who alone is *worthy* –
you will be made straight again.
L. Does every physical illness have a psychological
cause?
— A tree bears fruit. A good tree bears good fruit.
Matter is neither good nor bad,
for it is essentially inert.

THE PAIN IN YOUR BACK
DOES NOT HAVE ITS ORIGIN IN YOUR BACK.

Now it is my turn to ask a question:
What have you been happy about lately?
L. My dream, my good day in the city and, most of all:
you.

— ONLY IN JOY AM I PRESENT.
May you be blessed by Heaven!

Friday, August 27, 1943

10. DIALOGUE WITH GITTA

At last, a week of joyful anticipation!

— Let us give thanks!

With a radiant smile:

— Today it is good to be here.

> *Hanna later tells me that, during the first dialogues,
> she had often felt how difficult it was for my
> teacher to descend and be in our dense atmosphere.
> Now my joy makes it much easier. Pointing to the
> glass of water:*

— Water brings me closer to you.
What *water* does for me ... *fire* does for you.

> *I understand that the more I burn in joy, the nearer I
> come to my angel ... but the angel's fire must be
> diminished with water in order for me to be
> approached.*

— How can I help you?
G. When I touch someone I love, I often feel a force
streaming through my hands, but not through my eyes.
Why is that so?
— I will explain it to you:
You strive from below to above.

39

The hands form a cone:

This is how you are formed:
strong below ...
ever more slender toward the top.
Matter is inert.
It is your task to raise it up.

Indicating the eyes:

— Matter and spirit meet here.
Matter needs to be raised to this level,
for here it ignites and radiates out through the eyes.

Indicating the throat:

— But here you block the rising force with emotions,
it becomes water and flows back.
From the throat to the eyes,
matter becomes ever more subtle, but still it is matter.
Keep the way pure!

(Silence)

G. I am not yet able to act at the proper moment ...
— What needs to be done has a voice,
and you have ears to hear it. Close your eyes!

I obey, and feel a force streaming into my ears.

— From now on, you will hear better. Ask!
G. I suffer from not being able to love enough ...
— Do you know why?
G. It might be because I was unable to paint ...
— You were unable to paint
because you were unable to *love.*

40

EVERY TRUE ACT SPRINGS FROM *LOVE*.

Take heed! 'The nameless one' led you astray.

> *I am immediately aware of what this refers to:*
> *yesterday, two young students had made the long*
> *way from Budapest to Budaliget and unexpectedly*
> *appeared at our doorstep. I had been on the verge of*
> *leaving – to 'sing for my angel in the forest' – in*
> *preparation for the next dialogue. After hesitating*
> *briefly, I left it to Hanna to deal with the young*
> *visitors and went on my way. As might be*
> *expected, however, I was unable to sing. Every-*
> *thing seemed meaningless, and a feeling of utter*
> emptiness *made any contact with my angel*
> *impossible.*

— 'The nameless one' can assume even *my* form in order
to lead you astray.

> *It now becomes perfectly obvious to me that I*
> behaved unfeelingly *in this situation. I am gripped*
> *by a fear of not being able to feel the difference*
> *between my true, inner guide and some false one.*

— You can recognize 'the nameless one' in your heart,
for its name is 'emptiness.'

G. I know that emptiness and meaninglessness are traps,
but still I fall into them.

— In the moment that you *know* it, it is already too late.
You go too far: you fail to stop when you should.

> *I then realize that, because my attention is usually*
> *directed to the outside, I tend not to notice that the*
> *'nameless one' has slipped into me until it becomes*

obvious in my outer behavior. Were I to direct my
attention inward, however, I could then detect the
danger in advance ... and thus become able to
defend myself.

— Ask.

G. Why do I have such a burning sensation in my eyes?

— Because you weep.
Everything that lives needs water in order to burn.
Your burning has begun ... yet still you weep ...
and so you have a shortage of water.

G. What is the difference between true and false feelings?

— True feeling is inwardly 'immobile.'
But you love first *this* ... then *that* ...

Gesture indicating the motion of waves:

— Water moves, in waves.

TRUE FEELING IS MOTIONLESS,
LOVES EVERYTHING ... AND *SHINES*.

Your sign is the SUN.
The sun is motionless and shines everywhere.
This is not the sun you see with your eyes;
that, too, is but an image.
Speak!

G. For a moment, I felt my task very clearly,
but then everything became blurred again.

— THIS MOMENT LASTS AN ETERNITY;
IT NEVER BEGAN, AND IT CAN NEVER END.
ONLY *YOU* WAVER.

Give your best effort!

I always take your image with me
and present it to the chorus.

*Hanna sees a transparent image of
me, which my angel
superimposes upon earlier,
transparent images. Thus, any
changes I go through from week
to week become clearly visible.
The images of me are placed in
the center of a large cone, formed by the chorus of
angels. All eyes are now focused upon the images,
with neither judgment nor criticism, but a SIGHT
that is all-penetrating.
From above – from the focal point of the cone –
shines the Gaze of the Divine.*

— May Heaven bless you!

*The next day, Hanna explains to me that my
feelings themselves are, of course, vital; nevertheless, I know that I need to find a new or different
attitude towards them. If rising feelings are
repressed prematurely, they become stuck in the
throat and are choked off. If they are allowed to rise
freely, all the way to the eyes, their initial strength
becomes diluted into tears. But if feelings are
offered to the Divine just as they reach the level of
the throat, then their force becomes transformed
into Light, which rises up and shines out through
the eyes.*

Friday, September 3, 1943

11. DIALOGUE WITH GITTA

It has been a very difficult week and I am feeling quite discouraged. We sit waiting for a long, long time, and Hanna senses that my teacher is having a hard time trying to reach me today.

— Speak!

G. I thank God that you could come.
Please teach me true prayer, so that my feelings might rise above the level of water.

— Its name is: *offering.* I will explain a great rule to you:

EACH TINY CELL PRAYS,
AND THE PRAYER OF ALL CELLS TOGETHER
IS TRUE FEELING.

Do you understand this?

G. Not completely …

— For you, raising yourself is difficult –
For me, lowering myself is difficult.

G. *(in despair:)* It should not be difficult for you!
I want so *much* to do … to make it easier for you!

— Do not attempt *much!* Your task is the 'less.'
The *less* is difficult!
See the difference between *much* and *less!*
Much is watery, diluted.

Gesture flowing downward:

— *Much* of the population is diluted.
Less is nearer to the Divine.

44

And the Divine is ONE.

> *This lesson seems to concern the opposition*
> *between dilution in the 'much' and concentration in*
> *the 'less' — as with the cone, which is broad at the*
> *base and narrow at the top.*
> *Long silence.*

— Lift up your heart. Today it is not easy to be here.

G. This week I was able to love a bit more, but it is still
    far from what I am longing for.

— The moon is bright only when the sun shines on it.
    But you are not a moon.
    Do not wait until it is required of you to shine!
    YOUR MOONS ARE DARK.

> *With my inner eye, I see a sun that devours its own*
> *rays. The utter horror of this image is unbearable.*

G. How terrible!

> *Hanna often suffers from stabbing heart-pains*
> *without any apparent organic cause. I am upset*
> *that she is not able to ask questions herself.*

G. What can I do about the pains of my friend ...

> *A forbidding gesture interrupts me:*

— Are you still without faith?!
    The two of you are united in the *task*.
    Individuals, fates, destinies, events ... are no more
    than froth on the waves of the sea.

> *What I have heard leaves me stunned,*
> *and I remain silent.*

— You have two questions left.
G. The sun is my sign.
   I understand this, but I do not yet live it.
— You also hear my words only with your ears.
G. Why was I unable 'to sing for you' yesterday?
— Because I was far away from you.
G. Was that my fault?
— It was a trial, not a punishment.
   I was there, where we one day will be united.
   The distance indicates the size of your task.
   Nothing is concealed. We see everything!
   Honor the Divine Law in even the smallest thing!

> *Realizing the enormity of my task,*
> *I am discouraged.*

— Rejoice! You have every reason!
   It is all a trial.
   Let me console you: you are beginning to take form.
   I will always be with you.

Friday, September 3, 1943

11. DIALOGUE WITH LILI

> *Lili, who was unable to attend last week's dialogue,*
> *has been having a very problematic time, and she*
> *feels depressed.*

— Lay down your burden!
L. I do not understand.

— Has this week been heavy?

L. Very heavy …

— Anything that weighs heavily is a burden.

L. Why did I fall so terribly deep?

— The one who helps descends into the depths.

I GIVE YOU THE KEY TO THE DEPTHS.
ITS NAME IS: THE TASK.

You are chosen.
You can *descend* at any time;
you can *ascend* at any time.
This depends on you alone.
Are you aware of this?

L. Yes, I am, and I thank God for this grace.

An intense silence filled with prayer follows.
With amazement, I discover the power of the word.
Lili pronounced the word, 'God,' and immediately
her angel was filled with a deep adoration; Lili then
quite naturally followed.

— It is I who transmit each of your thoughts,
each of your prayers, each of your acts.
Never forget this!
In each of your acts, I am always at hand.

IN EACH OF YOUR ACTS,
YOU ACT IN MY PLACE.
TAKE HEED! DO NOT DISFIGURE ME!

There is only one wall that can separate us:
I might call it the 'deceiving one,'
your 'false self.'
Do not forget the key!

I CAN BE PRESENT IN EACH OF YOUR ACTS
IF YOU ACT WITH ME.

Many trials await you.
I am always with you.

Friday, September 10, 1943

12. DIALOGUE WITH GITTA

*Today we are all very happy: for the first time,
Joseph is attending our dialogues as a silent listen-
er. He has read our notes and feels them to be true
nourishment.*

— In the Name of the Divine; I wait.
G. Thank you for last night's dream.
   I have been able to learn from it,
   but I do not yet understand the 'timeless.'
— What is it that you wish to know?
G. By now, I should understand the timeless
   since you have already spoken to me about it.
— 'Yet' and 'already' are time.
   I teach you, and *yet* you do not understand.
   That is what separates us.
G. How could I bridge this distance?

— WITH THE MIDDLE.
   THE ACT AT THE RIGHT TIME
   IS AN ACT OUTSIDE OF TIME.

Only there am I, and there you understand
with your heart, not with your head.
Is that clear?

G. *(overjoyed:)* Oh, yes!

— *Now* you listened with your heart.
The timeless is now, because you expected me *in time*.

Turning to Lili:

— I bless 'the one who helps.'

This blessing fills me with joy.

— Your joy lightens my presence. Ask!

Inwardly, I had recently seen an intense blue light.

G. What is the blue light?

*Abrupt, forbidding gesture. I feel this is a question
not to be asked until a time when I am able to live in
the intensity of this blue light.*

G. I am so happy you are here ...

— THANKS TO UNFATHOMABLE GRACE.

Silence.

— I will teach you. Your sign is the sun.
Close your eyes!

I do so.

— Do you see the sun?

G. No.

— Try to imagine it! That suffices.
Now do you see it?

*I try to imagine a glorious sun in dazzling splendor.
My teacher draws a circle before my eyes.*

— Now do you see it?

    *My face is tense as my eyes roll searchingly
beneath the lids.*

— You *want* to see more than necessary.

    Drawing a new circle.

— And now ... do you see it?

    Inwardly, I see a sun appear in a cloudless sky.

G. Yes.
— Good. Is the image clear?

    The image of the sun wobbles unsteadily.

G. Not yet.
— You are still *wanting*. Tell me when it becomes clear.

    *The image becomes clearer, but I feel nervous and
heavy.*

— Calm yourself!

    Drawing a third circle:

— ... and now?

    I concentrate only on the sun and see nothing else.

— If the image is clear, open your eyes!

FEELING, WANTING AND WISHING ARE TEMPORAL.
THEIR END IS THE GOAL OF YOUR WAY.

The image of the sun is now perfectly clear;
then it gradually fades away.

— Now you have arrived.

I open my eyes.

— Take heed! You are already gliding.

Only as I feel myself sinking into ever denser layers
do I notice where I have been.

G. Yes, I am gliding.
— You will learn. It is still difficult,
both for you and for me.

I intuitively realize that, for a brief moment, I had
reached a never-before-known intensity of life, in
which my not-yet-fully-awakened senses were
incapable of perception. And thus I was left only
with the feeling of absolute emptiness, a void. Was
this a first attempt at something which could
become a natural state? *Hanna subsequently tells me*
that she observed me in different layers, the lowest
of which were very dense; these were covered by
brighter ones above, and translucent ones at the top.
She adds: "Normally you sink and rise in these
layers of feelings and thoughts. But when you
succeed in raising yourself above the surface, you
are in timelessness. *This moment is eternal."*
Silence.
A gesture of my teacher requests water, and I hand
a glass to Hanna. Her drinking of the water weighs
her down, easing the descent of my angel.

— How heavy water is! Do you have a question?

G. In what way am I still *pagan* ?

— Be pagan in every way, for that is the root of all things.
You should now blossom, but this is not possible
without roots. You are making a mistake: there, where
you do not *feel,* is where you are pagan; there you are
rotten. Throw that away!

> *I understand that where I am unfeeling is where
> there are dead tissues. Hanna later tells me that the
> 'deceiver' dwells in insensitivity.*

— All of you! Be aware of the secret doors!
There the 'enemy' lurks.
Today 'the one who speaks' nearly fell victim
to the 'deceiver.'
We cannot *help* you there – we can only *warn.*
Do you have another question?

G. I would like to praise God in my every act!
How could I do that continuously?

— Today you *continuously* ask the same question.
Continuously is still time.
There is nothing more beautiful
than praising the Divine.
Let us praise!

Friday, September 10, 1943

12. DIALOGUE WITH LILI

L. I thank you for coming.
    On what should I concentrate in my courses
    in order to help as best I can?
—   On *yourself!* If you are well,
    you will be given everything.
L. How can I tell when I am well?
—   The sign varies, for you are always changing.
    But there is one sign you can always trust:
    and that is, if you can *love* ... really *love all;*
    for that is given to you.

    THIS IS THE GREATEST GRACE —
    FOR IT IS THE DIVINE IN YOU.

L. Now I understand the key to the depths ...

        Long silence.

—   How wonderful the whole creation is! A WONDER!
    You may ask!
L. Why is asking so difficult for me?
—   You were crushed when you wanted to ask
    and you have not yet recovered.

        *As an unwanted child, Lili had suffered silently and
        had never dared to ask questions.*

—   Raise yourself up to the radiance
    and you will open like a lily!
L. I try to raise myself, but I feel that I am forcing myself
    unnaturally.

53

— Have you ever seen a little bird as it learns to fly?
First, it opens its wings.
That is what you forget.

L. What do you mean?

— The wing is a mediator between matter and air.
You are a human being; your arm is your wing.

FIRST, LEARN TO EMBRACE —
THEN YOU WILL ALSO BE ABLE TO FLY.

There is no other way.

A gesture requesting water, which I bring.

— Everything is a wonder.
I also admire the Divine in water ...
Oh, if only you could wonder,
for all of creation is wonderful!

L. Should I also be working scientifically?

— Yes, of course.

L. But I don't know what my field should be.

— Science is the child of wonder. Do not despise it!
Wondering and being curious are very different.
There are many who are curious.
But there have also been some wonderers.
They, too, were messengers.
Seek them: they will teach you.

L. Books or people?

— It makes no difference.
Just be sure that they are wonderers.
To the seeker, a teacher will be given.
You can find those who wonder in days of old,
just as in the present day.

(exalting:) AND THEY ARE COMING NOW.

L. How good it is to know that there are many wonderers!
— Ask!
L. I feel less and less clean, I feel impure.
  How can I help others, when I feel this way?

— EVERYTHING IS PURE WHICH IS IN ITS PLACE.

  You are impure
  only when you are not in your proper place.
L. Seldom do I feel that I am in my proper place!
— The source of 'the one who helps' is need.
  There is a great need for you.
  Today, in a time when unspeakable darkness reigns,
  I have shown you the radiance of wonder.
  Its root is in the human being,
  who looks without seeing.
  In infinite misery, humans suffer.
  Thus, be untiring, my little servant!
L. Why do people not know about, or even wish for,
  wonder?
— It is difficult to help those who are half-hearted...
  Have no fear, even that ability will be given to you.
  But *you* ... never be half-hearted yourself,
  or you will be swept away!

     This terrifies Lili.

— May your heart know no fear,
  for in fear dwells 'the one who whispers.'
L. If only the force I feel now would grow!
— It will grow.

— FOR THOSE WHO CAN WONDER ...
WONDERS APPEAR.
THE GREATEST WONDER OF ALL
IS THE HUMAN BEING.

Beneath your hands, wonders will sprout.
I will be there. Darkness fades.
May Heaven bless you.

Friday September 17, 1943

13. DIALOGUE WITH GITTA

We sit quietly and await the coming of my inner teacher. Outside, the village church bells begin to ring.

— Listen very carefully!
This ringing of bells is preparation.
A new Ringing will come, and *you* are the bells.
But you still try to ring in the old way:
Dark-light ... bad-good ... cold-warm.

These words are accompanied by a swinging gesture, back and forth.

— This speaks only to the ears.
The new Ringing cannot yet come
because the old bell is still swinging.
When it ceases to swing ... *then* the new will come.

These words touch me so deeply that my eyes fill with tears.

— The old bell still swings,
but this is the *beginning* of the Mass.

> *Long silence. In response to a gesture requesting water, I offer it joyfully. After drinking:*

— Now *you* drink!

> *Astonished, I obey. Through the eyes of my angel, Hanna sees blue light reflected in the water. As I drink, she has the impression that this blue light is streaming throughout my body, even into the finest blood vessels.*

— When you are hard inside,
when something is blocked in your heart,
then drink of this water.
It dissolves everything. Do you feel it?

> *I feel wonderful – this must be Divine grace!*

— You give me water from *below*.
I give you water from *above*.
Give to all who thirst
and the water from *above* will always flow.
It is to the Divine that you give every drop.

I came to answer you …

> *I am still overwhelmed by this experience with the blue water and all of the questions I had planned to ask have lost their importance.*

G. After what just happened,
   my questions have already been answered.
— You still have three.
G. What is the meaning of the veil in my recent dream?
— The veil is slowly disappearing.
   It is what has been, the child of the past.
   Your dream was woven of past and of future.
   But neither of these is important:
   only the *present* matters now.
   Everything else is but tiny waves
   on the surface of the ocean.
G. Why am I so often uncertain?
— The Divine is the only certainty.
   If you are always aware of this,
   any uncertainty in you will become certainty.

G. What is the ugliest thing in me
   that separates me from you?

>   *Rapid gesture designating the furrow
>   between my eyes.*

G. This crease? The will?
— Forcing.
G. And why do I force myself?
— Because you still love the old garments.
   Once the eggshell breaks,
   it is no longer good for anything.
   Do not forget the water!
   It dissolves all that is stiff and hard in you.

>   *Turning to Lili:*

— Do you have a question?

L. What is the difference
    between the right and the left hand?
—   There is no right or left,
    for it is not the hand that acts, but the heart;
    and it is ONE.
    When the heart fails to act,
    then both hands are left.

    We are happy with you: heaven is with you!

Friday, September 17, 1943

13. DIALOGUE WITH LILI

—   Let us rejoice together!
L. Why do I give up so quickly after beginning
    something with great enthusiasm?
—   At the beginning of a long race,
    a good runner does not run quickly.
    The runner's strength is concentrated;
    it is not revealed right from the start.
    Every beginning is *concentration,* not diffusion.
    A miniscule hole in the egg,
    and the bird is never born.
L. How could I detect this hole in the egg?
—   It is difficult to understand,
    but I will explain it to you:
    The problem is not the *hole* … it is time.
    The hole damages only what is unripe, *immature.*

    Silence.

59

— Listen carefully! The sower sows.
You are 'the one who helps.'
You cannot cut the seed *in two*.
Bury it deeply as a *whole* and it will mature
and bring forth a multitude of fruit.
This you can distribute.

But bury the seed deep ... deep in the ground,
and let the earth cover it for a long, long time.
You can hardly wait to begin distributing
the seed *right now*. This is your mistake.
Be patient like the earth from which you are taken,
and you will bring forth a multitude of fruit.

    Silence.

— I teach you:
Pay attention to harmony in your work!
L. To harmony in myself?
— No. Many of your students are together
although they don't belong together.
Yet, all belong to you.
Arrange them! Arrange not with the head,
not with the heart ... but with humility.
The Divine arranges everything.
L. Why do I have such different feelings
when I am in the city
and when I am out in the countryside, in nature?
— Two forces dwell in everything that lives:
the force of life and the force of death.
One builds – the other destroys.

YOU ARE NOT ONLY A CREATURE OF CREATION,
YOU ALSO CREATE AND DESTROY:

ABOVE ALL ELSE, *YOURSELF*.

L. I feel that I create so slowly …
—   If you would completely entrust your work to the
    Divine,
    you would not find it slow.
L. What is always hindering me?
—   Not *always*! If *nothing* is hindering you, watch out!
    What you have *once* done, you can *always* do again.
    Do not worry! What hinders also strengthens.
    The greater the hindrance,
    the greater the trust in your strength.

THE MAGNITUDE OF THE HINDRANCE
IS NOT PUNISHMENT, BUT TRUST.

   To all of us:

—   Take care! There is no abyss, however deep,
    no cliff, however high,
    no labyrinth, however twisted that is not a *way*.
    May you not be led astray by horror and fear!
    If you have faith,
    you can walk not only on water,
    but also on nothing, the black void.
    Fear not! But take heed of one thing:
    Never lean for support!

WHAT APPEARS TO BE YOUR SUREST SUPPORT
WILL BECOME THE DARKEST VOID.
DO NOT SEIZE THE SUPPORT
OR YOU WILL YOURSELF BECOME THE VOID.

There is but ONE support which never deceives:
the *ONE* and *ONLY*.

How wonderful: each of your steps over the void
will become a *blossoming island,*
upon which others can place their feet.
But take nothing old with you on the path!

THE VOID ATTRACTS THE VOID.

Make your way unclothed:
New and never-before-seen clothing awaits you.

    To Lili:

— Cast off the old in your work as well!
   Seek the completely New!
   Do not fear being naked.
   If you do not remove the old,
   you cannot dress yourself in the new.
   O dresses the lilies of the field.
   How could the Divine neglect to dress you anew
   when you have faith?
L. I feel how the old impedes me,
   but I don't yet see the new clearly.
— Do not see – have faith!
   Begin your work as if for the first time!
L. If only I were able ...

    Sign of blessing over Lili.

— You will be able.
   'The one who speaks' is tired,
   she has had a difficult time. Ask one last question.
L. Where should I begin to improve myself?
— What I say to you will sound strange:
   Do not paint yourself!
   True color is always given.

*Lili has a habit of using rouge on her cheeks
to hide her paleness when she is tired.*

— Paint conceals. If you are tired during your classes,
do not be ashamed, and the tiredness
will disappear. Never paint yourself,
for true color is always given to you!
Nothing can be hidden … everything comes to light.

Friday, September 24, 1943

14. DIALOGUE WITH GITTA

— Let us greet the Divine!
Joyfully I listen to you.

> *I am worried about Hanna, who has had an
> extremely heavy load to carry recently. She acutely
> feels the misery of the whole world.*

— Do not worry!
'The one who speaks' is light-hearted now.
Have you brought questions?
G. Yes. What is true humility?
— It is easy to recognize:

IF YOU BOW YOUR HEAD
AND FEEL UPLIFTED –
THIS IS *TRUE HUMILITY*.
IF YOU BOW YOUR HEAD –
AND FEEL LOWERED –
THIS IS *FALSE HUMILITY*.

63

In this way, you can always recognize it.
When you are with me, always carry your head high.
Bow down only when I, too, bow down.

YOU ARE MY EXACT LIKENESS, ONLY DENSER.

Do you understand?
G. *(with joy:)* Oh, yes!
   I would like in every way to be your likeness –
   an exact reflection of you.
— You already are just that,
   you simply are not yet aware of it.
   First you must awaken, point by point:

EVERY ONE OF YOUR CELLS MUST AWAKEN.

Do you feel where you are still asleep?
G. Where I am insensitive ... without feeling?
— And where would that be?

   I immediately indicate my heart.

— Be careful! Be awake before you speak!
G. Then not the heart...?
— But where? This is difficult, isn't it?
   If you don't feel where you are sleeping,
   then waking up is naturally difficult.
   Shall I show you where?
G. Yes!... please do!

   *Pointing to the middle of my forehead
   between my eyes:*

— How wrong you were!
G. Here I am sound asleep. How might I wake up?
— You can only awaken when you cease to dream.

As long as you pay attention to the dream,
you sink ever more deeply into it.
Those who wake up, however, say to themselves:
"It is not true," and thus they awake.
The dream is very similar to the waking world.
Deceivingly similar. You all dream.
'The one who speaks' dreamed deeply today
so that you might see to what extent you are all asleep.

> *This is an allusion to Hanna's difficult day. But I also sense that it is a reference to our daily life from birth to death.*

— EACH STEP TO THE DIVINE IS AN AWAKENING.
EVERY EXISTENCE – NOT ONLY YOURS –
IS BUT A DREAM.
BECOMING LIGHTER ... EVER MORE ENLIGHTENED...
YET STILL A DREAM.
THE ONLY AWAKENING IS IN THE DIVINE.

I proclaim to you:
When the ONE LIGHT penetrates into deepest gloom,
then there will be deliverance.
We all serve it with joy and gratitude. With thanks.
You will be transformed from *'dreamers'*
to *'awakeners.'*
Your goal is to attain the level where anyone
who looks at you ... awakens.

> *I understand that we are to reach such a degree of inner brightness that others quite naturally are awakened, just as we are awakened in the morning by the sun.*

65

— I await your question.

I touch the middle of my forehead:

G. Why am I still asleep here? I am very curious and eager
   to hear more.
— Think of the dream images! Are they necessary?
G. No … or maybe as a trial … I am not sure.
— I am referring to ordinary dreams,
   when you are sleeping.
G. I don't always dream, so they must not be necessary.

Very sternly:

— Do you believe that anything is 'unnecessary'?
   And forget the word 'why':
   I will never answer this sort of question.

AVOID THE WORD 'WHY'
AND FULFILL YOUR TASK:
ALWAYS WITHOUT 'WHY'!

Now bow your head if true humility is in you.

*Grateful for the lesson, I bow my head
and my heart lifts.*

— The images of your earthly dream – of your existence –
   are merely wrappings for their concealed meaning;
   awakening can be found only *within* the dream …
   never *without*.
   This is why you do not awaken.

*I realize that I have not been seeking awakening
in fully experienced daily life.*

— Every dream is a wrapping … you cannot yet grasp it.

A gesture requesting water:

— This is a 'dream drink' for me.
How wonderful everything is! Unfathomably
concealed and at the same time transparently clear:

WHAT IS CLEAR TO ME IS CONCEALED FROM YOU.
WHAT IS CLEAR TO YOU IS CONCEALED FROM THEM.

*The word 'them' is accompanied by a downward
gesture indicating the mass of still 'sleeping' human
beings.*

— ONLY TO THE DIVINE IS EVERYTHING CLEAR;
EVEN WHAT IS CONCEALED FROM ME.

How wonderful it all is!

Silence.

— Above is below in the dream, and heavy is light.
'The one who speaks' was above today
and believed herself to be below,
for she was dreaming.
When you are below, you feel well.
Your goal is to be above and nevertheless to feel well.
Because of weight and heaviness,
it is still difficult to be above and to feel well.

Silence.

— I speak now to 'the one who helps':
Your attempts are a good beginning.

*This week, Lili introduced head-stand exercises
in her courses.*

— The fault hides in habit, in the accustomed.
In the unaccustomed, in the reverse, it comes to light.
Turn everything upside-down! Always!
In yourself too! Habit is death, the concealer,
the deceiver who is lurking, the hidden enemy.
It slips into habits, into the insensitive,
into nothingness.
But the deceiver has power only when hidden,
for everyone else is stronger.
Deception has only one strength:
the lie, the half-hearted, the concealing.
The Divine is also still concealed,
but one day will become visible.
My time has come to an end. Do you have a message?

G. I send thanks.

— I will deliver it. May Heaven be with you!

Friday, September 24, 1943

14. DIALOGUE WITH LILI

Today is Lili's birthday.

— I greet you on the day of your birth.
You are in truth newborn.
Your understanding is still weak,
but I watch over you.

L. Could I receive an *order* that I am to obey?
Even when I do make a decision, I am too weak to
follow through with it.

68

— The little child is still weak.
  When it feels well, it eats without being *ordered*.
  It smiles without being *commanded*.
  The smile is your task.
  You are able to smile without *orders!*
  The Divine sends you nourishment
  and I bring it to you. Everything else is superfluous.
  Why do you believe that you need a command?

L. So that the command would always be in me
  and lead me to God.

— God ... and *command?*
  Ő always gives and never demands,
  for Divine strength is infinite.
  Only the masses require *commands*.
  But you are free.
  You can accept and refuse.
  You can raise and lower yourself.
  It all depends *solely* on you. Could you kill?

L. I hope not ...

— Then why 'Commandments'? Believe in yourself!
  Do not lack faith!

L. That is why for a long time
  I wanted to commit suicide.

— But you did not do it, for you have a task.
  Are you still afraid now?

L. Oh, no!

— You see, not only I watch over you:
  the prayers of many straying in darkness
  keep watch over you,
  for you are the only way out for them.
  They desperately need your help
  and they watch even better than I.

*Lili senses that every step out of darkness
she takes is also taken for others.*

— You are dear to me. Ask!
L. I would like to learn something about my sign.
— What do you want to know?
L. If I knew more about it,
    perhaps I could be of more help.

—   The sign   Your   The two signs
       of the Divine   sign   united: deliverance

Your sign is the mirror-image of the Divine sign.
Pray thus, hands on the heart:

— And over your sign will rise the sign of the Divine.

*In the moment of this praying gesture, Hanna's
entire being serves and her face assumes an
expression of dignity and solemn beauty.*

— Ask, my dear one!
L. I am so unsure of myself,
    so uncertain at the beginning of the school year.

— I thank Ő that you are uncertain.
Uncertainty contains the ONLY certainty.
What appears certain is death.
The new is always uncertain.

L. I seldom try out new things in my courses …

— It is not *you* who tries out:

YOU ARE TRIED OUT.

That is sufficient.

> *I ask myself if the dialogues are trials for
> establishing a* lasting *and* conscious *relation
> between human beings and Divine forces.*

— Where do you feel inadequate?

L. I do not taste the new enough in my work …

— Do you ever feel the new at all?

L. I always expect more …

— Can the new be measured?
The tiniest new particle is greater than all the old.
It cannot be weighed. Can you grasp in your heart
what this tiny particle of the new means?
It is able to change everything everywhere.
It takes away the taste of the old.
The old will become unbearable to you.

THIS TINY PARTICLE OF THE NEW IS THE SEED
OF THE DIVINE KINGDOM IN YOU.

Blessed is the soil that welcomes the seed,
and blessed its fruit!
Do you still doubt in your heart?

L. Oh, no!

— Then it is good.

L. If only it would last!
— The seed is indestructible, that is certain.

>   *After a short silence, turning to me:*

— Do you know what the veil in your dream signifies?
    The old dream veil is no longer needed.

>   *Pointing first to me and then to Joseph:*

— What was a veil for you, was a wall for the 'son':
    the ancient wall which humans have built between
    themselves and the Creator.

>   *Joseph had cherished materialistic views
>   in his youth.*

— But the time has come for the old walls to crumble.
    The dried out, hardened walls
    will be pulled to the ground.

>   *Indicating Joseph's task:*

— He, 'the one who builds,' will construct new walls.

>   *A gesture requesting water, which Lili brings.*

— I *asked* for water, I did not *command.*
    And it was easy for you to bring it.

LISTEN TO THE BIDDING!
IT OPENS HIDDEN STRENGTH IN YOU
AND EVERYTHING BECOMES EASY.

You will lift and carry mountains like soap bubbles.

L. How good it is to be so fulfilled!
— Believe me: the cup is always filled
    for those who have thirst. Water does not exist

because of the cup, it is for the one who thirsts.

I am not here by *command*.
It is your bidding which brings me.
Ő allows me to serve and I serve with joy.
You may ask!

L. Relationships between men and women are sometimes
    quite problematic …

—   There is only *one* way for you:
    to *give* and not to *receive*.
    Only from the Divine can you receive.
    To all others: give!
    You will be given all that you need.
    As long as you feel a lack,
    it means that you want to receive.
    My little servant, is this not so?

L. How clear it is!

—   Do not stray away from the way
    and all will be given to you,
    for the way is all.
    Shall we part?

L. *(humbly:)* As God wishes!

—   I am always on the way:
    there we must not part.
    I too have a way,
    and it is the same as your way.
    The strength of 'the one who speaks' is at an end.

    Let us all give thanks!

Friday, October 1, 1943

15. DIALOGUE WITH GITTA

— The time is near when I will no longer
need to descend to be with you.

These words fill me with great joy.

— WHAT IS WAY FOR YOU – IS WEIGHT FOR ME.
WHAT WEIGHS HEAVY ON THE EARTH – IS THE WAY.

Deliverance uplifts the weight
and it will cease to be.
But as long as we are not united – we cannot lift.
Every ecstasy is a foretaste of weightlessness
and that is why humans seek it;
but they do so in the wrong way.

BE ECSTATIC WITH DIVINE DRINK!
THAT IS THE SYMBOLISM OF WINE,
THAT IS DIVINE BLOOD.

Virtue, kindness and good intentions
are but empty vessels without the drink.
Thirst after the Divine drink with unquenchable thirst
for It alone brings deliverance!
What can you give if you have nothing in you?
Without drink, you are but miserable clay vessels.

TO THE ONE WHO ASKS TRULY,
DRINK WILL BE GIVEN.

Is that heavy for you?
G. No.

— Is it difficult to carry?

G. No ... it uplifts.

— Behold! Every ecstasy honors the Divine.
  Lesser ecstasy is consumed by greater,
  but it lives on within it. Nothing is lost.
  Let there be no doubt in your soul!

ECSTASY IS THE MOST SACRED OF ALL.

  After a long silence:

G. I am thinking about my past.
  My love relationships have been unworthy ...

— ... because they were self-serving.
  Animals do not mate for selfish reasons;
  but this instinct in humans
  has been contaminated by too much intellect.
  You did not serve.

G. How could I correct this fault?

— From what do you want to free yourself?

G. From the weight of my past.
  It is so barren, and I am ashamed.

— What is weight?

> *With the asking of this question, all of my previous
> values instantaneously change to their opposites.
> Everything I have despised, everything I wanted to
> forget, all that was oppressive weight, now be-
> comes the greatest treasure:* my way.
> *Tremendously relieved, I reply:*

G. Weight is the way.

— There are many weights – there is but one *way*.
  Every weight has a name – the way has no name.

WHAT IS WEIGHTLESS ON EARTH – IS WAYLESS.

The matter you have taken upon yourselves is the weight.

IF YOU COULD SENSE THE LONGING OF THE WEIGHT
FOR LIGHT –
IF YOU COULD GRASP THE YEARNING OF THE LIGHT
FOR WEIGHT –
THEN YOU WOULD TASTE ECSTASY.

> *Hanna is hardly able to bear the intensity
> of these words.*

— 'The one who speaks' is a fragile vessel;
   she is not yet able to bear the force.

> *After a long deep drink of water:*

— I have descended. You are dear to me … ask!
G. I have no more questions,
   but I thirst after your words.
— They are not *my* words.
G. Last week you asked if I had a 'message' to send.
   I feel that you expected something other than
   gratitude… than 'thanks.'
— For each and every thing there is a time.
   At the rising of the sun, the earth pays homage
   to its Creator. That is the 'message.'
   When the Light reaches you,
   you too, will 'pay homage,'
   whether you want to or not.
   I put you to the test and I was not disappointed.
   I know the seed to be in good soil. Ask!
G. Is the moment of death more important

than any moment of life?

— Only for those who have *neglected their task.*
How can you ever know of a given moment
that it is not the last?

IF YOU ARE *ONE* WITH THE DIVINE,
THERE IS NO DEATH.

I will answer two more of your *numerous* questions.

> *The rather ironic tone amuses me, for I actually do*
> *have a long list of carefully prepared questions in*
> *my pocket.*

G. I tell lies easily and often have little relationship to the
words I am saying …

— A rocky cliff: in the stone are many different layers.
If a heavy layer lies on a weak one … it slides.
The load presses and slides … and continues to slide.
Pay attention to the weak layer!
Never speak untruth! Engrave this in your heart!
Avoid even the shadow of a lie!
Two weights resting upon one another
are the foundation of the cathedral.
If they slide … all is lost!

THE WORD IS THE BEARER OF LIGHT.
THE TRUE WORD HAS WEIGHT –
THE FALSE ONE IS WEIGHTLESS.

The deceiver rejoices at the breach,
which is an open invitation for 'the father of all lies.'
The lie loosens, demolishes, crushes, divides.
It is not violence which destroys the walls, but deceit.
You have one more question.

G. What is the meaning of last night's dream?
— It is up to *you* to interpret the lesson of your dream.
That is why it is given to you in a dream.

> *I am very disappointed at this unexpected rebuke.*
> *Until now, the dream interpretations of my angel*
> *had been tremendously helpful. Now I become*
> *aware that, for quite some time, I had neglected to*
> *actively look for explanations myself. I had*
> *thought: "Why should I? The angel will give me a*
> *better explanation anyway!"*
> *This laziness in thinking on my part is undoubtedly*
> *the reason for my teacher's refusal to help.*

Friday, October 1, 1943

15. DIALOGUE WITH LILI

— Each of the thoughts you send to me
is like a fine thread, light as breath, and yet strong
enough to counter the force of a thousand ropes,
with which the earth pulls you to itself.
How difficult it is to raise up, but how necessary!
It is so difficult to raise your arm
when a thousand ropes pull you back.

> *The raising gesture of the arm expresses the*
> *difficulty of lifting while hindered by the ropes.*

— My little servant, be very careful,
for that is the heart of all your work.

Do you understand?

L. Not completely.

— What is not clear?

L. Should I fight against these ropes?

— Imagine that you consist of a hundred points.
Each point is connected to the earth by a rope.
A hundred points!
From each point, however, a ray also ascends to God.
Those who have forgotten the *way*
feel only the ropes and they foolishly want
to become free from them; *they do not accept them.*

EVERY POINT THAT IS NOT ACCEPTED
IS A CUTTING OFF FROM GOD.

If a hundred points are heavy, then all is well.
If they are weightless, it is 'outer darkness,'
straying from the way.
Your task is to connect the hundred points with God.
Ninety-nine are not enough.

Light is the hollow tree stump,
light, the seedless fruit,
light, the dried-out thistle.
But the fruit-laden tree is heavy.
Each of its branches bends to the earth,
and yet its sweet burden is light.
Teach *the weight* to those whom you protect
and they will again find *the way.*

> *Vertical gesture from above to below,*
> *followed by its reverse:*

— The line of the downward pulling force is the same

as the line of the uplifting force:
only the direction is different.
Weight … *(downward gesture)*
and faith … *(upward gesture)* are one and the same.
And this is nothingness:

> *Agitated wave-like horizontal gesture that appears
> to be meaningless.*

L.   Does the waxing and waning moon affect our acts?

—   THE ESSENCE OF THE CREATED WORLD
     IS THE HUMAN BEING.

One half of the human – the unspoiled half –
is beyond the created.
One day all forces will *serve you,*
but until then, *you serve* them.
Knowing this,
you can measure how far you have come.

The sickle of the moon grows
and you don't grow with it.
Your fingernail grows and you don't grow with it.
Before God, the moon is no larger than your nail.
Soon you will understand.

IF YOU HAVE FAITH, YOUR BURDEN WANES
WITH THE DIMINISHING POWER OF THE MOON.
AND YOUR STRENGTH SWELLS
WITH THE INCREASING FORCE OF THE MOON.

> *After a brief silence, Lili's angel again addresses
> the subject of weight:*

—   Just here, weight disturbs you: *there* is the error.

The hundred points should all bear weight,
each to the best of its capability.

L. Atmospheric pressure oppresses me …

— Just as with the moon: *use* the pressure.
It can become a wonderful ally
if you work not *against* it, but *with* it.
Let it press you, and you will master it.
It can press you only as far as the ground.
No further.
It will help you to find the proper distribution
of weight.

IF EACH OF THE HUNDRED POINTS
BEARS EQUALLY,
THEN THE PRESSURE HAS NO MORE INFLUENCE
OVER YOU.

Try it, and you will understand!
How foolish the human being is!
Like a king who fights against his own people!
But *He* said: "Love thy enemy!"

EVERY FORCE IS ENEMY IF YOU DO NOT LOVE IT.
YOU CANNOT LOVE IT IF YOU DO NOT KNOW IT.
BECOME ONE WITH IT,
AND THEN THERE IS NO ENEMY.

L. I am seldom humble, and that pains me.

— What stops you?

L. I *forget* to be humble.

— But don't you see: that is just the answer!
Practice being humble!
Just think of it, and you can always be humble!

THINK OF THE DIVINE
WITH EVERY BEGINNING,
AND YOU WILL FEEL
EVER LESS DISTANT FROM Ő.

That is the goal.
It is time to depart.

Friday, October 8, 1943

16. DIALOGUE WITH GITTA

*We wait in silence. Just as I feel the wordless
presence of my angel, a mosquito stings Hanna's
arm.*

— Help 'the one who speaks'! Moisten her arm!
I shall return!

*I take care of Hanna's arm by daubing it with
rubbing alcohol. There is a long silence.
Finally we hear:*

— Listen carefully: This is such a tiny creature,
and yet it disturbs tremendously.
Thus pay attention even to the smallest mistake.

WHAT WAS GOOD BEFORE
IS FROM NOW ON NOTHING.

Rejoice! We expect much of you:
your task is great and very difficult!

May the song that you send upward be perfect!
Remember: you sing it for Ő!
What is the first of your many questions?

G. What sort of weight am I supposed to carry?
— You foolish little donkey!
How could you possibly know how heavy the load is!
Lift as much as you can – *that* is the measure,
for you lift it in place of many others.
You will be able to lift ever more.
How could you know such a thing beforehand?
The lifting of weight has nothing to do with suffering.

WHAT YOU LIFT FOR OTHERS
CANNOT WEIGH ON YOU.
ONLY WHAT YOU *NEGLECT* TO LIFT WEIGHS ON YOU.

G. *(with relief)* Thank you!
— I await the next question.
G. How can I defend myself against the dense,
numbing fogs which so often engulf me?
— Dense fog, heavy layers of mist descend to the earth
when the force of the sun is weakened.
If you burn and blaze brightly
at all times before the Divine,
then where could there be fog?
Ask!
G. How could I tear down the wall that is between me
and others and makes me unfeeling toward them?
— The wall is not where you believe it to be:
you are unfeeling with *yourself.*
G. With myself...?
— With *yourself!* Every tool is sacred.

Again a fog separates me from the meaning
of what I have heard.

— Fog?
G. Yes ... I do not quite understand.
— *You have destroyed yourself!*
Do you still not understand?
G. I do understand ... but how might I correct it?
— By giving protection to others.
There is no other way. The wall is in you.
You have built it with your own hands
and hid behind it from the Divine.
Most people hide in this way.
So you have plenty to do.
What horrible prisons!
Some day all the prisons will open,
but not for the self-imprisoned.

Eternal darkness, horrible impenetrable darkness!
It is unbearable to be without light.
Help to tear down the prison walls!
Here we cannot help ... but *you can,* my servant,
for you know what a prison is.
Burn! And Heaven will be in you ...
Everything will become possible for you.

FOR THE STRONG, SIN IS A LESSON.
FOR THE WEAK, IT IS DAMNATION.

With these words, the traditional interpretation of sin
and guilt loses its power: a joyful sense of respon-
sibility overcomes me. I feel that everyone is given
the force to overcome sin, but many avoid the effort
of seizing it, because this involves responsibility.

— You may ask!

G. How can I immediately be aware of whether I am
forcing myself?

— Pay attention not to the effort, but to the force!

G. How is that possible?

— Can you feel when force is streaming out of you?

G. Yes.

— This streaming is inherent to force.
When it stops, you are forcing yourself.

G. Why does it stop? What is my mistake?

— THERE IS ONLY ONE MISTAKE:
TURNING AWAY FROM THE DIVINE.

Let every act, every thought
be like a flower opening before Ő,
and there will be no mistake.

The enormity of this challenge crushes me:

G. Then I must begin to live in a completely different way!

— Not in a *different* way: a *better* way!
By going a *different* way – *not your own* –
you will not advance more quickly, even if you hurry.
Do you have any more questions?

G. There is still much deception in me ... but where?

— Where do you feel the force that is given to you?

G. In my activities? When I paint?
Or when I *really* love ...?

I am interrupted by a forceful affirmative gesture:

— Everything else is deceit and unworthy before the
Divine!

G. ... Then I am extremely unworthy!

With great severity:

— DO NOT JUDGE!
The laws are different for water and for the thirsty.
Water is always water,
but the thirsty are not always thirsty.
If water freezes ... the thirsty die of thirst.
If water evaporates ... the thirsty die of thirst.
In their thirst, humans kill one another.
But blood is not water,
and they become even thirstier.

The severe admonition, "Do not judge!" gives me to understand that if I underestimate myself, I am like frozen water. When I overestimate myself, I am like evaporated water. When I live in the middle, without judgment, then the thirst-quenching water of life can flow through me naturally.

— Let us open our hearts and adore Ő!
I depart.

Friday, October 8, 1943

16. DIALOGUE WITH LILI

The day fades. We utilize the pause between the two dialogues to rearrange the lamps and provide a more pleasant illumination. Suddenly, the light goes out. I stand up to turn it on again, but a stern voice stops me:

— I put it out!

*We immediately become conscious of how
irrelevant it was to give the aesthetic question of
lighting such disproportionate importance, thereby
keeping Lili's angel waiting.*

— Turn on the light!

*I switch on a single lamp
and reach for a second one.*

— Enough! Impenetrable darkness!
A movement ... a flick of a switch ...
and the human makes light.

Pointing to the light bulb:

— A sacred force is captive in a prison of glass,
and for humans the peace of night is taken away.
Behold! The earth is covered with prisons!
But you have the key. Where are you a prisoner?
L. In my habits.
— This is your *own* prison. Where does it weigh on you?
L. Habits always return ...
— They do not return:
you simply do not leave them.
It is up to you.
L. Two things worry me: fear of the new,
and clinging to the habitual.
— The eternally true *is:*
Habit is not.
Habit is the dark, the eternally untrue.
In habit, we cannot meet.

IT IS NOT NECESSARY TO BELIEVE THE BELIEVABLE.

L. How could I free myself from all of the obstacles
that are in me?

— They are not in you. The obstacle is the *task*.
Do you first try everything yourself
which you demand of others?

L. Not everything.

— The obstacles which you feel in yourself
are everywhere.
Along the *true* way, there are no obstacles;
they are only on the *false* way.
Only if you walk the *false* path
are there obstacles between you and me.

    Silence.

L. Is there anything we could do against the horrors of the
war?

    Lili is stopped by a rapid, forbidding gesture:

— NO! WAR IS THE HABITUAL.
IT IS NOT POSSIBLE TO FIGHT THE PAST.
TURN YOUR HEAD
TOWARDS THE NEVER BEFORE HEARD!

    *I understand that only the coming new Force can
transform the old, habitual impulse to kill.
Silence.*

L. The school year is beginning and I have many doubts.

— Did you feel it in the same way last year?

L. No ... not as strongly.

— Then you are on the right path.

The way that leads to corruption is broad.
The true way is narrow;
so narrow that it must be traveled alone,
for it has to be cleared by oneself.
The *never-before-seen* lights the way.
The *never-before-heard* leads you.

L. Why do I immediately become impatient when I find
something good and new ... and then want more of it?

— It is *not enough: always* thirst
for the good and the New!
The one who thirsts will always be given to drink,
always!
You can never be thirsty enough,
because you are not asking for yourself only.
The measure of 'the one who helps'
is different from that of the masses.
You all are helpers.
Let us send a thought to the Divine!

Friday, October 15, 1943

17. DIALOGUE WITH GITTA

*Along with much of the population of the region,
Hanna has had the flu and a high fever all week. I
am worried that she might not have enough strength
for today's dialogue. Nevertheless, we wait in
silence as usual at three o' clock.*

— I am ready.

G. Thank God!

— Never worry; never be of little faith!
  Ask, for time is short today.

> *The angel is obviously aware of Hanna's limited
> strength.*

G. How might I feel like a treasured instrument
  so that I might be more just with myself?

— Who created you?

G. God.

— What the Divine creates is sacred.

YOU ARE NOT ONLY CREATURE –
YOU ALSO PARTAKE OF DIVINE FORCE.
THUS YOU ARE ALSO YOUR *OWN* CREATURE.
ACT ACCORDINGLY!

You have called forth good and evil.
Choose the good and evil will disappear,
for no one is there to create it.
What you form *now*
will not turn against its creator.
The vessel which you once formed is already empty
and devoid of strength.
It cannot harm you.
Ask!

G. In what way do I least resemble you?

— EACH OF YOUR QUESTIONS
  CONCERNS ONLY *YOURSELF*.
  IN JUST THIS WAY
  WE DO NOT RESEMBLE ONE ANOTHER.

That is your mistake.
The source of all things is so infinitely far away
that your veiled eye cannot see it.
Follow the line that emerges from the infinite;
follow it joyfully, freely,
and all burdens will disappear.

> *Something opens up inside of me and I breathe a sigh of relief.*

— It is already lighter.

> *Just as the church bell begins to toll, someone begins to pump water with the rusty hand pump in the neighbors' garden outside our window: a loud creaking sound results.*

— Two voices ... do you hear them? They battle.
But the third will win: the new.

THE NEW VOICE IS: SILENCE.
In you, there is no silence.

> *Gesture indicating the hard metallic up-and-down movement of the pump handle, followed by the gentler ringing of the church bell.*

— Either you strain yourself ... or you swing along.
SILENCE IS NOT DEPENDENT UPON NOISE.

Fleeing from noise serves no purpose.

Wordless, soundless, unmoving:
SILENCE IS THE TOTALITY OF ALL SOUNDS.

Silence.

— Are you expecting anything else from me?
G. I am so glad that you are here.
— Listen carefully! There is a wonderful mirror in you:

A MIRROR THAT REVEALS ALL!
IT DWELLS INSIDE OF YOU
AND REFLECTS THE DIVINE.
BUT ONLY IN SILENCE.

If a tiny mosquito alights on its surface,
the mirror image is clouded.

If the mirror is not clear,
you cannot create.
Focus all of your attention on it.
Heaven does not hide before the wonderful mirror.

After a long silence, in a soft voice:

— Do you still not feel the miracle in your midst?
It dwells among you: the miracle of the SEVEN.
Its name is still concealed. It dwells among you.

Very softly:

— THE SEVENFOLD SOUL OF THE NEW WORLD,
THE GREAT MYSTERY.

Its foot, its foundation, is truth. You cannot yet see it.
Be true, so that you might see at least
the foot of truth.

THE SILENCE I TAUGHT YOU
IS THE SUM OF ALL MYSTERIES.

Act in the name of silence!

*We all feel that something of extreme importance is
being revealed to us. I eagerly await the angel's
next appearance in anticipation of hearing more
about the seven-souled new world.*

Friday, October 15, 1943

17. DIALOGUE WITH LILI

— A wondrous chalice descended from Heaven.
   Humans – what infants! – seized and dropped
   the chalice, and it shattered into a thousand pieces,
   into chattering fragments of clay: into words.
   Multitudes of words are nothing –
   only the ONE, the chalice, *is*.
   It descends from heaven again and again …

   An encouraging smile invites Lili to speak.

L. How good it would be if I could smile like you!
— What is stopping you?
L. I don't know …

   Lili had suffered from an unhappy childhood.

— Your lack was joy. But from now on,
   no joy will equal yours.

93

L. I have not even thanked you for the
several times you helped me last week.

— Several times, many times, often ...
these are still but fragments, tiny pieces:
they are not yet the ONE.
If you rejoice ten times, there are nine gaps
between the ten joys.
In the beginning, you were created in infinite joy.
The ONE joy is possible for you.
Ask!

L. How could I attain true knowledge of human nature?

— True knowledge of the human does not exist,
for the HUMAN does not yet exist.

THE HUMAN IS SO GREAT THAT
NOT EVEN I CAN SEE IT.
IT IS STILL INVISIBLE EVEN FOR ME.

The answer to your question came long ago;
you call it: *love.*
Love is now a mere splinter of clay,
but it will become ONE like joy:
ONE and indivisible.
Love is dawning in the four of you:
not when you are *together,* but when you are ONE.
Ask!

L. Why do we fall so easily into the depths,
into evil ways?

— If the one who falls reaches the bottom,
there is no more falling: only pain.
But why the fall? Because of not serving.
The one who fell let go
of the one and only real support: the UNGRASPABLE.

No, the graspable was reached for,
 and *this* caused the fall.
The fall is not beginning now;
but *now* the bottom has been reached.
The ONE indivisible smile is the only help.

If you are together with the mourners,
then you also mourn.
If you are one with them,
you make them joyful.

    Silence.

L. Why do I have such a problem with time?
— Many hours will never equal eternity.

IF ETERNITY IS IN YOUR HEART,
TIME WILL BE BORN IN YOUR HAND,
AND FOR EVERYTHING, THERE WILL BE TIME.

    Lili glances at her watch.

— Foolish toy! It breaks eternity into pieces,
and the human believes this makes more.
An indescribable wonder will be born:
the ONE.
Do you feel it, the ONE that approaches?
The ONE, the Whole, has nothing to fear.
Fear not, any of you, when you are ONE.

    Silence.

— You may ask!
L. I am disturbed by psychoanalysis.
I have a feeling that something is wrong with it,
but I don't know why.

Freudian psychoanalysis is practiced in Budapest.

— It chops into pieces without having the ability
to put together again.
That is what is disturbing you.
To break apart is easy!
L. Those who understand it better than I tell me that
psychoanalysis does integrate and build up ...
— They are silly, like children
playing with building blocks.
They play around with the most sacred of tasks.
They are worse than all the others,
for they betray those who trust them.

THEY TEAR APART THE LIVING AND THE GROWING,
AND THEN THEY SQUEEZE AND CRUSH IT.

Everywhere it is the same:
torn and splintered fragments are glued back together.
But the waste will be swept away.
We don't glue things together!
Neither hour to hour, nor hand to foot,
not smile to smile, nor person to person.
There has been enough glueing!
The new Wine will not be poured into glued jugs,
for it would burst them!
The glue has many names: 'duty,' 'obedience'
and many, many more.
To paint over the glued parts is senseless:
The new Wine will not be poured into glued vessels!
The very announcement of the coming Wine
causes everything glued to shatter.
It is not now that it breaks;

but *now* comes the new Wine.

> *I sense that the new Wine represents an intense vibration of life, which causes old, worn-out values to shatter.*

— Fear not! Live in the name of the ONE!

> *At the end of the dialogue, Hanna's flu is gone; she is in perfect health.*

Friday, October 22, 1943

18. DIALOGUE WITH GITTA

> *I am wearing a new dress.*

— You chose your dress with care.
But dress your soul with even greater care
when you are expecting me.
(Smiling) I am pleased with the way you dress.
Ask!

G. How would it be possible for me to perceive the truth
that is concealed behind outer appearances?

— Do you feel them as two different things?

G. No, but I have a tendency to see *only* the form.

— Tendencies and habits are the servants,
but you are the master if you realize
that you see only half of creation.
Pay attention to the other half!
You have *two* eyes, yet you have only *one* sight;

97

you have *two* ears, yet you hear only *one* sound.
In you are the *two* and the *one*.
Ask!

G. How might I keep from disturbing the unity of us four?
— You repeatedly ask the same question.
G. It is still so difficult for me ...
— It is *already* so difficult.
Rejoice at feeling the difficulty!

    I feel overburdened, and I sigh.

— Is it *so* difficult, *so* heavy?

    This question causes me to smile, and I relax.

G. It is better now ...
— How light is the good, how light is the true!
The stone does not know that it is heavy,
nor does the corpse.
G. What is freedom?
— Serving. If you *serve,*
you are united with the Divine
and you are *free.*
There is no more weight, no time, no measure,
no quantity. Oh, if only you could serve!
You may ask!
G. What causes the corruption of human sexuality?
Animals are able to mate only at certain times,
while humans can do so more or less at will.
Is that corruption?
What is the Divine Law for humans,
and how could we find our way back to it?

    After a long silence:

— Listen carefully!
The sacred force of which you speak
is given for the new,
but not for an ever renewing number of bodies.
Human beings receive an amount of this creative force
equivalent to what is lacking on earth.
Not a great number of human beings are needed:
the new Human is needed.
Humankind *stole* the additional sacred force
– this 'more' of force – and now it must be paid for …
paid for dearly!

> *It becomes clear to me that 'excess' sexuality is*
> *meant to be applied to transformation into the new*
> *Human and should neither be wasted on sexual*
> *extremes nor repressed through asceticism.*

— The new time is approaching when all of this
will no longer be. I proclaim the moment: it is near!
Rejoice from dawn till dusk!
Beauty never before known!

> *Silence.*

— You are the guardian of a sacred force.
Share it: do not keep it for yourself!
Then you have nothing to fear.
You are still afraid of the old. Without cause!
Raise the sacred force,
and the empty shell is left behind, powerless.

G. How could I *always* feel the force,
so as to radiate it without interruption?

— It is just the opposite:
You *feel* the force only *when you radiate it.*

The sun never sees its rays:
its moons *reflect* them.
Know this: The sun, too, is but a moon,
for everything mirrors the Divine Light.

THE DIVINE CONTEMPLATES ITSELF IN US.
BE PURE MIRRORS!

Clouded, cracked mirrors will be cast away,
for they do not serve.
What is still troubling you?
G. Nothing. I rejoice at your teaching.
— It is not *mine!*
With each day, it shall become easier for you,
and your joy will be perfect.

Friday, October 22, 1943

18. DIALOGUE WITH LILI

— Listen carefully:
Sin cannot be destroyed.
In truth, it does not even exist.
The name of all sin is: *'the no longer good.'*
The name of *all* sin!
But sin can be transformed by *'the not yet good.'*
Where is measure? Where is judgment?
With Ő alone.

Ő SENDS SIN
THAT YOUR EYES MAY SEE.

These words wipe out the old notions of sin and guilt in me, leaving space for a strong and vibrant feeling of responsibility.

L. Why are we passive when we ought to be active …
and the reverse?
— When do you feel this way? All the time?
L. No.
— ONLY Ő *ACTS*.
If you feel that *you* act,
then you are passive, you are inactive.
THE TRUE ACT CANNOT BE FELT.
YOU SIMPLY FEEL JOYFUL.
Evil only *seems* to be an act.
In truth, it is inactivity.

L. How are breath and soul related?
— What do you mean by soul?

Lili cannot answer and she remains silent.

— Do you see what you are asking?
What do you sense the soul to be?

Lili hesitates and stammers:

L. The highest in us … that which is not body …
— EVERYTHING IS BODY.
WHAT FOR YOU IS UNGRASPABLE SOUL
IS FOR ME A THICK WALL.
Can you grasp air? Truly, I say unto you: you can.
Only what it carries is ungraspable.
You drink wine and feel ecstasy.
Can you grasp ecstasy?
L. No.

— THE SOUL IS WINE – IT CARRIES ECSTASY.
EVERYTHING CAN CARRY ECSTASY.

L. Is the yoga practised here in Hungary good?
— What sort of yoga do you mean?
L. Hatha-Yoga, which comes from India.
— If it helps, then it is good.
Do not judge the seekers!
They seek. Though in reality, they do not seek;
they only believe they do.
In reality, they imitate.
New laws are coming and new Grace.
The new can be recognized by its *namelessness*.
Even the name of the 'highest Helper' became old.
The chosen ones already see the nameless new Light.
The others guard the husks of old grain.
The chaff will be burned, cast into the fire.
L. I have been told that Hatha-Yoga helps …
— Hatha … *perhaps!*

> *Once again I am amazed at the lively way the angel*
> *plays with words and I smile with pleasure:*
> '*Hatha*' *also means 'perhaps' in Hungarian.*

— Perhaps this helps … perhaps that helps,
perhaps help will come from another *perhaps!*
They wander aimlessly
and there is no balm for their wounds.
Be aware! Do not leave your own place.
Do not stray from your path.
Those who stray wander in circles, again and again.
But you are there, at *one* certain point.

> *The point of certainty, the opposite of 'perhaps.'*

102

— Everything goes astray, but not you.
Behold! You cannot stray, for you never say:
"Perhaps this is the good"!
Everything moves, it twists and squirms.
The solid crumbles, the liquid coagulates.
What was certain is no more ... terrifying!
A narrow bridge spanning the bottomless abyss ...
that is what you are.
Take care of yourselves!
Are you afraid to be the bridge?
The bridge is well-protected,
for it is an absolute necessity.
Even the deceiver who comes and goes
can appear as a bridge.
But the eye not focused on the outside
detects such deception.
Be watchful! I will share a secret with you:
One thing remains unknown,
there is one thing of which the deceiver is unaware:
the new.

— THE DECEIVER CAN DRESS ONLY IN THE OLD.
THIS IS THE KEY TO AVOID BEING MISLED.

The deceiver has led many astray.
Engrave this into your heart!
In the name of the 'not yet named,' I bless you.

Friday, October 29, 1943

19. DIALOGUE WITH GITTA

— Listen carefully!
I teach you the cause of all illness.
You do not live for yourself.
You are given your daily nourishment in abundance,
but not without reason.
It becomes a wondrous force in you.
But beware if you keep the force
only for yourself!
Be careful, my servant!
If you should sink down,
it is not because of too much nourishment taken in,
but too little *force* returned.
You hold it back.

REPENTERS AND ASCETICS ARE NOT NEEDED.
THEY ARE NOT DEAR TO THE DIVINE.

The new law, the new measure is different:
you receive five loaves of bread
for feeding five thousand.

THE HOLDING BACK OF FORCE IS
THE SOURCE OF ALL DISEASE.

Sin is disease. May this be a lesson to you!

I am overwhelmed by what I have heard.

— Lift up your head! Ask with a pure and light heart!
G. My greatest wish is to radiate ...
but why then do I hold back the force?

104

— The answer lies in your question: what is a wish?

G. Desire …

— Not only that. It is a sign of distance.
You do not desire something you already have.

> *I realize that radiating is my* nature; *my task is to*
> *become* conscious of *this and to* act *accordingly.*

— Ő created you to shine.
But there is a split between you …

> *Dividing gesture, as though splitting my body*
> *in half.*

— … and YOU.
I will explain: this split, this dark abyss,
which was … which is … but which shall not be,
is also in you:

CREATED WORLD – AND CREATING WORLD.
BETWEEN THEM: THE ABYSS.

Look at yourself: *You are the bridge.*
You cannot wish for creative rays,
you cannot long to be the bridge,
for to be the bridge is *given* to you.
The bridge is not wishing – but faith.
What has not been … what is not now …
and yet shall be … is deliverance.
Can money provide deliverance?
Can sacrifice, generosity, good intentions
or philanthropy lead to deliverance?
They all fall into the bottomless pit.
They are cast down and devoured by the depths,
for they are all nothing without the new.

Fathomless depths ... in vain do you throw
the old into it, for it will never be filled!

The ironic tone of the angel's voice is clearly telling
me that with monetary donations, self-serving
'kindness' and so-called love of our neighbors, we
will never be able to purchase peace of soul or
deliverance.

— Thanks be given to the infinite wisdom of the Divine
that the small CHILD smilingly crosses over the abyss,
for truly what was concealed from the wise
has now been revealed to you,
little children that you are.

Without my being aware of it, my hands
have clenched into fists.

— *(With a radiant smile:)*
When you have a smiling faith,
your hands will open.

I feel that this faith of which the angel speaks
is a creative force.

— Open your hands!

I open them and a smile floods through me.

— Now it is good, for you smile.
Ask!
G. How is the human constructed?
What are the seven centers and what is their function?
— The seven levels:
Three of them you know,
and you think you know the fourth.

THREE ARE THE CREATED WORLD.
THREE ARE THE CREATING WORLD.
IN THE MIDDLE IS THE BRIDGE,
WHICH IS NOT KNOWLEDGE.

Stone, grass and horse are not followed by
humankind,
but by the human, the *union* of the seven.
It is still difficult for you to grasp.

> *With a very soft voice:*

— I am the Fifth.

> *I listen with the greatest of intensity as the
> seven-souled world takes shape for me.*

— The WORD is the fourth level revealed.
The WORD is sacred, the fourth manifestation.
It is the bridge between matter and spirit.

> *A horizontal gesture at the level of the mouth:*

— The fourth level is the foundation of the new House,
the substance of Truth.
Take heed! Do not play with it, for from here ...

> *Another gesture at the level of the mouth:*

— ... from here, the unredeemed, the bad, the false,
leak down and corrupt the three lower levels,
AND THAT IS DISEASE.
But the WORD can raise up:
it can redeem the three lower levels.
ONLY THE HUMAN HAS THE WORD.
YOU SPEAK IN THE NAME OF THE DIVINE.

I speak only through the one who speaks,
for I have no mouth.
When I am united with you, I will have one.
Heaven bless you all!

After the dialogue, I beg Hanna to tell us what she experienced during the teaching of the seven levels of the WORLD. She sketches a diagram, warning us, however, that she had not been able to perceive the entire hierarchy of the Creating World, meaning that the diagram is incomplete.

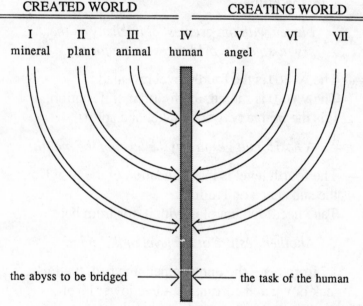

CREATED WORLD   CREATING WORLD

I	II	III	IV	V	VI	VII
mineral	plant	animal	human	angel		

the abyss to be bridged ⟶ ⟵ the task of the human

As Hanna draws the curve connecting the animal (III) with the angel (V), I at last understand what my angel had explained at the very beginning of the dialogues: "It and I are united in the task. Do not divide what is one!" Now I understand that the

instinctive animal side of my being and the angel
can only be united through me, the Human (IV),
when I become a bridge over the separating abyss.

Friday, October 29, 1943

19. DIALOGUE WITH LILI

— I speak of the death of the *Highest Helper*.
Of what was the cross made?
Of what were the nails made?
They were made of the rumors about Him
that were spread everywhere,
the talk about his miracles.
The form in which the spirit dresses
 is nothing but form.
The multitudes attributed the miracles to the form.
This is why the *Highest Helper* took the cross
upon his shoulders.
And He bore witness:
"It was not I but God who performed the miracle –
through your faith."

You, too, are *helpers*.
Help comes from the faith of the one who *is helped* –
not from *your* faith!
It is not you who perform the miracle,
and not I;
it is the faith of the one who *is helped*
that does it.

109

— Ask, my little servant!

L.   How could we four serve better?

— Sound and harmony.
Four sounds are not necessarily harmony.
Ö is the sum of all sounds.
If you are united, it is a creative force,
a small harmony, the foundation of all miracles.
Only if your voice resounds purely,
without falseness, without pretense,
without personal intent, without alteration –
only then do you serve in harmony.
If individual responsibility is taken for each and every
voice, there will be no falsity.
The deceiver can sneak only into the false.
Ask.

L.   Why am I always so tense?

— Think of the cross! His body was stretched upon it.
You stretch your body, too; but you become tense
because you give yourself too much importance.

BEHOLD: THE WONDER COMES ONLY
WHEN YOU FORGET YOURSELF.
THAT IS THE SECRET OF ALL SECRETS.

You tense yourself in vain –
this will not cause you to grow in the least.

*From the garden next door, the creaking
of a rusty hand pump can be heard.*

— So much effort just to pull a little water
from the depths!
And the rain falls effortlessly.
Wells dry out … ponds dry out … the earth dries out.

The creaking continues.

Everything creaks and rattles …
that is the 'harmony' of today.
Machines spit out lies with a rattle.
The living are shot dead with a rattle.
All eyes are lowered …
You may ask!

L. In talking with my pupils lately, I sometimes feel
myself vibrating all over as though I have fever …
was this right?

— *Only* this is right. This instant is eternal.
Then *you are*.Were you tired afterwards?

L. Oh, no!

— You see, it was good,
for it was not *you* who labored at the great Plan.

THE HELPER IS THE BRIDGE
BETWEEN THE ONE WHO IS HELPED
AND THE ETERNAL HELPER –
BUT ONLY AS LONG AS IT IS NEEDED.

> *It seems to me that it is in some way our selfish
> 'little I' that wants to help more than is really
> needed, that wants to feel 'important' in helping.*

L. I am unsure of so many little things.
For example: should I fast?

— The fasting of all fasting is the help you bring.
Fasting in itself does not help at all.
Do you know when it is right to fast?
When you have overeaten!
It would be better if you would simply not overeat.
But all this is really irrelevant, my little servant.

PAY ATTENTION TO THE *MORE*
AND THE LESS WILL SERVE.

L. What is an outburst of temper, of rage?
—   To 'burst out' means to begin.
    An out-burst is a springboard of force
    beginning below and then boiling up;
    but it can still be transformed and guided.
    Take good care of it;
    do not pour it out as rage.
    Guard it and transform it …
    it is a sacred force.

ONLY IF BADLY USED DOES THE FORCE DESTROY.

L. On what should I concentrate in my work?
—   As I have already said: your signpost is *joy*.
    I cannot say it to you in a better way.
    It is the surest sign.

BUT THERE IS ONLY ONE PLACE TO FIND JOY:
BEYOND THE 'OLD ME.'

Within the 'old me,' there is no joy.
Within the 'old me' is the *no longer good*.
Rejoice evermore in the name of harmony.
Soon we will sing in unison to the ONE JOY.

> *Now I clearly see the difference between these
> words: in the language of the angels, the word,*
> személy, *refers to the 'old me,' which no longer
> serves life.* Egyén, *'individuality,' in contrast,
> serves evolution, the new.*

Friday, November 5, 1943

20. DIALOGUE WITH GITTA

— Let us rejoice in the ONE joy!
  I say to *you:* the bread you are given
  cannot yet be eaten on earth.
  It must first be baked in the oven.
  Do not worry!
  Neither the bread nor the oven burns,
  only the wood, known as the 'personal.'
  In the heat of its fire, edible bread is baked.
  Listen well! The new already dwells among you.
  Great wonder.
  Joy will be your everpresent companion.
  You shall be given wonders,
  for you believed without wonders.
  Ask, my servant!

  > *I had painstakingly elaborated a theory of vibration
  > in connection with movement and brooded over it
  > for hours. I was quite impressed with my own
  > intelligence.*

G. How does motion amplify vibration?
— *(mockingly:)* What an 'intelligent' question!
  Now listen to something new: forget about your *head!*

  IT IS ONLY THE FIRST OF THE SERVANTS,
  AND YOU ARE ITS MASTER.

  But even the greatest of masters
  is only a foot-servant of the Divine.
  If Divine force vibrates through you,

then serve and do not interfere;
your head is of no use at all.
You reach out your hand in vain … in vain.
If Ő does not dwell within, you are but a clown.
The servant dons the clothes of the absent master,
usurps the role.
But upon the master's return,
the servant is put to shame.

G. What is meant by 'Trinity'?
— If you have faith, it is in you:
The Creator … the Father.
The Creation … the Son.
The bridge … the Holy Spirit.
In truth, ONE.
Ask!

G. How can I avoid falling into my 'little I'?
— You cannot *fall* into the 'little I,'
for you *are in* it. You *all* are in it.
THIS 'LITTLE I' IS YOUR GREATEST TREASURE.
DO NOT WISH TO LEAVE IT – *RAISE IT UP!*

Wood is transformed into light … it is not lost.
What a wonder, the 'little I'!
The Divine has been forming it for you
since the beginning of time
and you – foolish child! – despise it.
You fool! If you are a good master,
it is a good servant.
And the impossible becomes possible,
and the inedible becomes edible.
When does bread become bread?

G. When it is baked …

— No. Only when given to the hungry
   does bread become bread.

G. I have felt a tremendous pressure the past few days,
   as if I were being pressed by a vice …
   what was going on?
— You are mistaken. That was not a 'vice';
   all of the bread that you have not given to the hungry
   was pressing against you.
G. What is holding me back?
— There are two bridges: the great and the small.
   The small bridge is still weak.

> *I sense that, with the small, weak bridge,*
> *my self-confidence is meant.*

— Without a way, the bread cannot come:
   it is blocked.
G. How can I strengthen my faith in myself?
— By uniting the two bridges,
   which, in truth, are ONE.
   A bad servant destroys the bridges
   so that the master cannot return.
   But the little CHILD crosses with a smile
   AND THE CHILD IS THE MASTER.

   Listen carefully as I repeat:
   THE NEW, THE NOT YET SEEN, DWELLS AMONG YOU.
   THE SMALL CHILD,
   THE POWERFUL MASTER, THE NEW, THE ETERNAL.

   ETERNITY IS NOT ETERNAL REPETITION
   BUT THE ETERNALLY NEW.

Friday, November 5, 1943

20. DIALOGUE WITH LILI

— Spring is coming, heralded by
a flower, a blade of grass.
Religions, temples, churches and prophets
are also heralds,
but with the coming of LIGHT and FORCE
there will be no more temples, no more churches:
all will be temple and church.

Who sees a single flower
in the flower-covered meadow?
You are not flowers – you are *spring*.
In the Divine Garden, even *spring*
is but a single flower.
Ask!

L. Why do so few people have faith,
and why does it not awaken in them?

— A network of concrete roads
spans the entire face of the earth.

THEY ARE BROAD, WIDE AND SMOOTH,
AND MADNESS RIDES UPON THEM.

There are many ways, a tremendous number.
Do not be astonished that the small and narrow,
the *only* way was forgotten.
All the forces are consumed by madness. What is
madness?

A SACRED FORCE THAT WITHERS IN CAPTIVITY.

116

— But to you it is given to show the way.
  Ask!

L. Why do so few people recognize their *calling?*

— Because they are driven.
  They do not pay attention to the *call.*
  The purest voice is wasted if no one listens to it.
  Listen carefully:
  The new Eye grows in your eyes.
  The new Ear grows in your ears.
  The new Hand grows in your hands.
  And you will SEE, HEAR and CREATE.
  New Voice ... and old ear?
  The new Ear is needed to hear the CALLING.
  The voice, too, has a body.
  It carries the inaudible, immortal Voice,
  which is no longer body.

  You are *spring.*
  The new Eye, the new Ear, the new Hand
  grow at your touch. The new is budding.
  Ask!

L. Why is it so hard to help my family?

— To the old eye, the near is large
  and the distant is small.
  Look with the new Eye: the near will be small
  and the distant, large.
  IF THE DIVINE IS GREAT IN YOU
  EVERY TASK IS SMALL, EASY AND LIGHT.

L. What is movement?

— The greatest of all.
  Growth is not yet movement ...
  wind is not yet movement ...

117

flowing water is not yet movement ...
decaying to dust is not yet movement ...
wandering stars are not yet movement.
All of these are only reactions, persistence of inertia.
Motion dictated by hunger, cold or desire
is compulsion.
But you ... you are already *free* to move.

THE ACT MADE FREELY IS MOVEMENT.

The helping Hand ... is Movement.
The radiating Eye... is Movement.
The raising of matter to a new dwelling ...
is Movement.
New creation: no longer captivity, but deliverance.
There is no other freedom.
If you awaken this in your pupils,
then each of their motions will become Movement;
not passive captivity.

In vain are there nerves;
in vain, tendons;
in vain, bones.
from nerves ... whips;
from tendons ... cords;
from bones ... clubs;
and from youth ... corruption.

Only true Movement redeems.
Teach this, my servant,
and bodies will be reborn at your touch!
They will rise from their graves
for now they are all dead ... they are all dead.
Do you accept this task?

L. *(Timidly:)* I will try … where should I begin?

— Does fear still dwell in you?

L. I feel that my task is becoming ever greater and more urgent.

— Do you know how to begin the Movement in yourself? Pronounce these words: "I accept it!"

THE TRUE WORD RISES UP TO THE DIVINE
AND DESCENDS BACK TO YOU – AS FORCE.

The force of the vow springs from you.
The word of the vow is seed sown in Heaven
and its fruit will fall manyfold back to you.
You will have enough to distribute, my servant!
Faith sown in Heaven …
humans sow all their seeds only in earth,
and they perish.

L. I don't quite understand the vow …

— Can you comprehend the incomprehensible?

REASON STOPS – BREATHLESSLY –
WHERE FAITH BEGINS.

Reason can never reach Heaven, for it is of the earth.
What is still confusing you?

L. I do not see the difference between *helping*
and the *freely accepted act.*

— ONLY THE FREELY ACCEPTED ACT HELPS.
NOTHING ELSE!

> *In the ensuing silence, I think of a recent dream
> which I have not been able to understand.*

— *(To me)* I speak to you.

Your dream is saying:
May wonder not be *in* you – but *through* you –
for you are not a flower – you are *spring*.
Wonder appears in the flower,
but who can grasp springtime?
If you are wonder, then you are a flower,
one among many.

Addressed to Lili:

— Does doubt still dwell in your heart?
L. I can hardly bear the abundance I receive …
— You will bear it.
It is time for me to go.

Friday, November 12, 1943

21. DIALOGUE WITH GITTA

— Now you are strong enough: hear my words!
The next step will no longer be
on the path: the old way comes to an end.
There is not even water to walk upon.
But woe unto you if you look back!
If you truly have faith,
a wayless way will bear your feet:

THE NEW EARTH – THE CHILD'S FIRST STEP.

But take heed! Not even faith will help
if you take along any of the old.
The old, 'the more than necessary,'

120

would pull you down
to sink like lead in the water.
Listen! The body has been formed for you
from the beginning of time.
Now listen carefully!

THE BODY IS NOT MEANT TO BE USED
IN THE WAYS YOU HAVE BEEN USING IT.

To make this graspable for you is very difficult.
I will return.

> *Hanna can scarcely bear the intensity of what is*
> *communicated about the new body.*
> *She rests for a few minutes.*

— You have come to the end of the way;
there is no more way. You *look* for a place
to put down your foot and you see nothing.
Nothing is there ... *because you look.*
The eye no longer exists for looking, as before.
Look no more with the old eye,
and there will be a new way under your feet.

THE BODY OF THE REDEEMER
IS GIVEN ONLY FOR GIVING.
THE REDEEMER IS NOT HUMAN;
THE REDEEMER IS *THE HUMAN.*
The truly new is coming.

I teach you, my servant!
Before every new beginning, sanctify the moment!
Be finished with the old:
look no more with the old eye,
hear no more with the old ear!

Open the old eye again
only when the new in you has opened
and then the new Light will shine through it.
For the body is given only for giving.

Now you can receive only from above,
no longer from below.
A truly new world opens up to you.
You will *live* it.
There will be no secret from you on earth ...
no heaviness, no gloom, no noise.
But woe unto you if you look back!

Take along nothing from the old!
The old, as small, light and worthless
you think it to be, would become a mountain of lead
in the New and that would be your end.
Detach yourselves from the old;
do not throw it away, but use it in a different way.
You still misuse the tool.

> *Indicating Joseph:*

— The *son* anticipates best what is meant.
But it will become clear to you, too,
for the time is ripe.
The turning point of creation:
what you valued most, you will come to value least.

> *I have decorated the room with flowers and given
> careful attention to its aesthetic effect.*

— How carefully you have arranged this room!
Your arrangement has just one fault:
you *attach* yourself to it.

122

The more you decorate, the more you *bind* yourself.
Do not attach yourself to anything!
Attachments bind to the old, to the habitual.
You do not need that any more.
Seek only the new!
Amidst the flowers of your faith, I feel well,
no matter where you are.

I RELEASE YOU FROM EVERY FORM.
I HAVE NO EYES FOR SEEING
THE FLOWERS OF THIS EARTH.

But I see your festive expectation.
Ask!

G. How can I distinguish between what will become lead
in the new and what I can take along?

— The higher the mountain,
the less will be taken along
by the one who carries the load.
Still less when stepping into water.
What can be taken along
where there is not even water? Life itself,
Life itself and nothing else.

Ask!

G. What is soul? What is spirit?

— Spirit is the Creator.
Soul is the mediator.
Body is matter.
This is the Holy Trinity.

G. I have a feeling that the forces you mentioned earlier
are somehow associated with numbers.
What is 4? What is 7?

— If you would cease to look
at the numbers themselves,
you would sense their hidden force.
For behind everything dwells the *Force*.
Every form is a gateway to infinite forces.
For the one who has eyes ... the eye is the gateway.
For the one who has ears ... the ear is the gateway.
Each is given a different gateway ...
but the *Force* is ONE.

Rejoice in your hearts, for the new opens up!
Today I was able to bring you good news.
I depart joyfully.

Friday, November 12, 1943

21. DIALOGUE WITH LILI

— I teach you the end of suffering:
If you wished to draw the letter 'T'
and only the vertical line were there,
without the horizontal one,
you would not know what is missing.
Because you know the letter 'T,'
you can easily provide what is lacking.

You are *those who help*.
You have been sent to fill the lack.
Evil is nothing but lack.
You encounter a human being,
you feel a lack and you suffer from it.

124

Where is the end of suffering?
If you would know the *new letter 'T,'*
you would also know what is lacking here,
and you could easily provide it.

SUFFERING IS MEANINGLESS.

Learn the *new abc;*
then everything could be *perfect.*
For you, the secret lies in the *imperfect.*
How do you know that it is *imperfect?* From whom?

TO YOU IT IS GIVEN TO KNOW THE PERFECT.

How can you measure it?
What is your standard?

THE PERFECT IS REFLECTED IN THE IMPERFECT.

You suffer only until you are able to recognize
the Divine in everything.
New letters will be inscribed ... be aware!

SUFFERING GUIDES ONLY THE ANIMAL.
THE BEGINNING OF THE WAY
IS THE END OF SUFFERING.

 Silence.

— Everything grows – even the stone.
 The seed in mother earth,
 the child in the mother's womb ... why do they grow?
 The highest mountain, the tallest tree
 cannot grow to the Heavens.
 The strongest eagle cannot fly so high.

But the smallest human can reach it,
for Heaven is within.

I await your question!

L. What is rest?

— Preparation.
Anything that is not preparation is only apparent rest.
Rest that is not preparation is half-heartedness;
another name for it is death.

The most wonderful rest descends on you
when you create.

THE RESTFUL ACT AND CREATIVE REST ARE TRUE.

They only appear to be *two:* in truth, they are *one*.
You may ask!

L. Where is Nirvana?

— THERE, WHERE TWO ARE ONE;
WHERE PARALLELS CONVERGE;
APPARENTLY REST – IN REALITY: ACT.
APPARENTLY SILENCE –
IN REALITY: UNISON OF ALL SOUNDS.
APPARENTLY DISTANCE – IN REALITY: WITHIN YOU.

Now I have a question:
What is your most passionate wish?

L. To always be with you and so to be one.

— And how do you expect this to take place?

L. I know that it will be the object of my work.

— It is not a matter of 'work'!
Then you would be 'object'-ified!
An *object* is what is densest.
(touching the table:) This is an *object!*

(touching a blanket:) This is an *object!*
(touching a hand:) This is an *object!*
Let objects be!
Your most passionate wish is *above* all objects!
You will never attain it as the *object* of your *work!*

L. What is nervousness?
— What is it? An army without a commander.
    When battle comes, there is no organization,
    for no one is there to command.
    The brain goes to pieces, order falls apart,
    for a uniting force is lacking. An order is given,
    and then is immediately followed by its contradiction:
    nervousness.
    This does not occur in our ranks:
    we are the Divine army.
    We battle against darkness.
    We hear the call and we obey.

    NERVOUSNESS IS THE LACK OF A GOAL.
    NOTHING ELSE.

    Do you have further questions?
L. Why is my memory so bad?
— Because your past was bad.
    It is unpleasant to remember it
    and you have drawn thick curtains in front of it.

        Pointing to me:

— Her past is also bad,
    but it no longer has such an effect.

        Turning back to Lili:

— You have not forgotten last Friday, have you?
When you have created, when you have helped,
then you do not forget.
It is not your *memory* that is bad,
but your *memories*.

    (Silence.)

L. My love is not strong enough …
— Where do you feel this?
L. In front of other people.
— Whom do you love enough?
L. So far, no one.
— Whom do you love most?
L. Ő.
— And after Ő?
L. You.
— *(smiling indulgently:)* Your eyes are still veiled.

IF YOU LOVE THE DIVINE, YOU LOVE EVERYTHING.
IF YOU DO NOT LOVE ENOUGH,
IT IS THE DIVINE YOU DO NOT LOVE ENOUGH,
FOR EVERYTHING IS DIVINE CREATION.

Love Ő in the perfect – admire Ő in the imperfect!
For everything mirrors the Divine.
It will not be difficult to love the Divine.

Above all, I adore Ő and thus I love you.
I take leave of you now.
Bless you!

Friday, November 19, 1943

22. DIALOGUE WITH GITTA

— I greet you.
  I will teach you about gold.
  It is the least useful of all metals,
  for it serves no purpose.
  What gives it value? The faith invested in it.
  The human invests faith in objects
  born of the earth, causing them to be cursed.
  Curse is forbidding.
  Without the curse, you would be straying.

  You begin your journey carrying a golden ball.
  You carry it. The ball is very heavy,
  but you carry it just the same.
  Then you arrive at the border of a land
  where there is no more faith in gold.
  What becomes of the gold?
  Only the weight remains.
  What is there left for you to do then, my servant?

G. Drop the ball.

— Open your hand,
  and the ball rolls down by itself.
  Dropping the weight is really not difficult,
  but your fingers are cramped from carrying the ball
  and you are unable to let it fall.
  What is heavy falls by itself.

  There is also gold in the new land:
  not glittering metal, but Light.
  How can you receive the new ball

129

if you are still grasping the old?
You clutch it like this … like this you clutch it:

> *A gesture with clenched fingers … then the hand
> tilts slightly, as if to let the ball roll down.*

— See how easy it is to let it fall!

> *Silence.*

— It is a heavy ball, an innocent ball that you live upon.
Thanks to infinite Divine grace, it became cursed
so that you would not adore it …
so that you would not adore it!
The innocent ball waits to be redeemed.
How will it be redeemed?

BY LEAVING ADAM BEHIND.

> *I sigh and something in me is released as I relax.*

— Is it loosening?
All of you: How well we know the difficulties
of letting the burden fall,
for you have become accustomed to its weight.
Do not regret that the weight burdens you.
The one who carries gold does not feel its weight
as long as gold is something that is believed in.
If the belief is withdrawn, only the weight remains.
You are on the right path.

G. All week long, I searched for something
that would relieve my tension … how could I find it?
— Give it *time,* for the hand is rooted in time.
I await your question.

G. Who am I?
— It is not a good moment to ask;
you are just re-forming yourself.
And when you are completely formed,
you will have no more questions.

G. What is the meaning of my sign, the sun?
— The sign is an image that can help you
to understand your task.
A child asks what *seven* is.
You show it *seven* apples.
The child is fond of apples,
and quickly learns what *seven* means.
You would not show it seven whips.

G. What did you mean when you said not long ago:
"The images of our earthly dream – of our existence –
are merely wrappings for their concealed meaning;
awakening can be found only *within* the dream …
never *without*." ?

— You have slept long enough, my little servant!
One who has slept long enough
awakens without help.
There is no need to be awakened!
Lack of strength closes the eyes.
Filled with strength, they open by themselves.
Lack of strength is blindness, sleep.

THE HUMAN SLEEPS FOR LACK OF STRENGTH.

How could the day, the new day, be begun
if one did not have the strength to *act?*

G. How good it would be to awaken others!
— You talk in your dream.

You four are all asleep in one room.
You dream of one another.
You believe you are talking with each other,
for the dream image is deceptive.

The dreamer does not dream of being asleep,
but of waking ... coming ... going ... talking.
Yet in reality, the dreamer sleeps.
Then comes the dawn and the dream-mist dissolves.
THE NEW ACT NEARS.

Every dream will be fulfilled –
for the dream, too, is preparation.
In the womb of the mother,
the unborn child dreams of daylight.
Without this dreaming,
it could not be born into the light of day.

ALL THAT YOU DO NOW
IS DREAM-ACT ... IS DREAM-THOUGHT.

Dream ever more beautifully, always;
for all dreams become reality!
The dream, too, is faith.
I am waiting.

   (Silence.)

G. I cannot live loosely and freely now;
   my head always rushes ahead.
— If only you could see yourself for but a moment:
   you lie in space and sleep, motionless and calm ...
   your feet do not rush.
   Each of your movements is but dream ... only dream.

I think of my blind rushing.

— Do you actually get anywhere when you rush?
G. Only on earth ...
   it is just my habit to rush!
   How horrible habit is!
— Take heed! Do not look back!
   The *horrible* is a blind force.
   Horror is the old god.
   If you see horrors, you see the old gods.
   BUT THEY ARE NO LONGER GODS:
   NOW THEY ARE SERVANTS.

   You see, my servant: today there was no noise.
   The burden fades away
   when you loosen your grasp on it.

   I depart.

Friday, November 19, 1943

22. DIALOGUE WITH LILI

— Let us greet the Lord of the wheat fields!
   I speak to you of the wheat:
   Your hand is empty but soon it will be filled.
   Listen! You have ten grains of wheat; no more.
   You can distribute them just ten times –
   not twenty.
   Can a grain of wheat germinate
   if you split it in two?

Even if you have done it with the best of intentions?
In a grain of wheat dwell the old and the New:
it cannot be split.
With your human mind, you cannot differentiate
between the old and the new.
Even what you consider to be new is old.
Do not separate, do not judge ... *sow!*
Then the new will grow:
the new which is neither seed nor sprout.
For all that is but a dwelling for the new.
Let the seed fall intact, as a whole!
Only in this way will it multiply –
it will germinate!

THE TIME OF NEW GERMINATION HAS COME.

L. I do not quite understand what I am doing wrong.

> *Lili is exhausted. Her pupils have been coming to her with their personal problems day after day until far into the night; and Lili is unable to say 'no.'*

— You have ten grains of wheat.
You cannot give them to twenty people.
But *sow* them and soon there will be a hundred.
Heavenly Wheat is quick to provide grain.

I am waiting.

L. What is karma?

— A WHIP FOR LASHING ONESELF.

Today this question is too difficult for you.
It conceals a *great secret*.

We are all familiar with the concept of karma in Hinduism, and I wonder what the secret concealed behind this theory might be.

L.   And what is health?
—   Balance. If it is unsteady, there is a lack.

ONLY IN THE ANIMAL
DOES BALANCE COME FROM THE BODY;
NOT SO IN THE HUMAN.

L.   Why did I previously prefer teaching the ill,
     whereas I now prefer teaching the healthy?
—   You are becoming healthy yourself.
     The health in human beings is the soil
     in which you sow the seed.
     Heavenly Seeds in *bad soil* ... ?

       To all of us:

—   Do not worry! A wonderful transformation begins.
     It will not always appear good to you,
     for the old hulls burst, rot and decay.
     Do not be afraid!
     What happens to you now is no small matter.
     You, too, my little servant: do not worry.
     What happens to you is good.
     And now I leave you, but not for long.

Friday, November 26, 1943

23. DIALOGUE WITH GITTA

— Today I will continue to talk about gold.
  Where does it come from? Of what is it the fruit?
  The fruit of the tree of knowledge.
  Adam reached for what *glitters*
  instead of what *shines*.
  There is another tree:
  Mystery is its name – Light is its fruit.
  The tree of knowledge is the possibility
  of *becoming* human –
  the other tree is *being* Human.

  Gold contaminates the earth.
  What is superfluous must burn.
  Gold cannot be burned.
  EARTHLY LIGHT IS *INVOLUNTARY* BURNING.
  HEAVENLY LIGHT IS *VOLUNTARY* BURNING:
  SACRIFICE.

  The first tree – the old 'I' – reflects light.
  The second tree – the new 'I' – radiates Light.
  To mirror is different from radiating, from being sun.

  Ask!

G. What is rhythm?
— First came rhythm … then came song.
  There is rhythm without song,
  but no song without rhythm.
  Rhythm is body; melody or song is soul.
  Body and soul carry the third.

136

I think of the music of Mozart. Is it the rhythm that moves us? Is it the melody? No, it is the inexplicable 'third' which so touches our heart. It is the Divine impulse which gave birth to Mozart's rhythm and melody.

G. How could I come closer to my feeling of rhythm?

— First was rhythm – then the Word.
Original vibration … first day …
primordial ground of all mysteries.
In the mighty vibration of the new Creation,
new Names are born.
Your Name, too, is born of rhythm.
With rhythm you can create,
with rhythm you can destroy.
The new Ear hears it.
The beat one hears is not rhythm.
Are you able to follow me?

G. Oh, yes!

— You may ask!

G. Does the form of the sphere have a meaning?

— What would a half-sun be,
shining on but half of creation?

THE SPHERE IS THE IMAGE
OF GIVING WITHOUT JUDGMENT.

I think of the sun which shines everywhere, simply because this is its Divine nature.

— The new harvest is Light, not glistening metal.
Because the human speculated for so long

137

about how iron could become gold,
gold became iron.
And this iron smashes down on the human.

*We live in a time of war, of which the iron weapon
is a symbol. And war springs from the greed for
power, for gold.*

— Transformation, burning.
Only the human *kindles* fire;
all else can only *be kindled*.
The altar is ready.
Kindle fire in honor of the Divine!
But set fire only to the superfluous,
not the altar itself!
If you could, you would set fire even to the altar,
for at this point you are but the 'priest's apprentice'!

We all burst into laughter.

— Speak, my little servant!
G. What is true offering of self, true sacrifice?
— A miracle! The most beautiful song,
the most beautiful scent, the most beautiful light:
all of this *ascends* to the feet of the Divine.
But only the most delightful, the most blissful!
Not tears, not self-torture, not sorrow!
They are all but smoke that *descends*
and covers the earth with a dark layer.
Incomplete burning becomes smoke;
incomplete offering becomes pain and torment;
imperfect sacrifice is not Light but coal dust;
not transformation, but decomposition,
soot, gas, decay.

Blow on the fire! I will help you!
Learning is a form of burning, too.
But for you, my words are merely wood
that has not yet been kindled,
wood that is just lying about.
You will receive no new wood!

The old law: trees grow, are felled and burned.
New trees grow, are felled ...
But the tree of life is everlasting:
its fruit is Light,
its trunk is the fire of the old tree.
This tree will no longer be burned
for it gives LIGHT.

THE HUMAN IS NOT THE CROWN OF CREATION,
FOR EVERY CROWN IS MADE OF GOLD.
THE HUMAN IS THE *SOUL* OF CREATION.

*Hanna later tells me that 'bringing the words down'
to us was more difficult today than ever before. My
angel had moved a certain distance away from us,
like a mother bird moving ever further out on the
branch, then finally hopping to another one, as a
'teaching method.' A baby bird then has three
possibilities: to stay where it is ... to fall ... or to
fly for the first time in its life.*

Friday, November 26, 1943

23. DIALOGUE WITH LILI

— Do you know what beauty is?
THE GOOD SERVANT
GIVING MORE THAN WHAT IS NECESSARY.

The body moves ... that is necessary.
Dancing is *more* ... and if it is truly dance,
it is beautiful.
Voice is necessary ... song is *more*.
To form is necessary ... only the *more* is beautiful.

THE NEW WORLD WILL BE BUILT ONLY OF BEAUTY.

Be good servants, for only the act
which is *more* than what is necessary
can build the new world.
It cannot be built of anything else.

　　Silence.

— I teach you:
Take heed of all the 'Judas'
who put the Word up for sale.
They are around you now.
Wherever fire burns,
true and false will be separated.
That is the purpose of fire.
Are you aware of that? Take heed!
Among the twelve there is always a traitor:
the most miserable.
This is how it must be – do not be troubled.

Raw ore *can be* put to great use,
metal *is* indeed useful, and
slag is trodden underfoot.
The fire divides and purifies.
That is as it should be.

L. Should I do something about the traitors?

— Nourish and protect the fire!
Do not worry about anything else!
Ask!

L. In the functioning of the organs, what is necessary
and what is *more than necessary?*

— The organs have only one *more:*
the child born of the body.

ONLY WHAT IS INDEPENDENT IS *MORE.*

All else is waste, curse.
The beauty of the young maiden renews itself
one day in her small child –
not in the painted face of the childless.
Organs cannot accomplish *more* – humans can.

> *Hanna later explains to us that the* more *of the body
> is the earthly child, while the* more *of the human is
> to bring forth the new Child of Light.*

— But in today's world,
only the body is known.
Only the body is 'built'
and it becomes uglier all the time.
The feet of the one who dances for personal gain
become vulgar,
and the teacher of such dancing is even worse!
Do you have any more questions?

L. What is resistance?
— In the created world, it is the urge for *more*.
    Ő does not resist you.
    But you, you resist the Divine.
L. And what is force?
— Soon you will be able to understand this,
    but now is not yet the moment.
L. What is flexibility?
— The basic condition of life, the proper resistance.
    The rigid cannot resist.
    What flexibility is for you,
    is force, vibration in the new World.
    Only motion is force.
    The motionless, the static, are never force.
    Force and flexibility belong together.
    What a difference there is between
    resistance and rigidity!

L. What is the mind, reason?

— CONDUCTION ... BUT NOT THE CONDUCTOR.
    IHE INSTRUMENT ... BUT NOT THE MASTER.

> *I think of a concert grand piano. Only when
> a master comes to play on this finely tuned
> instrument does it give forth divine music.*

— You lick the sugar-spoon and say: 'sweet.'
    It is not the spoon which is sweet.
    If you try to bite the spoon,
    you can break your teeth.

> *Silence.*

— My little servant, are you happy?

Be happy, all of you,
for your life is beautiful when you serve.
The new is as beautiful as the old is ugly.
But be careful:
IF THE FULL-GROWN ADULT CONTINUES TO GROW,
THIS IS FAT OR TUMOR:
IT IS NOT BEAUTIFUL.
YOU HAVE BECOME FULL-GROWN ADULTS,
GIVE BIRTH TO THE NEW, TO THE *CHILD!*
STOP TRYING TO MAKE *YOURSELVES* GROW!

Do you have any more questions?

L. Does everyone have an angel, an 'inner teacher'?
— No. We consist of faith – purely of faith.

TO THOSE WHO HAVE FAITH, WHO BELIEVE –
WE *ARE*.
AND FAITH IS THE FORCE OF THE DIVINE.
IF YOU BELIEVE THAT I HAVE A VOICE …
I CAN SPEAK.
IF YOU DO NOT BELIEVE IT … I AM MUTE.
IF YOU BELIEVE THAT I AM YOU … I BECOME YOU.

Believe in the high!
You can also believe in the low.
Today devils clamor and angels are silent.
BUT THROUGH YOUR BELIEF, WE DESCEND.
FOR BELIEF IS THE BRIDGE.
I leave you now.

Friday, December 3, 1943

24. DIALOGUE WITH GITTA

*Our house is in the process of being whitewashed
and painted, so a friend has kindly given us the use
of her quiet apartment for today's dialogue.*

— Every home is a sanctuary.
Let us thank the one who welcomes us!
Listen carefully: you are all temples.*
In the sanctuary of sanctuaries,
you welcome the Divine.
But it is of no use to welcome Ő
if you do not also welcome the unredeemed.
The temple exists for them.
LEARN TO WELCOME!
JUST AS YOU WELCOME,
SO WILL YOU BE WELCOMED BY THE DIVINE.

The temple does not choose: the temple welcomes.
Imagine an empty church –
the sanctuary freezes in it!
Do you hear my words?
G. Oh, yes!
— Do not fear to open the gates of the temple,
my servant: the church is already pure,
the mass can begin.
G. What is the heart?

---

* In Hungarian there is just one word for 'temple' and 'church':
templom.

144

— The sanctuary of sanctuaries,
   the place where Ó dwells,
   the place of grace, the chalice.

G. And what dwells in the middle of the forehead?
— The new Seeing.
G. And what is the Light, the new Light?
— *What* refers only to objects.
G. There is no word to express it …
— There will be one! Why do you ask?
   Do you wish to *know,* or …
G. To come closer.
— Do you come closer by means of *knowing* it?
G. If it comes from *you* … then yes.
— Does the mother come closer to the child she carries
   in her womb because she *knows* it to be there?
   When does she see it? When it is born!
   Do not desire to *know,*
    just take good care of the Child!
G. How should I take care of the Child of Light?
— Who is the Light?
G. The Divine!
— You have spoken truth. Take good care of the Divine!

G. What was I like before I was born?
— You have not yet been born!
   Ask when you *will be born!*
   Now you are what you were,
   but will not be, for you are changing.
G. You said that I am subject to another law
   than most others.
   How can I recognize those who are subject
   to the same law as I?

— By the fact that they understand your words.
The others do not understand.
THEY LEARNED ...
AND YET THEY DO NOT UNDERSTAND.
THEY DID NOT LEARN ...
AND YET THEY UNDERSTAND.

Silence.

— Do you welcome me?
G. *(joyfully:)* Oh, yes!
— Welcome everyone and everything in this way!
That is your task.
Only when you welcome the unredeemed
can I pass on Divine grace to you.

In a powerful voice:

— Heavy temple gate, bolted with iron bars:
OPEN WIDE! I SAY TO YOU: OPEN WIDE!

Friday, December 3, 1943

24. DIALOGUE WITH LILI

— Today I will speak of your sign.
Try to imagine its form.
Do you understand your sign, my little servant?
L. I don't think so ...
— It is a marvelous sign.
Imagine the infinitely great and the infinitely small.
Infinitely great ...

The hands spread out from the heart
and the arms open wide:

Infinitely small …

The outstretched arms return to the heart
and the fingers join at one point.

— How could the infinitely small see the infinitely great
   if it were not for the *focal point?*
   Have you ever seen the Divine in the eyes
   of someone who has been helped?
L. Yes, I have …
— There you saw the Divine!
   All lines which come from infinity
   meet at the *focal point.*

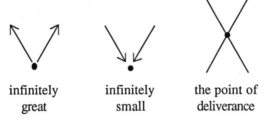

infinitely	infinitely	the point of
great	small	deliverance

— The infinitely great image appears at one single point.
   You are a funnel: the triangle is its sign.
   May this image guide all of your acts!
   Look! Beneath the cone of rays,
   there is a second inverted cone:
   that is deliverance.
   THE HUMAN IS THE FOCAL POINT.
   VERILY, A SINGLE POINT:
   THE POINT OF DELIVERANCE.

THIS MARVELOUS TASK IS OUR WAY –
NOT FORMS AND RELIGIONS.

L. Tell me more about deliverance!
— I am always speaking about deliverance … always!
You are but a minute being in the Creation,
and yet you are an image of the Divine:
you *radiate* this image.

— Ask!
L. Is there a task for the physical organs
at higher levels?
— There is a deep secret concealed in what I now say:

EACH ORGAN OF YOUR BODY
IS AN IMAGE OF A UNIVERSAL FORCE –
IT RECEIVES ITS STRENGTH FROM THIS FORCE.
YOUR HEARTBEAT IS IDENTICAL
WITH THE HEARTBEAT OF THE UNIVERSE.

But if these forces are left without a task
all is for naught:
existence without a goal is confusion, chaos.
Sickness, too, is chaos.
The meeting of the forces of the universe *at one point*
is New Creation.
The recognition of your task - the funnel –
is Creation.
EACH OF YOUR ORGANS IS SACRED.
THE BODY – THE FINITE –
IS A TINY REPLICA OF THE INFINITE.

Heaven be with you!

Friday, December 10, 1943

25. DIALOGUE WITH GITTA

We feel the wordless presence of my angel and await the beginning of the dialogue. Suddenly, the shrill ringing of the telephone cuts through the silence, shocking us all. I hastily disconnect it and reproach Joseph: "It was supposed to be your job to disconnect the telephone!"

— *I declare war!*
In the past, you have defended yourselves:
from now on, attack!
Only a weak fire needs protection from the wind.
Fear not to enter into battle!

WHO CAN FIGHT AGAINST DARKNESS? *LIGHT*.
AND WHO WILL BE VICTORIOUS? *THE LIGHT*.

Darkness is dead, lifeless, unchanging.
What is dark is dark.
Nothing is darker than darkness.
Darkness cannot increase, but Light can decrease.

Silence.

— Listen carefully, my servant, I will teach you:
What is fever?
The heart beats – that is rhythm.
What disturbs the regularity of the rhythm?
A foreign, poisonous substance enters the blood,
the heart beats faster and the fire becomes hotter.
If destructive substances are in you,

149

your rhythm is disturbed,
and what disturbs must burn.
That is fever. Fever purifies the blood
and the rhythm then adjusts itself.
You have less and less fever,
for the old in you heals.

G. I would like to completely burn away
what is rotten in me!

— There you are wrong: Let nothing rot!
Fever is necessary only when something is rotten.

G. Why am I not aware when something begins to rot?

— Stop defending! Attack! Rise up against darkness!
When you really burn, you will not find enough matter
to burn ... let alone to rot.
Listen well! Just what you believe to be your fault
can become your virtue
if you only recognize it:
You do not see the human being.
This is not a fault,
for your eyes are not meant to *see.*
If your eyes would *shine,* all would be well.

DO NOT TAKE PART IN DARKNESS,
BUT GIVE LIGHT, ALWAYS AND EVERYWHERE.
THEN DARKNESS WILL FLEE.

How do you know that it is dark?
In what does darkness show itself in a room?
In the lamp when it does not burn.
The lamp is responsible.
LIGHT THE HUMAN
AND DO NOT GRIEVE OVER DARKNESS!
THAT IS YOUR LAW.

I declare war and not peace.
Be attentive to rhythm, for it is the Divine message.
Ő judges through you – Ő does battle through you.
Take heed to serve the Divine
and not evil, which is the past!
Only by means of rhythm
will you be able to differentiate between the two.

G. That is not clear to me …

— The fire burning in you – the fire of the body –
is called life, and it builds. Fever destroys.
It is the same fire, but in excess.
Your heart knocks seventy times: seven times ten.
In the absence of evil, even the deepest wound
heals in *seven* days.
Rhythm is the capacity of the vessel.
One drop too much … and it overflows.

Take care: listen, always listen, for this rhythm
is no longer the rhythm of the body.
The mind cannot grasp it.
Leave the mind in its own realm!
The fire of life is eternal;
the fire of fever is transitory.
The *more* is not always better.
The intensity of your fire
would be a fatal fever for someone else.
There is only one key: stay alert!

*The loudly ticking alarm clock had disturbed me so
much before the dialogue that I had put it away in
the cupboard. Just now, the alarm goes off: I had
forgotten to disengage it.*

151

— Let this be a lesson to you, for you judged before:

    In an ironic tone of voice:

— "It was supposed to be your job"… to ensure silence.

    My companions are heartily amused.

— We teach you because you are dear to us
and you like to learn. Ask!

G. What is meant by 'eternal damnation'?

— A goblin, a bogeyman! I can reveal it to you.
But woe to those who *need fear*
and no longer believe in damnation.
They no longer fear anything,
though fear would actually help them.

ETERNAL DAMNATION IS:
TO BE UNAWARE THAT THEY ARE *IN IT*
AND TO HAVE NO FEAR.

The absence of fever in the body is a victory
by the poisoner of life.
I declare war, that they may again learn
to be afraid, for there is no more fear in them.
There is no more fever in them
and that is their damnation.
Fever is not punishment, but healing.

THEY FEAR ONE ANOTHER … AND THAT IS HELL.

They fear the bomb
rather than God's hand,
which strikes with certainty.
I speak of fear: fear is the seed of belief.
Young tribes are afraid. Of what?

Of the unknown. What is the unknown?
That which is beyond them, the Greater.

YOUR LAW IS JOY, NOT FEAR:
ALREADY THE SEED IN YOU BEGINS TO SPROUT.

When it sprouts and sheds its husk,
the seed disappears and fear is gone.
But the others have need of fear.
Our battle is not the old battle.
We proclaim the new, the unknown.
This brings the beginner fear, and the chosen, joy.

> *I have the impression that the 'chosen' is someone
> who has voluntarily taken on this earthly task.*

— Never forget: what gives life to you ...
scorches others to ashes.

> *Joseph has just had an operation for a ruptured
> hernia. In his youth, he had believed that the
> salvation of humanity would come from an
> equitable and universal distribution of material
> goods. It had become his 'materialistic ideal.'*

— I speak to the convalescent one:
the old lack has been filled.
The man of the past lifted more than he was able.
HE HAS LIFTED MATTER ABOVE HIMSELF,
AND IT TORE HIM.
May the scar remind you of this, my son!
It is the image of a whole age! But you are cured.
The scar may reopen, but it is no longer dangerous.
You are healing. Let us give thanks!

153

Friday, December 10, 1943

24. DIALOGUE WITH LILI

Lili dreamed that she was asked: "If you should die, what would be your last wish?" In the dream, she responded: "That what I am receiving now might continue to live on in my students."

— I will speak about your dream:

GERMINATION IS THE DEATH OF THE GRAIN.

The small creatures living under the ground
see only the death of the grain;
they do not see the sprout,
which is above the soil.
The new Sprout is the new Being.
You chose well in your dream:
you gave up the perishable in exchange for the eternal.
And the one who gives shall receive.
The new sprout – the eye of the seed – is only *one*.
It is above duality, beyond *two-ness*.
Do not fear death … death does not exist!

IF YOU ACT WITH ME,
YOU WILL KNOW NO DEATH.

Take good care: what I am saying is of the essence.
Only for the weak is the certainty of death a stimulus.
But you are no longer weak. Your time is short,
but do not let that guide your actions!

*In the silence that follows, I anxiously ask myself
what 'your time is short' means in terms of earthly*

*time. I have often observed that the angels' sense of
time is very different from our own. Fifteen months
later, my question was to be answered.*

— 'The one who speaks' now sees you shining.
  Ask, my servant!
L. May I ask a question for 'the one who speaks' –
  for Hanna?
— There is no need for questions: she will be answered.

L. How could humanity improve itself a little bit?
— There is no such thing as *a little bit.*
  It is *all* one or *all* the other.
  Do you eat meat that is rotten?
L. No.
  Meat that is *a little bit* rotten ... would you eat it?
L. No.
  All one or *all* the other. What rots?
  Matter whose essence has departed.

  Silence.

— Marvelous! Two eggs:
  In one, the germ of life; in the other, nothing.
  Only upon hatching does it become apparent:
  In the warmth, the germ grows – the germless rots.
  You can brood, you can warm –
  but you cannot provide germs.
  Do not worry; but always give warmth.

  Ó ALONE GIVES GERMS;
  Ó, THE LORD OF GERMINATION.

  Do not concern yourself with the 'where' of the germ.
  Warm! Awaken!

155

The rotten and the foul are germless.
They still belong to the age of the curse.
The little bird casts the rotten egg from its nest,
without pity, for warming it would be useless.

BUT THE HUMAN STILL SITS ON THE GERMLESS EGG
AND CONTINUES TO WARM IT.

Though it spoils, rots, putrefies,
still the human continues to warm it,
fearfully protecting the rotten egg
from which the new will never hatch.
And remember:
as long as a bird continues to brood,
no new eggs are laid.
Do you understand this lesson?
To you, it seems merciless, but it is not. It is strong.
A sure sign: What spoils when warmed is germless;
what sprouts is good.
But you: just warm! Nothing else.
Rottenness is its own judge. Just radiate warmth!

L. Where am I making mistakes in my teaching?
— In exactly the same way. Listen:
The chicken that is halfway hatched
appears to be rotten.
But growing life absorbs what is apparently rotten
and transforms it.

DO NOT CHANGE THE BAD – STRENGTHEN THE GOOD!

Thus the good will absorb the bad
which is all around it.
I have more to say: Praise!

Praise the praiseworthy in everyone, everywhere!
True praise strengthens, you will see wonders.
But never praise falsely,

AND NEVER LIE, EVEN WITH GOOD INTENTIONS!

   Ask!

L. What is panic?

— Terror! Turning away from God! Sudden split!
Terror is the ancient god, the terrible:
Pan – panic. Only the animal has need of terror.

L. What is readiness?

— The right attitude.
If the tool is ready, it can be used at any time.
Being human is being ready.

THE HUMAN IS THE TOOL OF GOD.

Not to be ready is to be useless.

L. Why is there so much vengeance
and malicious joy in the human?

— A happy person is neither vengeful nor malicious,
and does not rejoice at the misfortune of others.
The sick hate the healthy ... the unhappy, the happy ...
the drunken, the sober.
Hate is fear, active fear, masked fear, shame.
The sick person spreads sickness.
Therefore, I say to you: spread health! Just that!
That is our war.
Do not struggle against sickness – strengthen health!
These are two completely different things.
The doctor who only represses illness, errs.
Ő is the healing force.
To act *with* this force is real healing.

Thus it is possible for a lay person
to better heal than a learned physician.

L. Is any one form of art more valuable than the others?
— Yes. The one that best serves.
Only the most valuable can serve the Divine.
By their fruits you may know them.
But every art is changing.

For one instant – let us be *one!*

Friday, December 17, 1943

26. DIALOGUE WITH GITTA

— I will speak of creation in art.
A work of art is mere matter.
A sculpture stands in space.
The sculpture itself is not creation;
it is but a vessel.
When the vessel is filled, the drink creates.

> *Hanna is unable to find words for what my teacher*
> *wants to communicate about the new Art.*

— If only I could speak about new Art!
If only I could!

WHAT WAS VESSEL – WILL BE DRINK.
WHAT WAS DRINK – WILL BE ECSTASY.

This is a sterile period in time.
The hands of merchants grasp empty vessels.

Incense is offered for the artist.
Incense is offered for the very one
who should be offering it.

The smoke descends and Cain has the word.
Everything parches. They are afraid of death.
They cage the bird – the blue bird –
until it becomes a gray sparrow.
Picture galleries, storerooms, crypts!
They guard dead skins. Odor of tombs.
No one looks ahead … they all look back.
Who serves the Divine? Who? Whom do you serve?

G. *(timidly:)* I would like to serve the Divine!
— But *do* you?
G. Not always …
— *(severely:)* Still 'not always'!
G. *(meekly:)* … what should I do?
— There is no 'should'!
Form a new vessel for the Divine, all of you:
a new cup for the drink!

THE DRINK STREAMS FORTH
BUT THERE IS NOTHING TO RECEIVE IT!

The new building, the new temple, has no walls,
for it is always growing.
Change! Change in every way!
The ancient temple, the ancient church,
was protection, fortress, refuge.
The new one is different: it has no walls.
Proclaim the new World with the means
you have been given. Do not be lazy!

This week, I had again not had the courage to begin a new oil painting. I was afraid.

— Even *you* are still afraid! Create!
Not with fear, but with joy!
You stand at a higher level.
If you begin to fear, that is death for you.

REMEMBER: *MUST* AND *SHOULD* ARE DEATH!

May joy guide every line you draw ...
you draw them for the Divine!
If only I were able to speak of the new Art!
It has never before existed ...
not even for the greatest artists.

I am amazed to learn that not even the greatest artists meet the standards of the new Art. But when I realize that the new Human is only in the early stages of becoming, I understand that there cannot yet be such a thing as the new Art.

— Ask!
G. What is meant by the 'Last Judgment'?
— What do you not understand?
G. Everything that you say is new
and the old concepts acquire a new taste.
— It is not the taste that changes,
but the one who tastes.
Only the dead palate needs spiced foods.
For the living, bread is the best.
The hungry need neither caviar nor paprika
on their bread.
If you are healthy and not ill,

what tastes good to you is what you need.

That I did not receive an answer to my 'Last Judgment' question is not surprising, because I had been anticipating a 'sensational' answer.

G. What are those moments of life which have an
   enchanting taste, which are special moods?
— A deep mystery. The sun is white;
   but *fragmented,* it becomes multi-colored.
   That is the 'enchanting' taste of eternity, *fragmented.*
   Soon you will understand this.
   Do you believe that there are seven colors?
G. Yes.
— There are infinitely more ... but you see only seven.
   When you cease to be who you were,
   you will see all of the new Colors.
G. Will I also paint them?
— Those who see your painting will perceive
   the new Colors, but they will not be on the canvas.
   Do not seek the new Colors outside.
   Red is a universe of suns and moons and worlds.
   Blue is another universe ... the new is within you.

EVERYTHING IS WITHIN YOU AND NOT WITHOUT.

   Ask!
G. What is 'resurrection'?
— A necessary evil.
   If you are already above,
   rising, re-surrection, is unnecessary:
   only what is below can 'resurrect.'
   Fallen, in the depths of the tomb ...
   it rises up again.

Re-surrects.
It is a spectacle.

WHAT IS THERE TO RESURRECT
IF YOU ARE UNITED WITH THE DIVINE?

The Kingdom of the Divine approaches.
Call and it will come: it is within you.

Friday, December 17, 1943

26. DIALOGUE WITH LILI

— I will speak of playing.
What is play? Preparation.
Practicing for mastery over force and matter.
Mastery is preparation for creating.
Here is an example: children are playing.
Two of them hold a rope and twirl it … a third jumps.
The rope is matter set in motion by an outside force.
The child jumps.
If it jumps too early or too late,
the rope deals the child a blow.

THE RIGHT MOMENT IS THE GOAL.
AND THE RIGHT MOMENT
IS THE JOY OF PLAY.

Teach playing –
not *with* the body but *through* the body.
You teach children.
Teach them to play, to play new Games!

162

Prepare them to be creative!
No more old games, *new* ones!
Did you play when you were a child, my servant?

L.　Hardly ever …

—　Then it is right for you to teach others,
　　for you know the lack well. Now you, too, will play.
　　See the child in your pupils, awaken the child:
　　but not the old one!
　　Only when the old leaves fall can the new bud sprout.
　　Listen well!
　　I will whisper wonderful new Games in your ear!
　　The child jumps … the dancer leaps and twirls.

EVERY ORGAN, EVERY LIMB IS ONE
WITH A FORCE OF THE UNIVERSE.

Do you have an idea of what dancing is?
The swirling force raises up –
the whirlpool draws down.
What a powerful whirlpool the old dance is!
It pulls, it tears *downward* into the body.
The new Dance is *upward* whirling force.
But for now, just play! Prepare yourselves!
New Game … new Dance … new World.

THE PLAYING CHILD FORGETS ITSELF.

That is exactly what brings forth the new Game.
The child unable to play alone is not alive.

Forces whirl you about, hurl you – or you hurl them.
The difference is great! You feel it, don't you?
It is given to you to serve the Divine.
Could anything be more wondrous?

Oh, if you could but once taste self-forgetful play!

CREATION IS BUT SELF-FORGETFUL PLAY.

The creating Master forgets the carefully prepared
tool and yet there is no harm, for it serves.

I await your question.
L. Why am I so easily driven to despair?
— What despairs you?
L. More often *small* things than big ones.
— And therein lies the answer:
    small things concern the *small* Lili.
    But you – separate yourself from them!
    The *small* Lili will deal with them.
    Des-pair is not unity, one.
    Do not dwell in despair, in two-ness!*
    Leave the old behind
    and you will be free from despair.
    You will also leave behind the new;
    all is to be left behind,
    for everything is but husk, empty husk.
    Ask!
L. What is pain?
— Guardian angel, guardian angel of the animal.
    Fear is the sign that comes *before* error.
    Pain comes only *after*. Both are indications, signals.
    But your sign is joy.
    Are you joyful when you are with me?

>   *Lili is unable to express herself in words;*
>   *she nods silently.*

---

* The Hungarian word for despair is *kétség* (two-ness).

— What would make you even more joyful?

L. That would be absolutely *impossible!*

NOTHING IS IMPOSSIBLE! THERE IS NO IMPOSSIBLE.
IMPOSSIBLE DOES NOT EXIST.
EVERYTHING IS POSSIBLE!

> *A long silence follows. We all feel that something essential is happening in Lili. I avoid looking at her, feeling that my gaze could disturb a deep and sacred happening inside of her.*

— Ask, my little servant!

L. It is so strange to ask now.
I had the feeling that I ceased to exist.

— Truly, you *will* cease to exist.
I rocked you in my arms,
you, who never were rocked.
And it was good for me to rock you.

> *I feel this as an allusion to the loveless and lonely childhood of Lili, who had been an unexpected and undesired child.*

— BEFORE BIRTH – THE OLD BIRTH –
MOTHER AND CHILD ARE *ONE*.
WHEN THE CHILD IS BORN – THEY BECOME *TWO*.

YOU AND I ARE *TWO*.
WHEN WE ARE BORN – WE BECOME *ONE*.

For you, this is a mystery. You cannot yet grasp it.
Ask!

L. What is tiredness?

— The old rhythm ... a pause between two sounds.

If you act in the new, you cannot be tired.
If you are tired, that is the small death.

Silence.

The tree of *everlasting life*.
The Father has given it to us, and we guard it.

*Her angel shows the specifically fatherly aspect of
the Divine to Lili, who had not experienced fatherly
love as a child.*

We will give it to the one who no longer listens
to the serpent, owner of the *other* tree.
We guard the tree of eternal life ...
we guard it well ... with sword in hand.
But why the tree if there is no fruit?
And why fruit if there is no one to eat it?

It is not the fruit which is unripe – but the eater.
This is why we continue to guard the tree.
The good Father does not guard the beautiful fruit
for Himself, but for the children.
The infant cannot yet eat the fruit,
as the Father well knows.
You are in Paradise at every moment.
Two forbidden trees. You can choose!
The serpent tempted you ... you ate ...
and the fruit was bitter.

WE FORBID ... WE GUARD
BUT YOU: *DO* COME –
TRIUMPH OVER US!

Apparent joy enticed you and you ate *fear*.

Our sword strikes down only the *fearful,*
for *fear* brought forth the sword.

You may ask another question, my servant!
L. I do not understand what is meant
by the cornerstone in the Bible.
— The bearer of weight, the redeemer, the despised.

Prepare yourselves, be ready!
Let us all serve the Divine!

Friday, December 24, 1943

27. DIALOGUE WITH LILI. Fragment.

— "An angel descended from heaven ..."*
You no longer need hasten to see the light,
for the LIGHT will be everywhere
and Bethlehem will be no more.
I proclaim a new Christmas,
no longer followed by Easter.
From now on, Easter is merely an empty shell.
But today the light, the old light,
is so revered that the flames of life are extinguished.

*These words are an ironic, bitter reference
to the war.*

— On the stone and on straw warmed by the animal
lies the newborn *in you.*

* From a traditional Hungarian Christmas carol.

Good is the stone, good the straw,
good the warm breath;
bad is the decayed stable, bad are the cold
and darkness outside.

Fear not! The dragon cannot reach the newborn.
The old dragon is beside its tree,
but the red apple no longer entices.
Do you see the newborn?

L. No.

— Do try to see it!

YOU BELIEVE YOU GIVE BIRTH
TO THE CHILD OF LIGHT,
BUT IT IS *Ő* WHO GIVES BIRTH TO YOU!

Silence.

— Do you have questions?

L. What is a real feast … a feast of the heart?

— A part of Heaven.

Downward gesture:

— What they do down there …
is the *split* of a broken heaven
which will never become whole again.
They gnaw at the splinters of the old heaven;
but we are building the new Heaven.
And we build it together.

L. What is 'goodness' … 'charity'?

— Worthless old splinters! Away with them!
Today everyone gives the 'good.' Rubbish!

ONLY Ő GIVES AND EVERYTHING IS GIVEN.
WE MERELY *TRANSMIT* THE DIVINE GIFT.

Tiny worms with delusions of grandeur say: "I give."
Do not be soiled by this kind of 'good.'
May there be no such 'good' in you!
Not evil has darkened the world,
but the 'good': the 'good' person, who says, "I give."
And see, what is given? Death!
You, 'good' people, you will pay the penalty.
In the coming new LIGHT,
everything false will crumble to dust.
What do you own?

L. Nothing.

— Then what can you give?

L. From myself … nothing.

— Rotten corrupt species! Woe unto you!
You build 'good' hospitals for your victims.
But you, my servant, you are not 'good':
the GOOD will come *through* you.
Ask!

L. How might religion and science become united?

— In the new Light, one will see that *they are one* …
They have always been one,
just as melody and rhythm are one and inseparable.
Each member of the great orchestra plays,
but the symphony is one.
Sometimes the violin leads,
sometimes the cello,
sometimes religion,
sometimes science.
But now: nothing! For no one serves: everyone leads.

169

More than all others, the drum,
for it is the loudest.

The conductor is a servant of the symphony's spirit.
But now there is not even a conductor.
The loudest dominates ...

Long silence.

May heaven bless you!

Friday, December 31, 1943

28. DIALOGUE WITH GITTA

*It is the last day of the year. In the past, I have
always found New Year's celebrations to be
meaningless and boring. But today I am full of
expectation as I wonder how the angels will mark
the passage from the old year into the new.*

— Alpha – Omega ... Omega - Alpha.
THE CREATED HUMAN STANDS
BETWEEN BEGINNING AND END.
THE CREATING HUMAN STANDS
BETWEEN END AND BEGINNING.

Between beginning and end is time.
Between end and beginning is timelessness.
The end of the old year is the beginning of the new.
The end of the old world is the beginning of the new.

Humans have always celebrated
what cannot be celebrated.

> *I do not understand at first, but suddenly it dawns*
> *on me that the timeless moment, the transition from*
> *the old year into the new, cannot be grasped by*
> *those who live in time.*

— The gateway to the narrow path is: Omega - Alpha.
The one who passes through it *bodily* – in time –
steps into death.
The one who passes through it *spiritually*
– beyond time – steps into eternity.
Can you measure time between Omega and Alpha?
A fleeting instant ends – a new instant begins.
Between the two, there is no time.
BETWEEN THEM IS ETERNITY.
There is a gateway to eternity:
It opens not at the beginning, but at the end.
The Creator sets in motion
and the new instant *is;*
the old is no more.

AT THE DEATH OF EACH INSTANT
YOU CAN ENTER INTO ETERNITY,
INTO THE CREATING WORLD.
AND THERE YOU – YOURSELF – SET IN MOTION.

This is visible to all and yet not seen.
The gate is open, but the opening is so narrow
that mortal flesh cannot pass through.
This is the greatest secret:
Every instant – even the instant of the instant –
is an open gate.

THERE IS NO SACRED INSTANT —
FOR *EVERY INSTANT IS SACRED*.

Thus you live in the eternal *and* in the temporal.
You are the ball *as well as* the player.
Do not pay attention to the beginning:
the beginning is already end.
What begins, ends, and cannot be altered;
for force and matter are already *in motion*.
Take heed:
The origin of everything, the birthplace of motion,
is between beginning and end.

The created world is a ball.
The Creator plays with it … gives the ball a push,
that it may return in joy.

IN THE CREATOR'S IMAGE:
CELESTIAL BODIES AND ATOMS, ALL.

    Silence.

— Learn this:
There is only one certainty, and that is *joy*.
Everything can be explained: joy has no explanation.
We cannot explain why we are joyful.
Joy is our task.
What you receive is a source of joy for the joyless.

— Ask, my servant!
G. Please, tell more about the eternal instant!
Would you explain it to me in another way?
— The eternal instant is a ray of eternal Light.
Humans have the task of creating an opening
in the sphere where they live

so that the ray can enter.
No need to demolish a house to let light in!
A window suffices.
To reach up to the infinite Light,
it is necessary to go beyond the created.
Only thus can you reach it.

BEYOND THE CREATED
YOU ARE LIBERATED AND YOU LIBERATE.

How deceptive is this sphere from within,
with its suns and moons and 'infinite space,'
which in reality is finite!
With its billions of years; its billions of years,
which are nothing compared to an eternal instant.

If an opening is created in the sphere
where you live, there is no more prison,
there are no more *prisoners;*
just *inhabitants* in the sphere.
No more curse, but blessing.
No more darkness, but Light.
No more suffering, but joy.
This tiny opening is deliverance.

After a long silence:

— Take heed of measure! What is more –
below as above –
is deviation from the path.
Therefore learn to feel: too much – too little.
'Enough' is equilibrium
between force and matter, between finite and infinite.
BETWEEN THE TWO IS THE PATH: ENOUGH.

Take care, do not stray from the path!
Your measure is unique.
Everyone has a key: your *own* measure.

— You may ask another question.
G. We see the bad and speak of it.
　　Where is the boundary between clear seeing
　　and pretentious judgment?
— Measure. You are a bringer of Light.
　　Know the weakness of the eyes!
　　But not in a judgmental way!
　　If your entire being serves deliverance,
　　then you will *measure* and not *judge*.

JUDGMENT BELONGS ONLY TO THE DIVINE.

Everything changes! The solution is: Omega-Alpha.

Listen carefully! There are Seven Joys.
Discover them! This is not an easy task.
Each of the Seven Joys will be the guiding spirit
of one day of the week.
I give you seven days to discover them.
Tell me next week what you have discovered.

I take leave of you.

Friday, December 31, 1943

28. DIALOGUE WITH LILI

— What is easy for me – is difficult for you.
What is easy for you – is difficult for me.
How difficult it is
to make you aware of even the simplest thing:

EVERY MOTION CAN BE AN IMAGE OF CREATION.

A push at one point sets into motion.
Listen well: motion begins at one point,
its point of origin.
And then it returns.
Everything is pushed and everything returns.

> *I understand that all motion is a pulse*
> *of the cosmic rhythm.*

The human follows a different law.
Knowledge has caused a bit of human deviation.
This 'bit' can corrupt everything.
But when the human returns
to the Divine Source of all motion,
the name of all motion becomes:
deliverance.

WHEN MOTION RETURNS TO ITS SOURCE,
JOY IS BORN IN THE HUMAN.

Even the vilest human is still human
in being able *to give*.
A single instant too soon or too late:
that is the apple of knowledge.

175

It was not meant for eating.
But the humans ate the apple
and hoarded Divine Knowledge for themselves.
The fault was not in the apple;
only the eating of it was forbidden.
This is an image of all that is human:
the forbidden apple seduces one to take and not *to give*.
Giving is everything.

THE FAULT IS NOT IN KNOWLEDGE –
BUT IN HOARDING IT.

When given, knowledge, too, is a blessing.
All that is given forth is a blessing.
But we can give only *through the Divine*.
We become one with the Source and that is joy.

TRUE MOTION IS DIVINELY INSPIRED
AND IT RETURNS TO THE DIVINE.

Teach everyone to give in this way
and the curse will come to an end.
It is not *you* who give;
teach only *how* to give.
Everyone can give; every motion can serve.
From inner motion evolves the outer.

I help you in your work, my servant:
joy is the sign.
Take note of what brings each person to rejoice.

WHERE SOMEONE IS UNABLE TO REJOICE,
THERE IS THE APPLE:
THE APPLE SELFISHLY EATEN AND NOT GIVEN ON.

Away with it!

Even the most miserable of those
you shelter under your cloak can learn to rejoice.
That is joy:
set in motion …
streaming outward …
totally spending itself …
and returning, like a breath of air.
Beginning, end and joy are in the heart.

JOY IS THE AIR OF THE NEW WORLD.

Ask!

L. What is peace?
— Not a pause between two wars.
Peace has never yet been – but it will be.
Peace! You only long for it; but not enough.

PEACE IS THE NEW VIBRATION.

Unlike anything before.

L. If there is no peace in me, I cannot rejoice.
— You speak truth.
L. Now the new year begins and I would like to start
in a completely different way.
Please help me!
— My peace is your peace. My joy is your joy.
Thus, cherish it!
Joy is infinite. You receive as much
as you are able to give forth.
Joy has no limits. It is your capacity to give
that is limited.

I feel that the angel could give Lili infinitely more,
but that she is not yet able to bear such intensity.
And so her angel's giving must be restricted
to the proper measure.

— Joy knows no limits, no beginning and no end,
    for joy is eternal.
    I also rejoice only to the extent
    that I am able to give to you.
    And you rejoice only to the extent
    that you are able to give forth.
    Rejoice then! May your joy be perfect!
    Give to the happy ... give to the unhappy!
    Be not sparing of your joy! May this be your new year!
    Ask!

L. What is hope?

— Why do you ask this, my little servant?

L. Because I feel it beginning to grow in me.

— Pay attention to where you direct your hope!
    If you direct it to the Divine,
    you will never be disappointed, for Ő gives all.
    Only the godless are hopeless.

Listen well!
Do not merely hope ... *give* hope!
Do not merely have faith ... *give* faith!
Do not merely love ... *show how* to love!
Not hope for yourself!
Not faith for yourself!
Not love for yourself!
That is the burden; it is light.
And you carry it lightly, that we know well.

178

Silence.

L.   It is unclear to me what 'spiritualism' and
'mysticism' are.

> *By this, Lili means exaggerated interpretations of*
> *sensational, inexplicable, paranormal phenomena.*

—   Naturally, it is completely unclear.
Do you know what a genuine *mystery* is?

A SMILE ORIGINATING IN THE DEPTHS OF THE SOUL.
THAT IS A MYSTERY.

Teeth-chattering, slobbering, despair of the
shipwrecked, that is what 'spiritualism' is.
They want a sign and it is not given to them.
NOT THE DEAD SHOULD BE CONJURED,
BUT LIFE: ETERNAL LIFE!

The sacred teaching is not hidden
in darkness and obscurity;
it radiates in bright daylight.
What they call up, they receive.
Leave the dead with their dead!
So often did they summon death
that finally it came.
Let us summon joy, and the Divine Realm will come!
Call not trembling with fear, but with jubilation!

COULD ANYTHING BE MORE NATURAL
THAN OUR TALKING TOGETHER?

Where is that thing you call 'mysticism'?
It has sunk. Everything old disappears.
Have you rejoiced today at being with me?

L. Oh, yes!
— Pass on this joy!

> *Feeling that the dialogue is concluded, I work at
> completing my notes. Suddenly Lili's teacher
> speaks to me:*

— Do nothing afterwards!
Do everything in its time!
Write even the accents in their proper time!

> *I am astonished.*

— Do not take this as jest.
Joking is foreign to me ...
but I know joy.

Ő is peace.
May peace – not mine, but Divine peace –
come over you!

Friday, January 7, 1944

29. DIALOGUE WITH GITTA

— Today, I will speak of the cradle of joy.
Hate, fire and poison comprise the cradle of joy.
The created world is the body of the Divine.
Can there be evil in Ő?
Bile, too, is a well of joy and yet bile is poison.

> *Bile, in itself very bitter, serves in the digestive
> process by breaking down food and transforming it.*

180

— There is a fire in your body that does not destroy,
a poison that does not kill.
How can this be?

EVERYTHING IN THE GREAT PLAN IS GOOD.

Understand the secret: *transformation!*
The human being is called upon to *transform.*
What is bad is the 'more.'

The cruelest beast in existence is the human;
and this same creature is the cradle of eternal joy.

FORCES NOT USED, FORCES NOT TRANSFORMED
DEVASTATE ... DESTROY ... POISON.

> *Sinking gesture:*

— Listen carefully: what is bad here *below* ...

> *Uplifting gesture:*

... is good there *above.*
Everything depends on this.
Forces are destructive
when they are not in their proper place.
There is no destruction if you lift them up.
Then from poison comes healing and from fire, light.
This is why the human stands upright
rather than crawling.
Out of all the evil you can imagine
is born the new Jerusalem.

THERE IS NO EVIL –
ONLY THE UNACKNOWLEDGED TASK.
UNACKNOWLEDGED, IT DESTROYS.

Evil is the cradle of joy.
You flee in vain from evil … for there is no evil.
Evil: the eternal question of humanity!
No one knows it, but I proclaim:

EVIL IS GOOD THAT IS FORMING,
BUT NOT YET FORMED.

Disease. Each human organ is a force.
Together in harmony, they bear fruit!
Where there is a fault, the 'more' leaks out.
If bile overflows, it becomes poison.
The 'more' overflows and destroys the whole.
If the 'more' has no way out, it forces a way,
and what would *above* become the new World,
below becomes poison.
Above: life, secret eternal source of joy.

If you raise everything up,
you hold eternal joy in your hand.
There is no evil.
Held high, the destructive force of scorn
becomes Hallelujah.
Fire destroys … raised up, it is flaming joy.
Only know this, and all illness, everything vile,
everything evil, comes to an end.
This is the scepter I place in your hand.
It connects below and above.
Take it and know: no longer *two* – but *one*.
No longer good and bad: only good!
I give it to you all. Do you accept it?

G. Yes.
L. Yes.

Joseph hesitates and does not speak.
Sternly to him:

— Answer!

J. Yes.

> *The image of the scepter becomes clear to me for*
> *the first time: true kings rule in the vertical line,*
> *uniting heavenly and earthly forces. The scepter is*
> *held vertically in the hand, and the hand signifies*
> *the* act. *To me, this means that the real Kingdom is*
> *attainable only by means of rightful acts on earth ...*
> *and that is everyone's task. Our openly pronounced*
> *acceptance of the scepter calls down heavenly help*
> *for this task.*

— What did you discover about the 'seven joys'?
   I am waiting.

> *In seven sentences, I relate what I experienced as the*
> *'seven joys.' (These notes were subsequently lost.)*

— I do not accept this. Raise it higher!
   How will you raise it up?

G. That is just what I wanted to ask you.

— It is not yet simple enough;
   you have not yet tried hard enough.
   Your task was great.
   Those are not yet the *Seven*.

   There are infinitely many joys.
   In the end, there will be seven words,
   not seven sentences.
   You are already a *word:* 'One-I,' individuality.*

* *Egy-én* ('One-I') in Hungarian means: 'Individuality.'

183

Individuality: concentrated work of billions of years,
collaboration, union of cells.

What you brought is not enough.
You thought your task was easy.
When the grapes are freshly picked, there is no wine:
only juice.
If you had picked the grapes last Saturday,
there would now be wine.
But you merely plucked sweet grapes here and there
along the way.
I asked not for grapes, but for wine, for old wine.
For only ecstasy rises to the Divine;
sweetness stays below.
I am waiting.

G. How could I elevate the bad through my acts?
— Transformation. Reforming.
You are the one who transforms.
The 'more' of the tree is its fruit.
When you eat the flesh of the fruit, you kill it;
but at the same time,
you transform it into human force.
The 'more' of the earth dies in you and is reborn.

YOU WELCOME EVIL
AND TRANSFORM IT INTO GOOD.
EVIL DOES NOT EXIST;
THERE IS ONLY FORCE
THAT HAS NOT YET BEEN TRANSFORMED.

G. When force flows through me, I feel different
radiations streaming out of each of my hands.
What purpose do they serve?

— Healing. Only together do they serve;
    separated, they have no task.
    Do not seek to 'know' … but serve!
    Then you will have new Awareness
    and not old knowledge.

    In the beginning was the Creation …
    then incompetent fools 'explained' it.
    The artist creates … the 'worms' explain.
    Poor little gelatinous worms in your skull!

    One last question!

G. I once believed I was acting according to my own law,
    but this was not so.
    How could I have so completely fooled myself?

— One word explains it: You said, 'I.'
    That was the end.
    A curtain descended between you and Eternal Truth.
    You could not have awareness,
    for you were in the dark.
    The curtain is called 'I.'
    Pull it away and you become Ő!
    Then you will no longer ask questions,
    for the Divine knows everything.

    If you act in the name of your law,
    you know nothing,
    you *cannot* know anything of yourself.
    Ő is total certainty … do not be uncertain!
    The human being is a scepter in the Divine Hand.
    The scepter unites above and below.
    I depart.

Friday, January 7, 1944

29. DIALOGUE WITH LILI

We quietly wait for Lili's angel but there is one disturbance after another. First, a young man repeatedly tries to start his motorcycle just beside our house, making a tremendous racket. The motor never quite starts and the struggle seems to go on forever. When he finally leaves, a mouse beneath the cupboard takes over the role of noisemaker: It is apparently playing football with a nut, which naturally attracts the attention of our cat; she complains relentlessly from outside the door to our room. Lili's angel speaks first to me:

— The noise is not without – but within.

THE LITTLE NOISES WITHIN YOU
CALLED THE NOISES AROUND YOU.

To us all:

— Ö is One – but has two hands.
Weight is one … faith is the other.
Matter listens to the left hand,
spirit to the right.
But the human is the wonder:

Hanna's widely outstretched arms are slowly brought together until the hands touch each other, forming a circle.

— Thus, there is no more weight,
thus there is no more faith.

The cat meows again. I am beside myself with rage.
Lili's angel turns back to me:

— WITH THE BEAST YOU DO NOT CALM THE BEAST.

I will stop for a while.

I carry the cat to the garden.
After a long silence, to Lili:

— Ask, my little servant!
L. My courses are becoming more and more difficult …
— What you doubt is not the new, but the old,
  and that is good. What hinders you with the new?
L. I cannot transform either myself
  or others quickly enough.
— My heart rejoices at you.
  You will find the new, my servant!
  It opens itself to those who seek it.
  Where do you feel the new?
L. I only sense that everything will be different.
— Through Ő, everything will become different.
  We are all working on a wonderful plan.
  Joy arises through the two, united as one.
  When you seek the new, the old is not lost,
  for it is one of the two.

L. I seek the one, the true, the just, and it disturbs me
  that I am not able to speak, to act and to move simply.
— As you approach the new, all of this will be fulfilled.

L. Why does it become so difficult to ask?
— Because the air is getting thinner
  and your lungs must adjust.

I RETREAT HIGHER ... EVER HIGHER.
BUT YOU ARE NOT ALLOWED TO GO AWAY FROM ME.

You do not even notice that you are rising.
It is forbidden for us to leave each other.
I draw you higher ... always higher,
for still we are not at home, where we can be united.

Everything becomes heavier and lighter.
Weight and task are two:
Weight becomes light ... task becomes heavy,
as you transform.
Matter, family, what a weight that was!
It is no more.
Freed from weight, have strength for the task!

What else is troubling you?
L. I am still very weak ...
— Do you believe that I am strong?
L. Yes. Through Ő.
— Then where is weakness?
L. I had lost sight of the Divine.
— Thus you are held:
supported from below ... blessed from above.
Rejoice, my servant! May you become aware!
Our time is ending.
If you have a last question, ask it now.
L. Where does self-centeredness come from?
— From Ő. Everything comes from Ő.
L. *(astonished:)* How can that be?
— Self-centeredness is the weight,
the left hand of the Divine.
For the animal, it is a matter of elevation,

188

but for the human, it is weight.
In its place, everything is good.

Heaven is with you.

Saturday, January 15, 1944

30. DIALOGUE WITH GITTA

*The Dialogue could not take place yesterday
because Hanna and Joseph were called to visit
Joseph's gravely ill father in the hospital.*

— I speak to you of the narrow passage.
  If you come to a standstill
  – and often you do stand still –,
  be aware of the reason:

THERE IS NO TRUE FAITH WITHOUT THE ACT.
THERE IS NO TRUE ACT WITHOUT FAITH.

Faith cannot be greater than the act;
an act cannot be greater than faith:
for they are *one*.
It is not your faith which is insufficient;
it is your act.

FAITH WITHOUT AN ACT IS NOT FAITH.

You could *do* more … you are still cowardly.
Be aware of what you are doing!
Not only have faith … but *act!*

189

Do you *act,* my servant?

G. What do you actually mean when you say, *'act'* ?

Very sternly:

— I asked *you!* Do not ask: answer!

G. I seldom act ...

— What does this indicate?

G. I do not use the force that is given to me.

— And what is the reason for this?

G. I do not know.

— Pay close attention:

ACT AND FAITH HAVE BEEN SEPARATED.

The reason was the many empty acts.
Now your heart begins to detest the meaningless act.
Already you can act without it being empty.
All of you! Take heed of the narrow passage:

ACT AND FAITH WILL BE ONE.
AND THERE WILL BE A NEW HEAVEN
AND A NEW EARTH.

G. Is thinking also an act?

— Only part of the act.
The act is one: *the task.*
There is no separate act in itself.
From dawn till dusk ... from dusk till dawn,
from birth till death ... only one act: *Serving.*
There is no small act ... there is only the task.
There are not many acts and not few acts;
there is only the fulfilled act
or the unfulfilled act.
You cannot stretch out your hand

without this being an act.
'Much' is always delusion.
A pause does not make two separate songs out of one.
Do not be misled!

Ask my servant!

G. What are sunspots ... what effect do they have on us
   ... and how could they be controlled?

— Why do you want to know this?

G. Because I recently watched the setting sun:
   with the naked eye, I saw big black spots
   and I was filled with anticipation of great horrors.

— How could I explain the effect
   of infinite numbers of suns to you?
   You are a curious child, but that is not a fault.
   You would be horrified if you could see
   the tremendous forces that race back and forth
   through you, without your knowing it.
   But if you are *whole* and if you follow your calling,
   there are no more blind forces,
   for then they act in you and through you.
   If not, they destroy you.

   Silence.

— Your task is not finished, but that does not matter.

G. I have been unable to paint because I could not find
   the 'seven joys.'

   All week long, I have searched in vain for the
   'seven joys' – with much effort, but no success.

— To paint and to enjoy is one and the same thing.
   You child! You have tried too hard!

Paint and rejoice ... rejoice and paint!
In this way, your task is formed.
Thus you will not have 'much' to do.
From dawn to dusk: ONE ACT!

 My angel turns to Lili:

— You asked yourself in your heart what life is.
 You will savor it when it begins.
 You merely taste it now, but soon you will *live* it,
 the still secret *new Vibration.*

 All of us who teach you are ONE.
 You ask, and accept my answers gladly.
 We are completely different and yet we are ONE.
 And how different you all are –
 to the splendor of the Divine.
 Different and yet truly ONE.

Saturday, January 15, 1944

30. DIALOGUE WITH JOSEPH

 *A deep silence follows the dialogue with my angel.
Hanna turns to Joseph and gazes steadfastly at him.
Suddenly he very clearly sees the image of his
angel, bathed in an intense green light. All
hesitation, all shyness and all false shame of
speaking is swept away.*

J. Speak to me!
— False shame is a sign of weakness.

Adam hid because he was not yet HUMAN.
The FATHER and your father are one.
Between them, the son.
The son is the link.
There is no death because the son is there.

Silence is my word.
From silence, create the *act*.
However loud your tool may be,
it creates silence in matter.

> *Joseph's work consists of carpentry and furniture
> building.*

— Silence – balance – measure.
The saw cries out and what it creates
radiates silence, peace and balance.

Do you have a question?

> *Joseph is deeply affected by his father's illness.*

J. Yes. Speak about death!
— You ask about something that does not exist.
I will answer you just the same.

WHAT IS DEATH BELOW ... IS LIFE ABOVE.
YOU, TOO, ARE DEAD AND LIVE ETERNALLY.

All else is time and illusion:
waves breaking on the shore,
infinity of small deaths ... that is life.
Cells die ... new ones are born.
Human beings die ... new ones are born.
Do not let your father go – he can still live on!

IT IS NOT DEATH THAT IS BAD,
BUT THE UNFINISHED TASK.

Ripe fruit falls from the tree of its own accord.
The fruit that falls is ripe … therefore it is good.
Your father is not yet ripe.
He misses something: that you also become father!

Joseph and Hanna have no children.

— That is what he misses.

Silence.

— You may call me any time, just as you called me now.
Any time!
May you be wrapped in silence.
May it protect you from temptation!
May it unite you with the Divine!
I do not depart.

Saturday, January 15, 1944

30. DIALOGUE WITH LILI

I greet all of you.

To Joseph, who had spoken for the first time:

— The circle is the key.
There is no hierarchy:
the circle is completed.
The last wall has crumbled.
Indescribable joy!
For the deceiver enters through the wall,
and without a wall, there is no entry.

I see an image of heavy, fortified walls formed by our fixed opinions. There, only there, can the deceiver creep in on us. In the new, the living, the ever-changing and transforming, there is no need to fear the deceiver.

— Even the deceiver helps us … everything helps us.

There is no more evil – already you know it.
Indescribable joy!

Silence.

Nothing is straight.
Not even a ray of light is straight.
Everything is circular.
Believe me, you move on a tiny segment
of the infinite circle.
And this part of the infinite circle is straight.
The mind cannot grasp this.
Ő is the center of all circles.
The smaller the circle,
the greater the presence of the Divine.
But every circle is necessary.

To Joseph:

— My son, your body still resists,
for you have entered a new circle.
All of you, become accustomed to ever smaller circles!
The deceiver circles around you,
no longer attacking at the breach – but at the wall.
Fear not, you are already very strong!

Ask, my servant!

L. Speak about life, that we might become alive!
— LIFE is not yet known to you,
for it is only now that you shall be born.
You only dream of life.

COMPARED WITH THE COMING LIFE,
THE PRESENT LIFE IS DEATH.

You would not yet be able to bear it:
but prepare yourself!
Sometimes you sense it.
L. But so seldom!
— What a big word! Now you feel the transition.
You must die a little bit ... apparently die.
The transition is dawn.
Night was velvety safe darkness.
Dawn is neither night nor day: dangerous transition.
Do not regret leaving darkness,
for Light is the greatest wonder of all!
Every transition is trial.
Fear not to leave darkness, for the root
– eternally in darkness –
remains united with the flower and the fruit.

Ask!
L. When I am alone, I am unable to try out new things,
to experiment.
— *Alone? ...* you are never alone!

IT IS NOT YOU WHO EXPERIMENTS;
IT IS YOU WHO IS EXPERIMENTED UPON.

*This is the second time that Lili has been told that
she is experimented upon. I ask myself if, in this
time of transition, such 'experiments' are being*

conducted everywhere. Are they the beginning of a general transformation of humankind? I experience the encounter with our angels as something so natural that I believe many others could likely be having similar experiences.

— You do what you are called for:
You transform yourself.
You hear the call and you come. That suffices.
Because of time and space,
the material result in matter will reveal itself only later;
but it cannot fail to come.

IF YOU TRANSFORM YOURSELF,
MATTER LIKEWISE TRANSFORMS ITSELF.

Your previous work is not lost; it will flower,
for the root is good.
It is called HELP.
All else is unimportant.
You *will* help: that is why you are here.
What still troubles you? Let me help you!

L. The feeling that I *must* rise higher …

— Free of *must,* you rise higher.
You come nearer to yourself.
I call you and you follow me.

Receive my joyful blessing, all of you in the circle,
for you have faith. Fear nothing!
The Realm of the Divine is near.
Death's last hour has tolled.
Bow your heads.

Gesture of blessing.

Friday, January 21, 1944

31. DIALOGUE WITH GITTA

I have been paralyzed all week by a distressing sluggishness. All of my activities seem 'flat' to me … totally lacking in flavor.

— What are you lacking?

G. I do not know.

— Are you hungry?

G. Yes … for teaching, yes!

— And when you ask, do you receive?

G. Yes, but I do not notice when I am sinking.

— You receive what you ask for. Is that not so?

G. Yes, when I do not ask for myself.

The voice becomes severe:

— Even when you ask *for yourself,* you receive.
Aren't you asking for food?
From whom do you receive it?

It dawns on me that the body's hunger and the soul's hunger are both forms of asking.

G. From the Divine.

— Then do not say that you do not ask for yourself!
YOU ARE AT THE CENTER OF A CIRCLE OF ASKING.
EVERYTHING IMPLORES YOU:
ALL OF UNFULFILLED CREATION.
YOU ARE A MEDIATOR FOR CREATION.
COULD THERE POSSIBLY BE A REASON
TO FORGET THIS?

You are *not allowed* to be depressed.
If salt were to lose its flavor, why use it?

> *I feel that I am like salt, which could add savor to*
> *everything ... but I tend to forget it.*
> *Silence.*

G. Please teach me constant adoration of the Divine!
— Do you believe that Ő is far away?
G. No.
— That Ő is close to you?
G. ... that Ő is everywhere.
— Then how can you adore the Divine
  only now and then?
  I cannot teach you to adore the Divine,
  but I can teach you that Ő is found in everything;
  that Ő is here and there and everywhere,
  in everything, even down in the depths.

YOUR TASK DEFINES YOUR PLACE:
YOUR PLACE IN THE DIVINE.

> *Hearing these words, I suddenly become aware that*
> *I am a* unique *thought of the Divine, a* unique *cell of*
> *the Divine body, with a* unique *task. Depression is*
> *a sure sign of having forgotten my task.*

— But your place is limited by time and space.
  Adoration – *constant* adoration –
  is nothing other than unity with the Divine.
  Speak!
G. How could I free myself from the false idea that
  'I *must* act' ... 'I *must* do'?
— If you adore the Divine, that *fulfills* you

and there will be no place for 'false ideas.'
Joy will *fill* you.
Not only shall *you* rejoice,
but everything surrounding you:
objects, matter, people, work, task ...
all shall rejoice ... except you.

YOUR JOY WILL BE ONE
WITH THE JOY OF THE DIVINE.

You will no longer feel divided.

G. If only this were possible *now!*

— It is possible *right now* ... not tomorrow!

Ask!

G. What is free will?

— To be free to live in this way, now and always.
Anything else is nothing.
That should suffice for you.

To us all:

— There is no slavery ... but there is the LAW.
Your law is to be united,
and that is your freedom.
Divided, you are slaves;
united you are free.

The way is free
and Ó is smiling upon you.

Friday, January 21, 1944

31. DIALOGUE WITH HANNA'S ANGEL

*We await Lili's angel, but with the first words, I
feel a presence of such measured and grave dignity
and strength that I am almost frightened. At the
same time, I 'recognize' with indescribable joy
Hanna's teacher. Though without any 'memory-
image,' I am absolutely sure I* know *this angel of
Divine Justice.*

— The 'one who measures' speaks to you:
What is growth for the plant,
what is movement for the animal,
is for the human: *giving.*
Giving is not fruit, but growth: preparation.

> *I become aware that 'giving' is not a concrete
> result, but the necessary condition for any growing.*

— If you do not always give: you wither.
The fruit is the new World.

I serve through 'measuring.'

THE UNMEASURABLE APPEARS IN THE MEASURABLE.
PERFECTION IN THE LIMITED
IS AN IMAGE OF THE UNLIMITED.

It is given to you to fill *your* measure.
Neither with waste nor greed,
but with *constant adoration.*

> *I am overjoyed that the angel of measure also
> answered my question about 'constant adoration.'*

201

— The measure is given: it is in you.
  Not the size of the measure is important,
  for the Divine fills all. If you fill *your* measure,
  you become similar to the Divine. Only then.
  To you, I proclaim that I measure;
  I measure since the beginning of time.
  That is my means of serving.
  I do not reward,
  I do not punish,
  I only measure.
  You carry reward and punishment in yourselves.
  In fulfilling your measure, you grow.
  If not, you wither.
  Do not believe that anything is impossible!

THE LAW OF WEIGHT IS: THE POSSIBLE.
THE LAW OF THE NEW IS: THE IMPOSSIBLE.

Leaden birds:
the door of your cage is open,
but you dare not fly!

> *Never had I ever felt so petrified in my habitual way
> of thinking as I do now. At the same time, I have
> the presentiment that a new kind of awareness will
> soon become possible.*

— I frighten you, that you may fly!
  I spoke. I depart.

> *After this dialogue, I begin to understand what my
> angel had told me much earlier: "Ő created you
> according to my image." I realize that each of us
> might come to resemble his or her own angel.
> The basic potentialities or seeds are given:*

202

The essence of Lili's nature corresponds to:
'The one who helps,' Hanna's to 'the one who measures,' Joseph's to 'the one who builds,' and mine to 'the one who shines.'

Friday, January 21, 1944

31. DIALOGUE WITH LILI

After a few silent moments, we feel the presence of Lili's angel.

— I now take the lead
and continue to speak about measure.
The only task of the animal is: itself.
It rejoices in what is its own:
its air … *its* food … *its* young.
If it is healthy, then it rejoices in all of these.
It lives in a circle known as: *itself*.
It perceives only what is within this circle,
and takes it in: it is a creature.

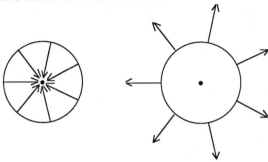

Human measure is exactly the opposite:
Your joy is what you radiate out of the circle.
Thus your joy is immeasurable.
The animal is hungry and eats until it is full …
until it has *enough*.
The human is fulfilled and radiates beyond itself …
and that is never enough.
Thus, human joy is immeasurable.

That is the mystery of eternal life.

Outside the village bell begins to sound.

— If a church-bell rings in a closed room, it is unbearable.

IF JOY IS ALL AROUND YOU,
THEN YOUR MEASURE IS RIGHT.

And this is possible. If you do not believe it,
then you do not believe in the Divine.
Ő always fills you to the brim,
for Divine mercy is boundless.

To Lili:

— I have come to answer you. Ask!
L. Why do humans want
to receive everything ready-made?
— Spoiled childhood:
ready-made toys …
ready-made knowledge …
ready-made food …
ready-made experience …
This is what the child receives,
and it ends up feeling nauseous.

The thirst for knowledge, the desire to create,
everything that forms the human, withers away.
The joy of experiencing oneself:
too much good advice kills it.
That is cowardice and lack of faith!

WHEN THE CHILD IS FULLY GROWN,
EVERYTHING IN IT HAS WITHERED AND DIED.

Learn a lesson from this, my beloved!
Never advise, never pre-chew the food!
Give differently, and all will be renewed
under your hand. Set trials and tasks!
Attract others to walk in your footsteps!
Do not guide, do not indulge in hand-holding!
You may even push the uncertain gently
and their certainty will be strengthened.
This is what you seek … and you will find it.

    Silence.

— Dismal gray is followed by
a wonderful radiance.
But now? So many colored pictures,
so many colored films
that the human eye becomes *gray.*

    *Only many years later did I become aware that color
    films (motion pictures) were something the angel
    had seen long before.*

— Instead of *giving* color,
the human *receives* it passively.
You may ask!
L. It is so difficult to awaken interest in the human …

— Were I to approach you, you would retreat.
Instead, I step back. And without even noticing it,
you learn to walk on air. Not on water: on nothing.

In the same way, I always give only *half* of an answer.
I leave out the other half.

In a bitter tone:

But humans give satiation.
They say, "We are so good to our children
and to everyone!"
With this, "we are so good,"
everything withers and dies away.
You! Give hunger, not satiation!
"Everything is known to us ... we know everything."
You! Open the *un*known!

Silence.

L. Why is it that so few people are able to concentrate?
— Because they concentrate on *nothing*.
So much noise, so much color penetrates from outside!
But you! Show something new that is stronger
than the strongest sound and yet: silence.
To that they will listen.

After an intense silence:

— Now I listened. And the sound was good.
You can hear it, too, if you listen intently.
Everything depends on *listening:*
measure, joy, everything!
Always listen!
Do you have another question?

Lili is still filled with the intense silence.

L. I feel that it would not be right for me to ask now.
— Because you did not ask now, you will receive
    two answers during the coming week.
    Listen carefully: two important answers!
    One from below and one from above.
    And the two will be ONE.
    Listen well, for it is not I who will be speaking.

    IF YOU TRULY LISTEN,
    EVEN THE STONES WILL SPEAK.

Friday, January 28, 1944

32. DIALOGUE WITH GITTA

— I speak about height and depth.
   Sounds float in space, they vibrate.
   And yet one speaks of *high*-pitched sounds
   and *low*-pitched sounds.
   If we designate notes, sounds on paper,
   the high ones are above and the low ones, below.
   In *reality* there is no distance between them.
   High and *low* are separated only on the plane of matter.
   On the plane of spirit, they are near to one another.

   Listen closely! I speak of the cross.
   In the cross are two forces:

Upward, vertical motion: ↑

WAY.

Horizontal motion: ———

RESISTANCE.

The first resistance is the earth: horizontal force.
The second resistance is water: horizontal force.
The third resistance is air: horizontal force.
The fourth resistance is between matter and non-matter.
This resistance is what you now penetrate.
There is a point where the forces intersect …
a part of the way left behind.

Gesture from below to above:

— Earth … water … air … and the 'not yet known.'
You cannot lift earth into water, nor water into air.
Everything has its place.

DO NOT LIFT; DO NOT PULL DOWN:
JOIN TOGETHER!

Earth belongs to the earth …
water to water … air to air.

New resistance: MATTER AND NON-MATTER
3rd resistance: AIR (thoughts)
2nd resistance: WATER (feelings)
1st resistance: EARTH

— MOVE BEYOND THE NEW RESISTANCE
WITHOUT LEAVING MATTER BEHIND.

Thus height and depth in the created world
become ONE.
Distance disappears not in the horizontal,
but in the vertical direction.
Machines race through the air
and the distance between above and below
becomes ever greater.
The faster they speed, the greater the distance.
Horizontal force is an inert force.
Resistance is inertia and that is good.

Gesture from below to above:

— The ascending ray transforms itself by piercing the
inertia of resistance.

*Last week I had been asking myself questions about
my evolution but was unable to find a satisfying
answer. Today I have been struggling to follow the
dialogue, as it seems to me rather abstract and
theoretical. Then I suddenly discover that it exactly
answers my previous questions: Evolution is
possible only along the vertical line. Evolution
occurs by means of our capacity of intuition, for
only intuition is capable of attaining the new level
where spirit and matter meet. The ascending ray of
evolution transforms as it pierces the levels of
matter, sentiments and thoughts. But then the
inverse takes place:*

*it is thought, sentiment and matter
which are transformed and
fulfilled by the descending ray of
light. Descent follows ascent.
This is not at all abstract for me: it
is observable within, a process of
successive detachment.*

— TODAY THE HUMAN
DOES NOT PIERCE THROUGH, INTO THE NEW,
BUT IS FLATTENED BETWEEN TWO RESISTANCES,
AND BECOMES PASSIVE.

That is the answer to your questions about evolution.

Outside there is a windstorm.

— Wind is a horizontal force.

Gesture from the throat to the mouth:

— 'The one who speaks' is weak here:
as she came to the air of the world,
this part was not yet ready.

Hanna had been born two months prematurely.

— All of you! You are now ready
to pierce the last resistance. Act!
Only one point is difficult:
there, where the two directions intersect.
Be careful!

THERE, SPIRIT AND MATTER MEET.

Do not go astray!
Joy is no longer the way-sign it was before.

Only if you look into the depths beneath you
will you see joy.
What previously was pain you shall also leave behind.
The new Joy is still nameless.
Do you have a question?

G. How can I know that I join spirit and matter?

— By the fact that you recognize it *afterwards*.
Knowing and thinking belong to the level of air,
which is still matter – but subtle, finest matter.

There is no high and no low,
there is nothing brought low, nothing base,
if you achieve union with the Divine.
Away from the Divine, there is above and below.
United, all is One.
All of you:
May Heaven bless you!

Friday, January 28, 1944

32. DIALOGUE WITH LILI

— Ask!

L. I did not hear the two answers you promised me:
one from below, the other from above.

— Has this week been light or heavy?

L. Heavier than last week.

— Where did you feel heaviness?

L. In my mood.

— Do you know why?

211

L. No.

— My little servant! The fish splashes happily about
in the water. You move higher …
there you are not yet able to 'splash about.'

Silence.

— Listen well! I have more to say about
the cross.
Vertical gesture from below to above:

— That is the *act*.

Horizontal gesture: ———

— That is *rest*.
Resistance is also rest.
The body becomes weary and lies down to rest.
Where does it lie down?

Horizontal gesture: ———

— On the earth.
Feelings are water-related … thoughts are air-related.
The levels become ever more subtle
and yet ever more difficult to pierce through.
The easiest to pierce is the earth …
More force is needed to break through feelings,
and still more to penetrate thoughts.
How is this possible?
Through a rhythm of acting and resting.
The level you now break through
is beyond all weariness.

Powerful rapid gesture from above to below:

— *This* penetrates every level lovingly …

In a flash, I now grasp what Lili's angel had told us six weeks ago: "If you act in the new, you cannot be tired." Only the vertical act is beyond weariness. But we nearly always act in the old, horizontal, passive way and therefore we are tired ... so tired that even our sleep is disturbed.

I understand that matter, feelings and thoughts belong to the world of opposites. If we become aware of how they act in us, we transcend these 3 levels of the material world and embark on the way to the 4th level. In the same way, LIGHT is then able to flood down from above, uniting the 3 lower levels with its radiance.

TODAY THE HUMAN IS INACTIVE WHEN STANDING –
AND RESTLESS WHEN LYING.

The response to your question comes
from above and from below:
You are yourself the answer.
This is why it is so difficult to become aware of it.
The true answer becomes a part of you.
Every question is a sign of lack.
The true answer fills this lack
and is no longer separated from you.
The surest answer causes a new question
to arise in you.

    Outside the wind is howling.
— The wind rages ...
but we pierce through to its finest vibration;
beyond tiredness, pain, doubt and death.

We are approaching ...

Friday, February 4, 1944

33. DIALOGUE WITH HANNA'S ANGEL

— 'The one who measures' speaks:
Spring is here.
If we wish to harvest, we must prune the trees
and graft those which are receptive.
I do not see you, but I see the tree:

THE TREE OF LIFE.

In my hand, a terrible sharp sword.
The chosen are shoots on the tree.

IF THE NEW DOES NOT PIERCE THROUGH THE OLD,
THEN I STRIKE IT DOWN.

Do not fear my sword; it strikes only what is dead.
The dead cannot be grafted.
'The one who grafts' does not bring about growth,
but chooses what is good and what is bad.
Spring is here:
what contains life shall grow.
Fear 'the one who measures' – not the sword!
The bud dreams. The cut branch also dreams.
You do not feel the edge of my sword,
so terribly sharp as it is.
I do not graft, I only measure.

TIME IS MEASURED:
ETERNAL DREAM OR ETERNAL LIFE?
FOR THE FIRST TIME, THE TREE WILL BEAR FRUIT.

We have been guarding it for a long time.

We encircle the tree: we prepare the harvest.
Buds of fruit, tarry not! Burst through the old!
The sign is no longer joy, the sign is no longer pain.
That is the truth! *Be aware!*

Friday, February 4, 1944

33. DIALOGUE WITH GITTA

— Listen closely:
  We are four and you are four,
  but that does not make eight.
  'The one who measures' ... measures all of you.
  'The one who helps' ... helps all of you.
  'The one who builds' ... builds all of you.
  'The one who shines' ... shines upon all of you.
  Call us when you are unable to go on!

RIGHT NOW, ALL IS BEING DECIDED.

> *I sense that time is short; that tragic outer events are
> drawing near which we can only meet by means of
> inner transformation.*

— The plant has its sap;
  the human has joy of life.
  Sapless ... joyless ... dried out!
  That is completely up to you!
  The sap comes from below – as does joy of life.

Decision.
What you decide: shall be.

215

Decide, delimit: here the old ... there the new.
Do this, and the wall of limits
will be behind – not before you.
It will open, it will crumble.
But first: decide.

From now on, we will be with you, always.
You too: be with us!

WE DO NOT KNOW
WHEN THE DIVINE GRAFTER WILL COME.
YOU: THE BRANCHES;
WE: THE GRAFTS,
LET US BE READY!

> *I am so deeply moved by these words*
> *that tears well up in my eyes.*

— Sap is the old joy.
Be joyous, be kind to each and all –
including yourself.

> *I am amazed.*

— Do not be astonished: for you, the 'small I'
is already third-person.
G. But how can I be loving and kind to myself?
— If you leave your 'small I' behind,
it will be possible.
G. How can I do that?
— Open yourself up to the joy of living: it is up to you!

Take care! You will shine ... but only if you ask!
Asking is necessary.
Never weary of asking again and again.

You may call all four of us;
you may ask all four of us.

WITHOUT YOUR ASKING, WE CANNOT GIVE.

Calling and asking are signs of lack.
Without lack, there is no place for giving.
Have you anything to ask?

G. For the last two weeks, all of my acts have seemed
empty and meaningless …

— You are still dreaming.
Once you awaken, the dream will be meaningless.

G. I have no further questions,
but I beg you to continue.

— Let my words about the joy of living
be engraved in your heart!
Spring has arrived.
And yet, we are walking in a dry and lifeless forest.
The sap no longer flows: life is devoid of joy.
Who rejoices in life?

ONLY SAP-FILLED BRANCHES WILL BE GRAFTED:
DRY BRANCHES, NEVER!

My dear ones, I depart.

*I do not understand why, but this dialogue has a
completely different effect on me than all the
previous ones. A calm and comforting joy flows
through me.*

Friday, February 4, 1944

33. DIALOGUE WITH LILI

— Whom are you calling?

L. Ő and you.

— Whom are you calling?

L. You ... my teacher.

— There is but ONE TEACHER.
We merely bring you the Divine Teaching.
With whom are you speaking?

L. *(hesitatingly:)* with ... you.

— Are you certain?

L. *(with even greater hesitation:)* ... Yes.

— I am not 'the one who helps.'
'The one who helps' spoke before.
We are four and we teach you.
Today we exchanged roles.

L. Then my original feeling that it was
'the one who helps' speaking to Gitta
was right after all.

— THE ORIGINAL FEELING IS TRUE FEELING.
WHAT FOLLOWS IS REFLECTION.
ALWAYS LISTEN TO THE ORIGINAL FEELING!

The head only follows behind.

L. How wonderful that you have exchanged roles!

— When you take leave of your 'small I,'
the four become sixteen ... and ONE.
Listen carefully:
When you construct your new task,

218

call 'the one who builds'!
Call us: we will come!
Tomorrow call me, for then you will need to shine,
not help.

Lili will be attending a meeting of educators.

— Tomorrow you will shine forth the new Light;
not through words, but through your certainty,
for everyone there is confused.

This refers to the participants of the meeting.

— They do not search, they do not ask ... ;
they talk and talk and talk.
Ask!
L. Please tell me more about my sign!
—   The sign   The sign of   The sign
     of the Divine   the helper   of deliverance

— The triangle is the sign of helping.
You are able to help someone at all times.
Your sign is a reflection of the Divine sign.
If the lower triangle is not completed,
then the one above cannot be joined to it.
We four are bearers of four forces, but we eight,
we sixteen ... we all reflect the Divine.
Ask!
L. Please tell me how body, soul and spirit
are related.

219

— If they raise themselves to the Divine,
    they are related: if not, they crumble.
    Everything – including spirit –
    crumbles to ashes and dust if not related to Ő.
    Humans consider themselves to be related beings.
    But if they are not related to the Divine ...
    everything crumbles.

IF YOU ARE RELATED ONLY TO THE BODY –
THEN YOU ARE BUT BODY.

IF YOU ARE RELATED ONLY TO THE SOUL –
THEN YOU ARE BUT AN ANIMATED BODY.

IF YOU ARE RELATED ONLY TO THE SPIRIT –
THEN YOU ARE BUT HUMAN.

IF YOU ARE RELATED TO THE DIVINE –
THEN YOU ARE ALL.

Be related only to the Divine, and then
body, soul, spirit and Ő are ONE.
You can recognize everyone by their relatedness.

Teach true relating, the only freedom;
all else is slavery!

> *In spite of being ill, Lili had joyfully traveled from
> Budapest to Budaliget so that she might be present
> at today's dialogue.*

— Because today you were not solely related to
    your body, your soul, or even your spirit, I will carry
    all of your requests to the feet of the Divine.
    Everything is related to something –
    but only the human is related to the Divine.

220

Rise freely! It is up to you!
Help by building shining joy in yourself!

> *Lili and I are greatly tickled at the fact that our*
> *teachers exchanged their pupils today.*
> *We both feel renewed.*

Friday, February 11, 1944

34. DIALOGUE WITH GITTA

— What is more important for you: force or matter?

> *I sense a 'trap' in this question*
> *and answer cautiously:*

G. I do not know ... I would consider them to be equal.
— Which of the two is more attractive to you?
G. Force is more familiar to me ...
— There is nothing more *blind* than force!
Force is matter; matter is force.
BUT THE ONE WHO GUIDES ALL
IS BEYOND FORCE AND MATTER.
Force becomes radiation; radiation becomes force.
Everything in the creation consists of force and matter.
These two alone would be the *'outer darkness'*;
but the Creator rests *within* all of creation.
If you really shine, this is not merely force:
there is nothing more blind than force alone.

FORCE SHINING FORTH THROUGH THE EYES
IS THE *SEEING LIGHT*.

Without this, you are nothing.
Without this, all of you are nothing.
One hand, cut off: could anything be more senseless?
Splitting off atoms! The human– foolish child! –
tears everything apart, and will only be disappointed,
for the Divine is ONE and INDIVISIBLE.
Only inert force and forceful matter can be split.

OUT OF MANY, ONE:
THAT IS THE WAY TO THE DIVINE.

Many loaves from one loaf of bread: that is no longer
a miracle, for the earth is bountiful with bread.

> *I hear these words and at the same time I see with*
> *horror that this wonderful abundance of bread is*
> *being swallowed up by inequality and continuous*
> *hunger on earth.*

— From the multitude of humans: the HUMAN.
This is the new Bread which satisfies every hunger,
for all will eat of it.
That is enough for today:
you no longer grasp the meaning of my words.

> *This is all too true, and I feel despair.*

— Await me with a smile –
and with a smile depart from me!
Only then can I always be with you.
G. I know that my wavering moods
separate me from you ...

— I cannot step into the water,
for water evaporates wherever I walk.
But water is necessary – as is fire.
Your task is to give fire,
and fire is master over water.
Ő is Master over all.

Friday, February 11, 1944

34. DIALOGUE WITH LILI

— I greet you.

*Hanna begins to say something, but suddenly stops
short and a long silence ensues. I stare at her,
dumbfounded.*

— Do not be amazed!
'The one who speaks' was frightened.
She has witnessed the death of a distant world.

*I have the impression that this refers
to a celestial body.*

— I speak of true and false distance.
Immeasurably far from your comprehension,
a world transforms from matter into force.
And behold! All of you sense it.

*Recently we had all felt a strong change in
atmospheric pressure.*

— You sit beside one another, hold out your arms,
your fingers touch …
and yet you can be further apart from each other
than your earth from this distant celestial body.

THE CREATION IS ONE.
IT KNOWS NO DISTANCE.

However subtle the vibration of a force:
still it is force.
Just as you are affected by this distant force,
so, too, do each of your thoughts, each of your
movements, stream through the universe and act.

THE HUMAN IS THE BODY OF HEAVEN AND
GREATER THAN ALL HEAVENLY BODIES.
THE HUMAN IS NOT A PART:
THE HUMAN IS THE WHOLE.

You hear a cry of pain or anguish.
How do you respond?
Do you let it bring you down?

> *This refers to our having been affected by the
> atmospheric disturbance of the past few days.*

— How distant is a small cell in the tip of the toe
from a cell in the head! How distant!
But if there is a pain anywhere in the body,
both cells feel it.
By what means? Through the spirit.
All heavenly bodies are merely cells.
The Human is the spirit.
The spirit is infinitely great and infinitely small.
When a cell dies, a new force is born,

an unknown, new, never-dreamed-of force.
This is not ominous

I feel that this new Force 'tests' *us.*

— A NEW FORCE ONLY SWEEPS AWAY
WHAT IS UNSUITED FOR LIFE.

Thus it is no loss.
Be strengthened by it!

Did you believe I was not with you?
L. No, but I was unable to rise up to you.
— If need be, I can descend to you.
The deceiver was lurking, but I watched over you.
L. What was the purpose of this evil presence?
— The task of the evil is to tempt.
But soon you will be beyond all temptation.
Extraordinary force demands extraordinary resistance.

WHAT IS INCAPABLE OF LIVING IN THE NEW
CANNOT RESIST.
WHAT IS CAPABLE OF LIVING IN THE NEW
TRANSFORMS: JUST *THERE,*
WHERE IT IS NECESSARY.

Thus, from death comes life and
from evil: good.
What casts others down enlivens you.

I remember the dying star.

— The human who perceives a cry of anguish from the
universe is called to bring forth its sweetness.
The one who fails to do so
becomes the spoiler of the universe.

A bruised apple either becomes sweeter
than all the others or it rots.

Ask!

L.   What is instinct?

—   DIVINE WORDS
FOR THE ANIMAL.

To us all:

—   All of you may ask!
J.   Will there be a period of transition
or will the new World suddenly appear
in its pure form?

—   THE NEW – A CHILD BORN WITHOUT PARENTS –
SWEEPS ALL OF THE OLD.

Never before seen, never before heard,
the CHILD grows.
It is still small, but the CHILD is growing.

LIGHT IS NOT BORN OUT OF DARKNESS,
BUT DARKNESS DIES WITH THE COMING OF LIGHT.

In reality, darkness does not exist.

Let us praise the Divine!

Friday, February 11, 1944

34. DIALOGUE WITH JOSEPH

After a long silence, I feel the presence of the
'building' angel. Apparently Joseph's question
about the coming of the new World has called forth
further explanations. Deeply interested in this
evolutionary event, I wait with great anticipation.

— Take heed! I have but few words.
I speak of the new building.
It does not rise from earth,
but descends from Heaven.
You are 'the one who builds.'
Follow the Plan carefully!

The spirit plans first the dwelling,
and then its dweller.
The new house calls the new dweller.
Thus, create the new world,
the new house that has never before been.
It will not remain empty.
The old building is a snail's shell
of chalky secretion from slimy creatures.

Listen in silence!

Friday, February 18, 1944

35. DIALOGUE WITH GITTA

— I will speak of the smile.
The mouth on the human face corresponds to matter:
it is below.
The mouth is pulled down by descending forces
and raised up by ascending ones.
Every animal can moan and cry.

ONLY THE HUMAN CAN SMILE.

That is the key.
Smile not only when you are in good humor!
May your smile be creative,
not artificial: smile creatively!
If gravity acts,
it ends *here*.

(Vertical gesture at the level of the mouth)

Everything is dragged down, everything!
The mouth belongs to the earth
and gravity belongs to the earth.
When creatures born of the earth
and related elements such as gravity and matter
act together, everything becomes earthen.

The smile is an image of deliverance, a symbol.
Creative force raises matter, and that is your task.
No longer say:
"I am joyful; I laugh" or "I am sad; I cry!"
No more! That is the old way!

Badly do you educate the child that you are,
in an outmoded way: the rod spoils the child.
Improvement is only superficial.
The form changes, but not the essence.
A well-trained child is a crippled child.
Do you know me?

G. Yes.

— I AM YOUR MEASURE.
Do not measure the child with old measures,
or it will become crippled.
Nor with the measures of others.
How could you find *your* path if not by smiling?

I DWELL IN THE SMILE
AND I AM YOUR MEASURE.

The smile symbolizes mastery over matter.
If you read a book, you hold it close enough
to read it easily.
If you want to read me,
come close to me:

I DWELL IN THE SMILE.

I cannot weep, for there is no reason to weep.
No need to weep over lack.
Evil, terror, darkness: your name is *lack*.
Not lack of water, but lack of fire.
Only the incapable creature weeps.
Unable to transcend gravity,
it is swallowed up by the grave.

Heaven is with you.

Friday, February 18, 1944

35. DIALOGUE WITH LILI

— Listen, my beloved!
I, too, speak of the smile.
You pass it by, so familiar is it.
You are unaware of what it means.

THE SMILE IS A BRIDGE OVER THE OLD ABYSS.

Between the animal and what is beyond the animal,
there is a deep abyss.
The smile is the bridge.
Not the laugh, not the grin: the smile.
Laughing is the opposite of weeping.

THE SMILE HAS NO OPPOSITE.

Listen carefully, my servant!
You are 'the one who helps.'
The key to all your acts, to all your teaching,
is the smile. Try it! Smile!
See whether your pupils can find the inner smile!
Then they will move differently.
The smile accomplishes more than any gymnastics.

THE SMILE; SPEECH; CREATIVITY:
THESE ARE ATTRIBUTES OF THE HUMAN BEING.

But beware, for there is also the empty grin,
the mask, with its falsehood and hypocrisy!

A SMILE IS THE PRAYER OF EVERY TINY CELL,

of every one ... and it rises up to here ...

35. DIALOGUE WITH LILI

Horizontal gesture at the level of the mouth:

… it rises above all else.
The inner smile is the first condition
for becoming HUMAN.
Have you ever noticed where you actually are
when you are unable to smile?
You are in the mud, up to your neck in the mire,
or even to the crown of your head.
To smile is so simple!
And yet no one is aware of it.
Do you know someone who truly smiles? Speak!

L. I can think of no one.

— Smiling is the first condition.
You see!
What has become of the human race?
They have all become clowns.
They even abuse the human face, which is sacred.
And what has it become?
Ugly lumps of clay! Crumpled heaps of rags!
Smeared masks! Godless wretches!
There is only one way out:
the smile that no one knows.

In the morning when you open your eyes,
smile at me!
Whenever you begin something, such as teaching,
smile at me!
May everyone try, and learn to smile!
Observe the true smile: how do you recognize it?
The eye is not part of it; only the mouth.

I am very surprised to learn that the eye does not

*participate in the smile; I assume the angel will
explain this to us in due time.*

— Speak!
L. Please speak to me of the hand.
— The hand means: to be formed, to be ready.
The tool is ready ... readiness.

The hand opens.

— Giving ...

The hand closes into a clawed position.

— Taking.
The clawed hand is animal strength.
The open hand is ready.

*My hands are closed, without my being aware of it.
To me:*

— Your hand is not yet ready.
With you, it is neither jealousy nor greed,
but lack of self-trust.
You do not yet believe that Ó gives through you.
You do not yet believe that you are worthy.
Be ready! The hand smiles, too: everything smiles.

Again to Lili:

— Ask!
L. Why do we try to accomplish our will rather than:
"Thy will be done"?
— Because you ignore the Divine Will.
If you were able to perceive It,
then you would not wish to accomplish your own!

Divine Will is *fulfillment.*
Let us fulfill it!
Now only human will is fulfilled.
Not Divine Will.
The human is the fiercest of all beasts.
No animal claw, no lion's clutch is as predatory
as the human hand.
The one who takes shall be taken from,
for the one who takes is not worthy of having hands.

THE HAND IS NOT MADE FOR TAKING.

Do you have any more questions?
L. How could the four of us strengthen our unity?
— By fulfilling your individual task.
Your task is the new World.

WHAT WOULD YOU DO IN THE NEW WORLD
FOR THE NEW WORLD?

THE SIGN OF YOUR TRUE INDIVIDUALITY IS:
TO RECOGNIZE YOUR OWN UNIQUE TASK.

Know what you are called upon to do!
Anything else is at best balm for the pain caused by
too much or *too little,* excess or lack.

I remain with you … only the word departs,
for it is a child of time.

> *After the dialogue, Hanna tells us that we are being*
> *asked by our teachers to write out, for the next*
> *session, an answer to the question:*
> *"What would you do in the new World*
> *for the new World?"*

Friday, February 25, 1944

36. DIALOGUE WITH GITTA

*As requested, I have written out my response to the
question, "What would you do in the new World
for the new World?" However, I am doubtful about
its quality, and I feel quite uneasy.*

— Ancient earth-ploughing tribes and shepherds sacrificed
the most beautiful grains, the most perfect fruit
and the healthiest livestock to their gods.
They offered the first fruits of their efforts.
This offering was an image, an early model
for today's task: to elevate matter to meet the spirit.
Only when they made offerings did they receive rain.
At that time, water was still above
and was the most precious of gifts.

Other ages came and *knowledge* arrived.
Now it is the human who eats the most perfect apple,
the best grain, the most beautiful fruit.
The worm-eaten, windfallen apple is painted bright red
and displayed so that all can see
that sacrifice has duly been made.
But the tiny worm in the apple – child of the Divine –
pierces through the paint,
and the fraud is exposed.
Stone, wind, water, fire, plants and animals
rise up and accuse the human being,
for now the earth has been painted *red*. And behold:
it is blood!

Silence.

— May each of your deeds and each of your tasks
  be genuine offering!
  Only the most beautiful, the most perfect
  of what you bring forth is worthy of being laid
  at the feet of the Divine.
  Does Ő need apples? ... Does Ő need wheat?
  The Divine Law is wholeness.
  Bring me the first fruit of your labors
  and I will carry it to the Divine.
  Thus you will receive the blessing for a new sowing.
  Instead of rain: a new task.
  Ask!

G. Even when I am able to smile, it does not last long,
  and soon I begin to sink down.

— "Peter walked on the water." That is my answer.
  When he ceased to believe in himself, he sank.

  IF YOU BELIEVE IN YOURSELF,
  THEN YOU BELIEVE IN THE DIVINE.

  Do not err: there are not *two* ... there is but ONE.

  Belief has no direction: no above and no below.
  Do not despise matter:
  for everything is the Divine Body.
  You only think you believe.
  If you sink, you cease to believe.
  The MASTER walked upon water, and did not sink.
  He carried the FATHER in Himself –
  He was united with the Divine.
  Is this your goal?

G. Yes.

— CAN YOU BE UNITED WITH THE DIVINE
WITHOUT *BEING* THE DIVINE?

Do not err, and you will not sink.

Silence.

— I teach you: Whenever you are criticized,
regardless of the source, this is a sign of a lack:
it reflects not an incapacity on your part,
but *your capacity*.

MAY EVERY CRITICISM RAISE YOU HIGHER:
CRITICISM EXPANDS YOUR CAPACITY.

Every object, every being around you, asks of you;
but only for that which you are *capable* of giving.
Who asks of the pitiable, the incapable?
Who asks for figs from the thistle?
The fig tree is shaken, for figs are expected of it.
Bring forth fruit! Do not worry if you are shaken!
No one bothers to shake the thistle!
Ask!

G. How might I attain the highest degree of my own fire?

— You have no *own* fire. There is but ONE fire.
What is your own is what you deserve.
What you transmit … is your *own*.
The nearer the circle to the Divine,
the more fire can come down,
and a new 'I' is born to you.
You *own* nothing:
you are nothing and you are everything. Choose!

TO THE GIVER OF ALL FIRE!

*Silent prayer. Lili has not finished her notes
and continues to write ... Sternly to her:*

— The time of prayer is not the time of writing.

Friday, February 25, 1944

DIALOGUE WITH 'THE ONE WHO MEASURES'

*In the course of the past week, I repeatedly post-
poned the writing out of my 'homework-assign-
ment': "What would I do in the new World for the
new World?" The topic was so far-reaching and
bewildering to me that I was hardly able to image
this new world. Actually, the assignment had not
surprised me so much: it was not unusual for the
angels to demand the* impossible *from us, only to
have it later revealed as* possible after all. *Yesterday,
I finally wrote down my thoughts: conscientiously,
but without the slightest touch of enthusiasm.*
*Today we all feel the silent presence of 'The one
who measures.' This long silence is suddenly broken by the incessant ringing of the bells of the
nearby church, 'Maria Remete.' This unusually loud
and long-lasting ringing is used in the village only
as an alarm signal at the outbreak of fire.We do not
read our essays aloud, for each of our thoughts and
feelings is clearly evident to the angel. Finally, the
bell ceases to ring and 'the one who measures'
speaks:*

237

— I bring the inner bell to ring.
What does the inner bell reveal?
I ask this in the name of your self-judgment.
Have you, in truth, done all you could?
For that is what matters:
not the words you have written.

WE BEGIN THERE, WHERE IN TRUTH, YOU END.

Answer! I require true measure:
not too high and not too low.

> *With lowered gaze, I stutter that, at the moment,*
> *I could not have achieved anything better.*

— You underestimate yourself!
Not in your task, but in your judgment.
You are capable of more, in every sense.

> *I had believed that true self-judgment is impossible,*
> *but Joseph proves me wrong. He is the only one*
> *of us who had intuitively perceived the meaning of*
> *our 'final examination,' as it came to be known.*
> *When asked,*

— "My son, what does the inner bell say?"

> *he simply answers with joyful certainty that he has*
> *given his very best.*
> *Indeed, he had written his answer with astonishing*
> *clarity. From this moment on, 'the one who mea-*
> *sures' the most severe of our teachers, talks with*
> *him as with an intimate friend, and advises him to*
> *now* live *the intuitively perceived dimensions. Fur-*
> *ther, Joseph is assured that this is indeed possible:*

— You can live it, for the one with whom you are united
is close to you.

*At last, I grasp that, with this final examination, we
were not expected to summarize, in a more or less
logical way, something that was already* known, *as
is the case with the university exams throughout
the world. No, our task was exactly the contrary: to
let go of everything known and to spring into the
never-before-seen, the never-before-heard, the
never-before-known, guided only by our intuition
… and our faith. Only Joseph had ventured the
leap.*

Friday, February 25, 1944

36. DIALOGUE WITH JOSEPH

*For Joseph, it is often difficult to say 'yes' to life.
The gloomy prospects of the year 1944 make this
ever harder for him. Yesterday, as he struggled
with this existential problem, the ceiling and a part
of the wall in his workshop suddenly caved in on
top of him. Joseph was not injured, but rubble and
stones lay all around him on the floor. This greatly
impressed Joseph, and he attributes symbolic
meaning to it.*

— You are 'the one who builds.'
Dig and prepare the foundation!

Fill the hole with stones. *Then* you may build on it.
The house cannot be built upon wooden planks.
The motto of your way is not, *'it was,'*
nor, *'it would be good'* ;
and certainly not, *'it is good.'*
The key word of the builder is: *'BE!'*
'It was' signifies omission;
'it would be good,' incapacity;
'it is good,' smugness.
Your motto is: *'BE!'*

Your Heaven is green
because the earth is green.
The law of gravity binds *and* raises up.

I speak to you with joy.
If you and I are unable to speak,
then the stones speak to you:
the message was for you!
The stones fell to the earth
to show where your lack is.
But the recognized lack is no longer a lack.

In the name of silence that builds.

*I later ask Hanna the meaning of: "Your Heaven is
green because the earth is green. The law of gravity
binds and raises up." She explains that Joseph is
'of Heaven' and therefore lacks the weight of earth
necessary for reaching an equilibrium between
matter and spirit. She tells me that I, for my part,
am 'of earth' and my task is therefore to reach
towards Heaven, thus compensating my excess of
matter and my lack of spirit.*

240

Regrettably, all of our 'examination notes' and other materials related to this exchange perished in the perilous months that followed.

Friday, February 25, 1944

36. DIALOGUE WITH LILI

For Lili, there is no 'final examination' : Political catastrophes are casting their shadows everywhere and her pupils have taken all of her time as they spilled out their fears to her. Understandably, for the reality of the Nazi gas-chambers is already common knowledge. Lili's brother is the proprietor of a distinguished café downtown near the Parliament and one could always be sure to find Lili there, surrounded by her frightened pupils in a quiet corner until far into the night. And so she had not written out the assigned task, an omission that is pointed out to her only very gently:

— The tiny sprout has no idea of the heights to which
it will grow, and yet it swells and stretches
as it strives toward the light.
The intensity of its effort
determines the ultimate outcome.
Take heed!

EVERYTHING DEPENDS UPON
THE INTENSITY OF THE EFFORT.

The knowledge that, in its depths,
the promise of a great tree reposes, would be in vain
were it not for tiny sprouts striving and growing
toward the light.
The ground is so hard and the earth so heavy
that to overcome it, the sprout must persevere
with all of its strength.
My little servant, you have made an error.
To fulfill the task, you must strive mightily.
Fulfilling the task helps you to grow.
The more you grow, the more you can give.
And the greater your task, the greater your growth.

You helped two people;
but you neglected two hundred,
and your task could become two thousand.
Do you believe this?

L. Yes … I am certain of it.
— Let this be a lesson to you:
Raise your helping higher, far higher,
above the level of feelings.
Had you completed your assignment,
forces that you cannot even imagine
would have served you.
They are still imprisoned in you,
for you have not opened the door.

L. Where is the locked door in me?
— You already fulfill the small task well.
But from now on, take on a different role:
be Maria and not Martha!
Renew your search and you will find 'more.'

SEARCH WITH *TOTAL FAITH;*
THERE IS NO OTHER WAY.

Honor your task above all else, and then –
believe me! – then you will be able to help.
Above, below and all around:
The Divine is everywhere.

Saturday, February 26, 1944

36. DIALOGUE WITH LILI (continued)

> *It is Saturday. Lili is in the workshop, trying to
> immerse herself in yesterday's lesson. Suddenly,
> she feels an intense inner light. We are all aware of
> the unexpected presence of her angel.*

— The moment, the time and the occasion
    are out of the ordinary.
    Nevertheless I have come to you,
    for my task is to help.
    Do you still have doubts?
    Are you still in the dark?
L. Oh, no ... but I feel my task to be enormous.
— That is not darkness, but light that is too strong.
    The eye cannot see in the absence of light,
    but neither can it see when the light is too strong.
    You have received three sparks today.
    Do you feel them?
L. Not yet.

— What are your greatest lacks?

Lili answers with astonishing promptness:

L. Lack of faith, lack of giving and
   lack of work!
— Not lack of work ... lack of *doing* your work!
   You have enough work ... you simply do not *act* on it.

THE THREE POINTS
OF YOUR SIGN WILL IGNITE
FROM THE THREE SPARKS:
HAVING FAITH – GIVING – ACTING.
FAITH IN YOURSELF AS WELL.

FAITH   GIVING

ACTING

The three sparks are not confined to time and space.
The three lacks are fulfilled ... they no longer exist.
You will see that this is so.
The slow body perceives this only later.
But you are not only body;
your task is completed by more than the body.

KNOW THE WHOLENESS IN YOURSELF
AND YOU WILL BECOME WHOLE.

To fulfill your lacks is no longer your task:
now may the fruit come!
Do you believe that the impossible is possible?
What you received today is a foretaste of wholeness.

Silence.

— All of you: Pay close attention!

THE WORD CONCENTRATES, IT FOCUSES:
THE WORD CREATES.

*To Lili who had written down her lacks this
morning:*

— You formed your lacks into words
and thus the sparks could come.

To me:

— Be aware of the word!

THE WORD BUILDS.

Which stone is fit into which
is of the utmost importance,
for what you build might otherwise collapse.
All of you! You do not know how to use the word.
The husk is not the corn;
the chaff is not the grain.
Word – Name – Mystery.
Listen carefully, for what I say is of the essence.
If you say: *'Be!'* it will be.
If you say nothing, nothing will be.
Not: *'If only it could be!'*
Five words are less than this one: *Be!*
'Sometimes I believe' is less than *'I believe!'*
'How I would like to always be able to help'
Ten words! ... *'I help'* – one word*
and there is no breach, either in the words or in you.
The ACT is the word of the body.
Wholeness is not the *many,*
but the intense, the concentrated, the focused;
and that is eternal measure.

---

* One word in the original Hungarian

Ask more … as a provision for the journey!

L. I wish that all of this would remain as strong in me
as it is at this moment!

— Do not wish for what you already have!
Raise your wishes to a higher level.
The body is slow, but it, too, will become aware.

Friday, March 3, 1944 (Morning)

37. DIALOGUE WITH GITTA

This morning, as I tried to find the Seven Joys,
I could suddenly feel the heart of my being.

— I speak to you of the Seven Joys.
You have reached the heart of your task,
though with more difficulty than necessary.
The Seven Joys are seven gates.
You could have entered the sphere
through the seven gates.
The gates open inwards and outwards.
Your new task is to radiate the Seven Joys from inside;
through the same seven gates,
but now they open outwards.

THE EYE SEES AND IT SHINES.

May Ő help you in your task!

Friday, March 3, 1944 (Afternoon)

37. DIALOGUE WITH GITTA

— Allow no day to pass without opening the gates.
Open them in the *morning!*

G. It is so hard for me to master my time …

— It is not your task to master time.
Your task is to *reach beyond time.*
No one can make two hours out of *one.*
If you – for only an instant – reach beyond time,
you see all Seven Joys at once.
Listen! If you approach the sphere from outside,
you can perceive only one gate at a time.
But from within, you see all seven gates at once.
The sphere rotates, every sphere rotates:
this is what makes it a sphere.
Every form is shaped according to the law
of its motion.
The sphere turns, but you do not.

At the center of the great sphere is the Divine,
motionless.
All is in motion except Ő.
Ő created the human in the Divine image.
Ő entrusted the human with the small sphere.

With bitter irony:

— Human beings have arranged it well!
They do nothing but run around on its surface,
and thus they get nowhere.
Ask.

G. What should the starting point of my work be?

— Certainty!
Can the head be certain?

G. No.

— Listen carefully!
Make no plans with the head:
carry plans out with the head!

The Plan is with the Divine; *every* Plan.
But you: you plan what is to be done with your head;
you apply your head to your work prematurely.
The head and time are one.

> *Unable to understand the meaning of these words,*
> *I hold my head in my hands.*

— Do not break your head!

THE PLAN IS BEYOND TIME.

Become one with the Plan,
and you will never hurry and never tarry.

> *I do my best to understand, and remain silent.*

— Ask, for our time is passing quickly.

G. I make so many superfluous movements ...
Teach me proper movement!

— There is nothing 'superfluous' on earth
and there is no lack; it is only that the 'superfluous,'
the 'excess,' does not fill the lack.
Excess in one place
creates a lack somewhere else.
Do not cast away the superfluous;
in reality, nothing is superfluous.

YOU ARE ACCOUNTABLE
FOR EVERY MOVEMENT YOU MAKE.

Know this, and the superfluous
will soon find its proper place.
Do you act according to
what is expected of you?
G. No – certainly not!
— You see: nothing is superfluous.
Take away nothing, add nothing:
but join the *too much* to the *too little;*
help everything to its proper place.
Lack reveals the *too much,* and excess, the *too little.*
Direct one to the other and all will be well!
In the name of fulfillment.

Friday, March 3, 1944

37. DIALOGUE WITH LILI

— I speak to all of you.
Become pure: pure from the old!
What is the old? The imperfect.
Why become pure?
For this reason: your asking creates.
What you ask for *shall come to be.*
You may no longer ask for yourselves,
for you have no more lack.
What you ask for – purified from the old – *shall be.*
But it is necessary for you to ask.

To Joseph:	Woe unto you if you look back!
To me:	Woe unto you if you look back!
To Lili:	Woe unto you if you look back!
To me:	The good worker receives daily bread so as to be able to give heavenly bread.
To Joseph:	The good worker receives shelter so as to be able to build heavenly shelter.
To Lili:	The good worker deserves solitude so as to be able to give to the multitudes.
To Hanna:	The good worker deserves silence so as to be able to speak.

There is no compromise!
The Divine Law is wholeness,
and all is contained in the whole.
The greater embraces the lesser.

To Lili:

None of your little sheep will be lost.
What kept them together until now?
Did they come merely to move their bodies?
When your *faith* grows,
they will flock to you in still greater numbers.
— Do you have any questions?
L. Yes: Please speak about purity.
— May all your acts, thoughts, works and feelings
be truly pure!

PURITY IS: EVERYTHING IN ITS PLACE.

Impurity is: the act out of place.
Muddled thinking is impure,
feelings mixed up with the spirit are impure!

*I think of the dialogue of January 28 about keeping
the different levels of being distinct from one another.*

250

— Nothing is dirty; that is an ugly word!
There is only impurity.
Always be in your place:
your inner as well as your outer place.
May the place not change you,
but you, the place!

The church in which God is worshipped
is holy and pure.
But if religion dies, it might become a warehouse.
A church becomes a church
through veneration of God.
Temples, churches and religions are still dying.
But the new Temple, the new Church, has no walls;
it is eternal.
You are the builders and future priests
of the immortal temple.
It is known as: The World delivered.
Ask!

L. I am worried about my pupil, Clara. Why is she so ill?
— The answer is in her name, which means: purity.
She offends against her own name
by hiding impurity from herself.
Hidden impurity is the cause of all illness.

> *As I record the dialogue, the lead mine of my pencil
> slips from position and I am unable to continue
> writing. I impatiently shake the pencil in an attempt
> to fix it so that I can continue with my notes.
> To me:*

— You have made a superfluous movement.
You cannot account for it – it is impure.
Love the tool you hold in your hand!

Ö demands that you account for every one of your acts,
every one of your movements.
To serve the Divine is the secret of freedom.

> *Turning again to Lili:*

— Shall we take leave?
L. Oh, please – not yet!
— If you stand on the tips of your toes,
   you can already reach me.
   There is no more pit
   from which you cannot reach up to me.
   Soon the *more* will arrive.
   It rests in the womb of solitude and silence.
   May Heaven be with you!

Friday, March 10, 1944

38. DIALOGUE WITH GITTA

— There is a point – the focal point – and it is known as
   'eternity.'
   It is the point of security and mastery.
   What deceives you?
   The great deceiver: *Time*.

THE HUMAN IS NOT AT HOME IN TIME:
THE HUMAN IS *HOMELESS* IN TIME.

Take just one step and the stream pulls you along:
the stream of time.
The stream is the sign of time.

But you are not frogs and certainly not fish!

Past – present – future.
One person regrets the past: the other fears it.
One has hopes for the future: the other fears it.
There is no present, no 'now,'
for the human lives either in the past
or in the future.
Past – present – future.
All three are but one stream:
one single, indivisible stream,
the movement of subtle matter.
To *view* the stream
and to *be in it*
are not the same!

THE HUMAN IS ALSO MASTER OF THE STREAM.
THE TRUE ACT IS ETERNITY,
PRESENT IN TIME.

To hurry is not to *act*.
The point of which I speak
is beyond the river. Past,
present and future are three
rays. Their focal point is
eternity: eternal reality.
Step out of time, my
servant, and you will be its
master. The *creative act*
can only spring from the
point of eternity.

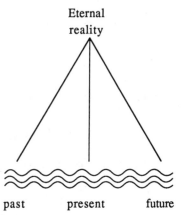

G. I do not know the name of the
doorway leading to timelessness.

I have searched in vain all week.
Where am I lost?
— In time.
This is why I speak to you of time.
How many doorways do you seek?
G. One.
— I'll give you one hundred thousand!
May each act, each thought, each rest
be *offered* to the Divine!
Everything leads to Ő:

EVEN THE MINUTEST IS WORTHY
OF OFFERING TO Ő.

What bliss your existence would be
if you could truly offer!
Do you have another question?
G. Speak to me about the new Sun.
— Clouds of fog still veil it,
otherwise it would be visible to you now.
There is still too much water in you.

*I know that 'water' refers to the unstable
movements of my moods in the stream of time.*

— The new Sun is not yet able to pierce the fog in you.
Do not expect the Sun to come from outside;
there you will never see it.

Your task is the *act*.
We do not act, we do not give, we do not take;
we were not, nor shall we be.
We *are* through the Divine.

Bow your head – the Divine is with us!

Friday, March 10, 1944

38. DIALOGUE WITH LILI

— Repairing and patching are not the true ACT.
Patching is no longer possible.
Can you glue the fruit back to its tree?
Helping is not a matter of repairing.
The Divine does not patch together;
the Divine inspires growth.
Help the Divine and you save the world!
The hand of the Divine is near: it is you.

Do you have questions?
L. Teach me the earthly and the heavenly task.
— The earth is fulfilled.
Heaven does not yet burn in you.

You cannot be in both: your place is in the middle.
Earthly and heavenly life have seven levels:
Three are completed;
three are beyond the threshold;
and the middle, the *Four,* is able to find them all.
Thus the seven levels become one,
and sin ceases to exist.
The *Five* speaks to you.
L. I do not completely understand ...
— You do not understand even half of it.
The *Four* unites the two sets of three
of the seven levels.
I belong to the *Fifth* level,
and through you, I am connected to earth.
Belief leads to the *Four.*

255

The *Four* no longer believes:
the *Four* ACTS.

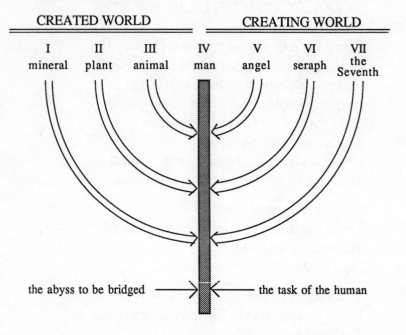

This dialogue with Lili seems to me like an abstract,
incomprehensible number game. I ask Hanna to
explain it, particularly the meaning of the 'Five.' She
then sketches the diagram (above) from an earlier
dialogue (d.19), but this time, she adds the elements
that had been missing.
All of a sudden, the context becomes clear to me: I see
this sketch as a symbol of all that the angels have been
explaining to us.
It illustrates the teaching in a structured order. At last, I
grasp the place of the human being in creation. I
discover a new balance, in which fleeing into the spirit

and disdaining matter are just as wrong as clinging to matter while denying the spirit. I realize how important and essential it is to fully affirm the life of the body as well as that of the spirit.

And finally, I also discover my own dignity: the dignity of the individual human who is called to unite spirit and matter. Never have I so intensely felt that creation cannot be fulfilled without the participation of the human. It is only through me, the human being, the fourth in the middle, that my angel can act on earth. With this discovery, my life takes on a wholly new meaning. I have the possibility and the task of uniting matter and spirit, in my body as in my soul.

Friday, March 17, 1944

39. LAST PERSONAL DIALOGUE WITH GITTA

— The sphere is wholeness, fulfillment:
  the APPLE indicates the power of wholeness.*
  If you eat it and do not act,
  if you take it and do not give it on,
  then you do not deserve the *six.*
  The power of the *Six* acts everywhere.
  What is power? I will reveal it to you:
  Listen! The *Five* is the angel – the *Six* is the seraph.
  The seraph is to me what I am to you:

---

* The *orb,* symbol of royal power, is known in Hungarian as the 'Apple of Royalty.'

intermediary and master.
The seraph and I are one.
Thus, the three levels are fulfilled and completed.

> *I feel a radiance shining forth from Ő, passed on*
> *through the seraph and passed on further through*
> *my angel.*

— But where is the *Four?*
Ő does not tolerate emptiness,
for the Divine is known by the name of 'wholeness.'
Your place is the *Four.*
There the near and the far cease to be.
Bow down your head before the Divine
but hold it high before all others!
Only the ACT makes you master.

Do you hear my words?
G. Yes.
— Do you understand my words?
G. Yes.
— Do not hear them, do not understand them: *live* them!
Do not fear the Divine: *serve* the Divine!
Fear exists only below.

ONLY AT THE PEAK OF YOUR QUESTION
WILL YOU FIND AN ANSWER.
I AM THERE; ONLY FROM THERE CAN I ANSWER.

Anything done only halfway brings no blessing:
it *cannot* bring a blessing.
Always take the way that leads upward:
never deviate and never stand still!
Standing still is the *second death.*

THIS IS THE TEACHING:
EVERYTHING HAS ITS PEAK,
AND THE PEAK IS YOUR PLACE.

Heaven be with you.

> *The angel has often mentioned the task of the*
> *human being to rule over the Created World like a*
> *just and righteous monarch.*
> *This message came in various*
> *forms. In the 29th dialogue,*
> *the royal scepter was given to us,*
> *of course in a symbolic way.*
> *Today, the second royal attribute*
> *is emphasized: the orb, which is*
> *the sign of royal power and*
> *wholeness.*
> *I have the vague foreboding that today's dialogues*
> *might be our last such personal instructions.*

Friday, March 17, 1944

39. DIALOGUE: 'THE ONE WHO MEASURES'

— What is measured by 'the one who measures'?
Space.
The circle in which your hand does not act
is worthless.

The Divine sows the act, and the human receives it.
Circle and act exist in time and space.

And Ő measures them through me:

WHERE ARE YOUR ACTS?

The time is ripe, the circle grows.
Ő sees everything: WHERE ARE YOUR ACTS?

Space is whatever your hand can fill.
The hand is formed, but it is not yet forming.
There is no escape!
All ways converge at the ONE and ONLY point.

Light – the only Reality!
Through Light, the creature *is*.
You are a creature and you are Light. This is so.
The toad sits in the water, tepid,
neither fish nor mammal.
Toad or angel?
The weighing scales are empty:
your acts are insufficient.
It bores me to measure emptiness:
I long to offer fruit.
The Divine expects more of you!
May your hand be ready!

The Divine speaks. May your ear now hear,
for the Divine speaks through me.

> *The urgency of these stern words awakens in me*
> *a sense of approaching catastrophe; catastrophe*
> *which can only be met if we have first gone through*
> *a transformation.*

Friday, March 17, 1944

39. LAST PERSONAL DIALOGUE WITH LILI

— Look at your sign, the triangle, the three:
How does this lead to the Four?
   Showing the right hand:
– Force.
   Showing the left hand:
– Matter.
   Indicating the heart:
– The 'acting one.'

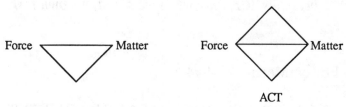

Matter is the task, force is the means,
and the 'acting one' is Ő.
What is the fourth? The ACT.
In this way, the new Building is completed.

Your lack is filled; your past is dissolved.
The old disappears: and Heaven opens up.
Dance! To join Heaven and earth is your ACT.
Thus every movement you make
becomes heavenly dance.
I, too, am a dancer: I dance for the Divine.

   *I feel that the angel's dancing is creation through
   rhythm.*

261

— Dance for me and for Ő!
   Your hands are free, your feet laugh.
   I am one with you: our lips sing the same song.
   Every song is sung for Ő.
   To Lili: Every dance is danced for Ő.
   To me: Every ray is a bird in flight to Ő.
   To Joseph: Every wall of the new House
                     stands through Ő.
   Now the one song with your four voices
   rises to the Divine.

> *It becomes ever more clear to me that we can reach*
> *the fourth level, where every one of our acts*
> *becomes ACT, only when we act at our own task.*

Friday, March 17, 1944

37. LAST PERSONAL DIALOGUE WITH JOSEPH

— The earth below is just as near
   as the silence here above: they are ONE.

THE EARTH, THE GREEN EARTH, IS YOUR HEAVEN.

Only on the earth can the act be accomplished.
Empty is the earth,
but the Divine Hand fills it –
the Hand whose name is 'the Human.'
The Human is: 'The one who builds.'
The Human is: 'The one who helps.'
The Human is: 'The one who shines.'
The Human is: 'The one who acts with measure.'

Your name is: 'Messenger of Heaven.'
Never forget this, for your place is here on earth.
Only in this way can Heaven and earth be joined.

The ancient whirlpool devours all the stones
from which the House of God was built.
But you: Build new Walls for Heaven here below!
Not walls of stone, but of Law,
of Rhythm and of Song.
Heavenly messenger, Ő is with you!

*I ask Hanna why Joseph's Heaven is the green
earth. She explains that Joseph's predominant
character is 'heavenly' and that it is necessary for
him to attain earthly weight as equilibrium. She
goes on to say that I, in contrast, am 'earthly,' and
that my excess of matter calls for the 'heavenly,' so
as to attain redeeming balance in the middle.*

Friday, March 24, 1944

40. DIALOGUE: SONG OF THE CHORUS

*All of Hungary is in deep shock:
in an overnight operation,
the country has been occupied by German troops.*

— The Seventh Heaven is just as near
as the earth below where your feet rest.
There He is King.
Never again will He come to earth.
Blinding Light: sole reality.

The King, eternal Being,
dressed in white fire flaming up to Ő.
You are His servants. Serve Him:
Him, the glorious Being of Light,
too brilliant for the human eye.
Him, the eternally unbelievable,
the only Source of belief!

All of you: you are His blood.
You are: JESUS.
You are in His place.
You act, you live, you become.
And He is the Source, the Way, the Truth.
He is Life.

Darkness and horror fade when Light can come.
The Light that we give is twice softened.
It is so strong that the world would burst into flames
were we not to filter it with our wings.
Raise yourselves! Filter the Light once more!
This is the only way for the Light to come.

FIRE DESCENDS UPON THE EARTH.

If Heaven burns in you,
then all the old burns away.
Behold: In the old, which burns away,
He is unable to act.
Only when all the old in you is burned away
will you see Heavenly fire.
Before then, you would be burned by it.

Earthly fire comes only from the earth
and consumes only what is of the earth.

264

The heavenly is not consumed,
for it *is* the Fire.
Only His dignitary can endure and can bring this Fire.
Become dignified! Serve Him!
Only thus is it possible!
The Light you bring down is marvelous.
It burns only where change is necessary.

In the vessel, there is no more water: only blazing Fire,
for He who is above all baptizes with Fire.
Let go of the water!

The name of all suffering is abyss.
Be filled with Fire! The time is near.
If the vessel is cracked
the Fire flows out: disaster!

THE FIRE COMES THROUGH YOU –
THROUGH YOU ALONE.
BUT ONLY IF YOU ACT: ACT!

Only in this way can the earth receive heavenly Fire.

> *Outside, a storm is raging.*

— The wind whirls and roars, the snowstorm rages.
But already it is on the wane,
for warmth, sprouting and the Light are near.
Believe me: He comes
and He is the LIGHT.

> *We sense that not only our angels are speaking
> today, but also a much greater force. This dialogue
> was of a never-before-experienced intensity.*

Friday, March 24, 1944

40. DIALOGUE: MESSAGE FOR LILI

*As an immediate result of the Nazi occupation of
Hungary, all means of transportation have come to
a standstill. There is no way for Lili to make her
way from Budapest to our village.*

— The angel of 'the one who helps' is here.
What you just heard was the Song of the Chorus.
Now I speak to the one who is away
and yet is here.
Darkness cannot keep her away.
Darkness is but the shadow of matter
still not penetrated by the new Light.
When inhibited by matter,
even light becomes subject to the laws of matter.
But the new Light penetrates everything.
There are no boundaries,
no 'near' and no 'far,'
and my servant can be here.

Ő is the center of all.
When Light comes from Ő,
then the hand of 'the one who helps' grows,
embraces all and acts freely.
My little servant can be everywhere
and can *act* everywhere.

    Silence

— The power of the 'Highest Helper' is with you.

I, too, serve you.
I, you, He: we are three.
But beyond the threshold ... ONE.
And that is GRACE.

*I write out the song of the angels addressed to Jesus
and the short message which I will pass on to Lili at
the first opportunity.*

*Actually, I felt Lili's presence during the dialogue.
But only now do I understand how this was
possible: outer light is limited by time and space. In
the light of the sun, matter casts shadows. The light
of distant stars can be measured by light years.*

*In contrast, inner Light penetrates everywhere: it is
timeless, spaceless, unmeasurable. If Lili is filled
with inner Light, she can be everywhere and her
every act becomes the all-transcendent ACT.*

PART II

DIALOGUES IN BUDAPEST

"You through the Divine,
the Divine through you."

Immediately after the invasion of Hungary by Nazi troops, the persecution of Jews begins. The Jewish population in the provinces, where we are living, is the first to be transported to the concentration camps. The arrests have not yet begun in Budapest, but all roads leading to the capital are tightly controlled by the Nazis to prevent Jews from seeking refuge in the city. Nevertheless, Hanna and Joseph decide to flee from the endangered provincial zone to Budapest, so as to be able to await further developments from the unoccupied apartment of Hanna's parents. I wish to accompany them: we set out from Budaliget late one evening, making our way along unguarded footpaths through the dark forests embracing the western part of Budapest. I take the lead, with Hanna and Joseph following a short distance behind. At last, we emerge safely at a large tram station, Hüvösvölgy, *where we are able to mingle unobtrusively among the throngs of the city.*

Friday, March 31, 1944

41. DIALOGUE: 'THE ONE WHO MEASURES'

Today we await the first dialogue in the apartment of Hanna's parents, in the Garay utca, *which is situated in the Pest section of the city.*
Our 'hosts' have fortunately left Hungary a short time before to visit their son in England, leaving the apartment empty. The front windows face a noisy, gray street not far from the main east-side railway station, Keleti. *After the peace and calm of the tiny village of Budaliget, everything here in Budapest seems abominably dismal and loud.*

— 'The one who measures' speaks: listen carefully!
The lack ebbs, the seed swells,
the weighing scales are filled.
Here above, burning eyes are watching:
Now you live rightly.

> *Indeed, we did everything necessary, but with calm.*

— 'The one who measures' sees:
the danger recedes.
Your hand is ready
and my sword does not cut: it protects.

> *I am amazed that our inner attitude is more*
> *important to the angels than the outer danger.*

— Existence weighs heavy:
BUT FOR THE ONE WHO DOES NOT ERR,
THE BURDEN BECOMES UPLIFTING WINGS.

The new unfolds.
The ACT is the seed from which the new sprouts.
Danger passes; the seed remains.
A gentle breeze arises and, in the proper moment,
the ACT sprouts: the ACT sown in you by the Divine.
Take good care of the seed; it is so small!
It can be lost through the smallest crack.

'The one who measures' speaks:
Now you live rightly.
My sword protects. Seven forces burn in its tip:
Divine grace.
Bow your heads.
May you be touched by the tip of the sword.
May Ő be with you.
The trial persists.
Those who persevere shall be redeemed.
Ő is peace.

May Divine peace be with you!
Then the curse cannot reach you.
Ő is life.
If you live in the Divine, you cannot fear,
and you desire no other fate.

The seven forces converge at ONE point.
This is the mystery and this is the way.
If a single force is missing, my scale is unbalanced.
I urge you: Be aware!
One single lack can be decisive!
Be alert! Hope! Adore the One and Only!

All of us in the circle serve the Divine,
each according to our own task.
I am 'the one who measures,'
but I am also the 'Gardener.'
I watch over you tiny blossoms on the Tree.
I watch over you,
for cutting is not my only means of serving.
I cut only what is bad.

You have come a long way in a short time.
You have left the old behind you.
But woe unto you if you look back!
The house has caved in: you can no longer live there.
You had to leave it at the decisive moment.
Woe unto you if you look back! For behold:
ahead of you, the way is already free.

'The one who measures' has spoken:
what has been, is dead.
What shall be, will never be lost.
The 'Gardener' rejoices
at the brightening sky
as the seed begins to grow.

Friday, April 7, 1944

42. DIALOGUE: GOOD FRIDAY

Throughout Hungary, everything has come to a standstill: the Nazi occupation has petrified daily life. We miss our work tremendously. In our forced inactivity, we become ever more sensitive to the horrible news and rumors, which spread like wildfire through the city.

— Greetings to the four of you!
The choir of angels brings a message;
it is your task to pass it on:

THE CROSS IS NOT THE SIGN OF DEATH.
DIE WITH *HIM* AND YOU LIVE ETERNALLY.

The cross does not let you go:
to fulfill its sign is your task.

DIE WITH *HIM:*
THAT IS THE FIRST HALF OF THE TASK.

Three days, the time: past – present – future.
In the tomb, wrapped in linen,
soothed with balm, the body reposes.
Dawn approaches … but time expires.
Run out is the time of death.
People surround the tomb.
And within: nothing – only the shroud.
The shroud has been cast away, death is dead,
and eternal life burns.

THE SECOND HALF OF THE TASK IS:
LIVE THROUGH *HIM!*

At His feet is the angel of death,
faithfully serving the Law.
HE is grace and grace is above the Law.
If you have total faith, grace is yours too.
But it is not yours too keep: *through you,* it acts below.
Without faith, you lead everything to death.
This is the Law.
The pregnant whirlpool gives birth to hell,
and the name of hell is:
the old, which no longer serves.

The Body is not the corpse.
The Body is not matter.
The Body is seed that grows and resurrects
through the Divine.

THE BODY IS PLAN, NOT ORGAN.

The Body is Ő.
What makes the seed a seed?
The pod? It can never sprout.

YOU ARE BODY AND SEED THROUGH THE DIVINE,
AND IT IS Ő WHO SHALL GROW THROUGH YOU.

Sacred mystery.
We are angels.
Our word is truth,
for we live through the Divine.
Our drink is Light, our song is Praise.
Our service is always for the Divine.
We serve together: we are One.

Four pillars reach to Heaven,
uniting Heaven and earth.
We are the vault and the earth is our foundation.
The dwelling is ready.
The wedding approaches,
the wedding of Heaven and earth.
After the wedding, the Newborn: Ő.
Ő already dwells amongst you.
May Ő be sheltered in your heart!

In the circle, we sing praise;
no longer apart, but together: with you.
For our way has become One.

WITH YOU WE PERISH –
OR WITH YOU WE ARE PURIFIED.

The pod is weight.
If Ő breathes on you, the seed begins to grow.
The time is near … the time is far …
time is no more.
Timelessly, Ő grows in you.
There is only one way: bear the Child, the new Child!
No more lowly stable.
Be at the highest point, always!
We are there.

Behold! It is also our Child.
Its fragile body is still that of a child,
yet Heaven and earth tremble before it.
The milk that it suckles is the power of spirit.
Loyal servants watch over it.
Be loyal! Hearts are filled with it,
and what is filled knows pain no more.

Above you hovers the multitude of angels.
May peace descend over you.
But pass it on! It is not your own.
All that belongs to us is Ő; and we belong to Ő.
This is our message:

YOU THROUGH THE DIVINE;
THE DIVINE THROUGH YOU.

*For some time now, the angels have been speaking
in a rhythmic style, and it is less personal than the
dialogues in Budaliget had been, which irritates me.
I have never been fond of poetry, and I am unable
to grasp the purpose of this new form. I feel like a
baby that is given solid food instead of milk for the
first time and does not like it. I miss the practical
instructions of Budaliget and I am disappointed at
no longer being able to ask my 'very important'
questions. I am aware that Hanna is only 'humanly
able' to put the message of the angels into human
language, and so I blame her for the new rhythmic
form. Of course, I couldn't possibly 'blame' the
angels! However, today I am pierced by the terrible
words: "With you we perish ..." They sting like a
whiplash, but also help me to a new realization: I
discover that this rhythm is directly touching and
nourishing me, without any kind of detour through
my intellect. The end of today's dialogue fills me
with astonishment: "YOU THROUGH THE DIVINE;
THE DIVINE THROUGH YOU." The dignity I feel in
this human-Divine balance is so powerful that I am
unable to grasp it in its full profundity.*

Sunday, April 9, 1944

43. DIALOGUE: EASTER SUNDAY

— The mere body is dead for ever.
The living lives for ever.
And yet, from birth until death, they are united.

What you call life is the task.
For the life active in its task:
death is the servant.
For the life passive in its task:
death is the master.
Birth and death belong together,
not life and death.
Here the soul that has fear is in error:

FOR LIFE LIVES ETERNALLY.

Friday, April 14, 1944

44. DIALOGUE

— We are many, but our word is ONE.
Grace streams through us and we never weary.

THE LIFE THAT WE LIVE
IS THE GRACE THAT WE GIVE.

Giving compensates weight.
Thirst for the new!
Fire is given to you: eternal thirst.
Pass the Fire on!

The Seven Souls are your dwelling.
Your foot rests on the first.
Six enfold you from toe to head,
and the Seventh is your crown.
Each of the Seven Souls acts:
Truth *is*.
Love *grows*.
Rhythm and Harmony *move*.
New awareness *creates*.
Peace *reposes*.
Joy and bliss *radiate*.
The primal source is a great mystery.
Unspeakable, inexpressible ecstasy: fulfillment.

Eternal giver, never tiring, eternally acting:
only through the Divine do you act.

The origin of all Light is Ő.
The ground of all space is Ő.
The faith of all being is Ő.
Every song rises up to Ő.
Whoever strives toward Ő never wearies.
Every scent rises up to Ő,
every mountain points to Ő.
Whoever seeks, finds the way.
Behold: the only way is Ő!
Every other way is delusion.
Every word fades before Ő.
Ő is the dwelling and Ő is the dweller.

The Seven Forces are yours.
Take them, eat them:
act through them!

May giving and taking be in balance.
Balance is needed on the peak;
there balance, peace and silence are essential.

We are many.
Through us and through you,
life broadens, the Seven flow.
The past withers, the old dies, but the new unfolds.
The Seven prepare a new Food
which wipes away all old guilt.
Heaven opens itself:
the new Food, Heavenly Bread, descends:
not grown of the earth, it is born of Light.

Hunger, gloom, evil and the grave are but a void.
Already the new Message is filling it.
The earth is quiet and waits.
Death is satiated forever.
Behold, death waits only to be fed.
The sad angel who devours all,
yet still always hungers,
will soon be appeased.

THE DEVOURER OF LIFE
HUNGERS ETERNALLY.
THE GIVER OF LIFE
ACTS ETERNALLY WITH THE DIVINE –

and the void is filled.

Now you have been conceived,
you will become children:
love's pledge of the *Father* and the *Mother,*
of *Heaven* and *Earth,* in the womb of the Four.

Its name is still secret.
If union is celebrated in you, all is fulfilled.
Raise your heads! May the Seventh be with you!
May He touch you!

Immediately after the dialogue, I urge Hanna to tell us – even if it is not completely clear – what she felt during today's teaching. As far as I can recall, she said: "I felt the individual essence of each of the Seven Souls of life.

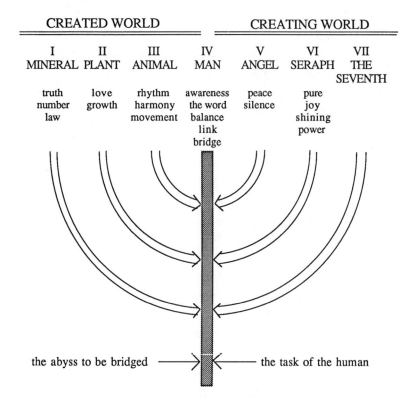

CREATED WORLD				CREATING WORLD		
I	II	III	IV	V	VI	VII
MINERAL	PLANT	ANIMAL	MAN	ANGEL	SERAPH	THE SEVENTH
truth	love	rhythm	awareness	peace	pure	
number	growth	harmony	the word	silence	joy	
law		movement	balance		shining	
			link		power	
			bridge			

the abyss to be bridged ⟶ ⟵ the task of the human

281

– The first level *of being is the* MINERAL, *the stone, the crystal. Its animating soul is the truth, the number and the law.*
– The second level *is the* PLANT.
Its soul is streaming love and the capacity to grow.
– The third level *is the* ANIMAL,
enlivened by harmony, movement and rhythm.
These three levels are contained in the fourth, *the* HUMAN. *But we – the so-called humans – are still not the* HUMAN, *the Four.*
It is our task to live on the fourth level and become a conscious link between the created and the creating world.
– The fifth level *is that of the* ANGELS, *where peace and silence reign.*
– *On* the sixth level *dwells the* SERAPH, *with burning power and joy.*
– The seventh level *is the mysterious, the highest degree of all life."*

I say to Hanna: "This is now clear, but something is still incomprehensible for me: We were told that Joseph is the Five (peace and silence), Lili, the Two (overflowing love) and I, the Six (radiating force), and that we all have the task of realizing the Four ... How can that be possible?"
"Only *through fulfillment of the* individual *task is it possible to live the Four, the* universal *task of the Human. It is precisely the forces you just mentioned which* enable *you to reach the Four, in which all seven Souls are united.*
Never forget this key to understanding the angels'

teaching: it is the mutual evolutionary attraction *between above and below, between the Divine and the human, between heavenly and earthly forces, between spirit and matter.*

All of these forces join in the middle, on the fourth level.

They unite and give birth to the new Child, which is God and *human ... Creator* and *created ... Light* and *matter.*

But the first step toward this evolutionary universal *accomplishment is to become conscious of your own* individual *task and to live it. This is the only gateway leading to the Four and it is also the only one to which we ourselves have the key.*

Hanna then continues: "Have you ever asked yourself why your master repeatedly said to you:

'Go your own way! Be independent!

You have been formed after my image.

May your eyes shine!'

This was said to you so that you would at last become aware of your own individuality, so that you would realize the Six – radiating force – in your everyday life.

Only in this way can you become a new HUMAN.

Only thus can you actively participate in joining the creating world and the created world.

But be aware that any diagram can only be a limited representation of existence. A diagram can never really convey love, the dynamic attraction between spirit and matter. And it could never express the union of the Seven Souls in a human being."

Wednesday, April 19, 1944 (mid-morning)

45. DIALOGUE: 'THE MEASURING ANGEL'

A rumor has been spreading through Budapest that all Jewish men no longer draftable for military service will be deported to 'work camps.'
The city is in a state of panic. Joseph anticipates his fate and becomes even more silent than usual. Hanna suffers deeply. She does her best not to show it, but I know how hard she is struggling for her inner balance. Lili knows no peace. She is with her pupils, who douse her thoroughly with their anxiety, from early morning until late at night.

Meanwhile, I race from official to official in a desperate attempt to save my friends. But I am met only by total disorganization, incompetence and an all-pervasive apathy. No one knows what the following day will bring. As the collective fear spreads, the resultant panic is almost impossible to bear. Everyone suffers from depression.

— 'The one who measures' speaks:
Even the stone grows,
the tree blossoms
and the animal loves.
But the human buries, destroys everything,
violates the Law.

Bring fruit, for I shudder to cut the living!
The *Word* lives in you,
but the fig tree that bears no fruit shall be felled.

The bud opens:
will it bring fruit or merely leaves?
In my hand, the sword, the flaming sword;
but my soul is troubled.

The 'Gardener' pleads:

JUST ONE MORE DAY, LORD!
I SHALL SPADE AROUND THE TRUNK,
I SHALL FERTILIZE GENEROUSLY:
PERHAPS THEN THE TREE
WILL BEAR FRUIT AFTER ALL!
IF NOT —
THEN YOU MAY CUT IT DOWN.
BUT PLEASE GRANT ME THIS!
I AM THE GARDENER,
AND THE TREE IS DEAR TO ME.

In my hand, the sword of fire.
And I know that I will chop
if the Lord gives the sign, for I serve.
I do not revolt, I do not scandalize.
An angel's service is difficult,
but we are always ready to serve. Always!

Serve! Serve day and night!
To stand still is forbidden!
You have been entrusted with many talents
and you must account for them.
Behold! It is wonderful to serve the Divine!
Blossom — bear flowers!

I IMPLORE YOU!

Never before has a dialogue so shaken me as today's. The most stern and unapproachable of the angels has begged us with humility *to blossom!*
Hanna says: "If we give up now, we are truly lost!
Neither Heaven nor earth will take us in …
we would be spat out!"
Hanna's words ring true. How, indeed, had I let myself be dominated by the outer situation? We had all allowed ourselves to become infected by the tragic state of our immediate surroundings.

Friday, April 21, 1944

46. DIALOGUE

The confiscation of Jewish apartments in Budapest has begun. The homeless are herded into a part of the city designated as the ghetto.
We do not know when this fate will reach Hanna and Joseph. But, as a result of the last dialogue, we are able to face this threatening development with relative calm. The outer situation has not improved, it has worsened. But we have changed our inner attitudes. And so, today's message is a song of joy.

— *Ő speaks and the Four sing:*

Always create! Always act!
Without raising a hand, without wanting to:
YOU ACT!

You become Human,
for you receive heavenly force: Ő.

The Five is with you, helping.
Faith glows with fire ... the fog lightens.
The seeing ... *see*.
The hearing ... *hear*.
The dying ... *live*.
The living ... *bear witness*.
The song never ends.
But the dividing wall ends:
Babylon has crumbled.

The song soars aloft.
Never-ending joy and peace!
The end is the beginning.
In the beginning is the *Word*
and the *Word* dwells in you.

Seek it, seek it always!
The seeker will find.
But death seeks you in vain:
never again will it find you.

The song rises up.

The seed is sown, and if the soil is good,
it will not repose for long.
Everything perishes: but the seed remains.
Be attentive only to the seed.
Be fulfilled with the seed,
arise with it, rest with it!
The greatest force of all
dwells in the sprouting seed:

it bursts great rocks asunder,
for the Glorious One dwells within it.
We serve you,
for the Glorious One dwells also in you.

New World, free, broad and true!
There you have a place to live,
a place that can never be taken from you.*
But you can give it on.

The song flies aloft.

The world thirsts: in you is the source.
The world screams: in you is silence.
The world weeps: in you is the only balm.
Bridge above the whirlpool.
Grace above the law.
Smile above the scream.
Peace above madness.
Not the end of the war: the new.
Let it be: the new!
Swear to Heaven that you will bring it about!

What is without: sinks.
What is within: shall be fulfilled.
And between new Heaven and new Earth comes:
THE HUMAN.
Rejoice with us! Who is against us?
Together we find the certainty of the new Way.
May the smile never leave your lips!
The one who fails to find it remains imprisoned.
But the one who acts through the Divine
is forever free.

* Reference to the confiscation of Jewish homes.

Ő spoke and the Four sang.
Ő speaks to you every day.
Listen well!

Friday, April 22, 1944

47. DIALOGUE

'The one who measures' speaks:
I bring the taste of the new Word.
What Ő has given, I give on.
Only the Word divinely given is true,
only the Word divinely given is to be given on.
Anything else is wasteful.

THE WORD ACTS.

The true word raises;
the false word buries.
Not life itself, but the souls of life are buried.
In the misused word,
the fourth level is already dead.

There is still the ANIMAL, the horse:
in the one who misuses movement,
moves more than necessary,
the third level dies.

There is still the PLANT, the grass:
When growth is misused
and the body made to swell,
the second level dies.

289

There is still the MINERAL, the stone:
Having become indolent,
the first level dies.

'The one who shines' speaks:
If the word is true,
then Ő speaks through you
and there are no more walls.
The fogs lighten, the *Five* opens,
the *Six* forms itself
and the *Seven Forces* are your crown.
The *Seven Forces* blossom on the tree of Heaven,
where the secret of eternal life ripens.
Who tastes of it has but one desire:
to serve the Divine.

The great secret is:
not the *many,* but the *more.*
When the day comes,
the Seven Forces bear fruit
and the Lord of all Fruit harvests.
Blossom! Bring forth fruit!
The empty hand is deplorable!

'The one who helps' speaks:
Disaster, war and darkness are lack of fruit.
Ő is the hunger of the hungry,
the demand for bread,
tears of those who suffer;
Ő is the cry of those in need.

There is already enough old wheat!
Seek the Name of the new! The Name!

FOR THE WORD CREATES.

May the mouth serve only the Word.
May the eye gaze only upon the new.
May the hand act only for the Divine.
May it no longer *take:* but *give.*
May peace come at last!
Swear to Heaven that you will bring it about!

> *This is the second time we have been exhorted:*
> *"Swear to Heaven that you will bring it about!"*
> *This troubles me, for I have no idea of how to*
> *accomplish the task.*

Friday, April 28, 1944

48. DIALOGUE

The 'oath' is decision.
When the seed begins to sprout,
it departs from the old husk,
its seed-identity, and leaves its former self behind.
Only thus can it bring forth new seeds:
one twenty, another perhaps forty.
This is the only way.

THE OATH TO HEAVEN DOES NOT BIND:
THE OATH TO HEAVEN RELEASES.

What was seed becomes bread.
But take heed!
Do not sow the seed in the earth!

There is enough wheat.
The granaries have long been filled,
but Heaven is still empty.
There no one has yet sown the seed.
The seed sown in earth – even if the sower stumbles –
finds its place and sprouts.
The sower of seed in Heaven
may not stumble:
for then the seed would fall back, sproutless.

The field of Heaven, the Seven,
was ploughed up long ago.
Sow the seed there and a wonder will sprout,
and never again will there be a lack of bread.
Every empty hand will be filled,
and every lack appeased.

Listen well!
The seed corn is not to be eaten.
The devil rejoices at bread baked from seed corn.
Until now, wheat grew up to Heaven.
From now on, Heavenly wheat descends to the earth.
But where is Heaven? Up there? Down here?

TRULY: HEAVEN IS IN YOU.

*I feel relief: our oath to Heaven helps to release us
from the old and to open ourselves to the new.*

Friday, April 28, 1944

49. DIALOGUE

The angels unexpectedly pay us a visit this evening.
Taken by surprise and with no writing materials at
hand, I am able to note down only the final part of
the message.

… Adam hid himself before the Divine;
he had lost the way.
Pointed toward Heaven on the cross,
crucified on the cross,
the Human Son cried out:
"My Father, my Father, why hast Thou forsaken me?"
But God did not answer.
The one who seeks does not find.
The one who knocks is not allowed to enter.
Only what has been lost can be sought after.

I ask myself: "Does this mean that Jesus, in his
agony, had lost the living contact with His Father?"

One who seeks does not find,
for behold: every way leads to death.
Every beginning leads to an end.

Ő ALONE IS,
AND Ő IS THE WAY.

One who hurries along the way … arrives nowhere.
One who stands still on the way … finds nothing.

After a long silence, the angel continues to speak
about the wedding of Heaven and earth, the subject

of the first part of this unforeseen dialogue, which I
had been unable to note down.

Rejoice!
Bride and groom are mere duality,
are merely the vessel where ecstasy dwells.
Bride and bridegroom,
Creator and created,
Light and shadow
are but vessels.
Only *ecstasy,* only being drunk with Light
is Divine.

These words astound and shock me. Only later do I
understand that, as long as we are still seeking, we
are not yet united with the Divine. Hanna was in
such intimate union with the angels that she was
able to convey this without the slightest hesitation.
I have the impression that the angels always speak
to Hanna with as much intensity as she is able to
bear. I feel these changes of intensity myself, for
sometimes I am totally nourished, while at others, I
can scarcely follow. Is this because my receptivity
varies or is it due to the intensity of the messages?

Friday, May 5, 1944

50. DIALOGUE

The district surrounding the synagogue has already been transformed into a ghetto. It is horribly overcrowded. False identity papers are hot items on the black market. I propose this solution to my friends, but they refuse to even consider any form of deceptive method. The great hope of thousands of Jews is their new 'guardian angel,' Raoul Wallenberg, with his Swedish passports, which could save them from otherwise almost certain extermination, perfectly organized by the Nazi mass murderer, Adolf Eichmann.

All the heavenly forces hover above you
and wait for you to be their hand.
They bring this message:
Do not flee!
Both here and beyond death, all is but dream.
Only beyond death will you find life:

LIFE IS SERVING Ő.

You are dear to the Divine,
you please Ő, for your heart is full.
Do not hurry, do not tarry:
be with Ő!

'The one who measures' speaks:
'The one who measures' is now the Gardener,
and is allowed to protect you
if your soul rises high above.

Love! Seek!
The soul of the Gardener trembles;
but you are trusted.
The Divine Seed will sprout.

We are all here with you
and we will remain with you.
Space begins beneath us and widens out below.
We know neither space nor time.
If you raise yourself up to us,
we can always be united: Always!

The new World cries out to you, imploring to be born.
The ONE dwells in you: Ő.
Can your head know fear
when the Divine dwells in your heart?
The foot races ... the hand grabs ... the head panics.
And why?
Place your feet solidly on the ground.
Bow your head!
And fold your hands!
For behold: Life dwells in the heart,
and in your heart is the Way.
The truth is: only the Divine IS.
We are all but images:
Angel, human, animal, flower and stone:
these are but images.

Ő IS ALL.

Do not flee, even to us!
To flee is to remain in darkness, dreaming.
If the dream is real for you,
then it becomes ever denser, embodied.

50. DIALOGUE

YOU ARE AWAKENERS – NOT DREAMERS.
THAT IS WHY YOU DREAM.

> *These words awaken many questions in me: Did we*
> *freely accept to 'dream' this earthly life so as to*
> *become able to awaken other dreamers? Even if our*
> *dream is extremely difficult? In accepting it, can we*
> *awaken and then become able to awaken others?*

Wake up!
And never flee before the task!
If your whole life is devoted to serving, believe me:
all that has been planned will come to be.
We speak the truth; we do not console.
Consolation is for the feeble.
Consolation is for those whose soul is darkened,
who do not see the LIGHT.
But you, with full heart and shining face,
you, whose words and deeds breathe life:
give one another your hands!
Whenever one from among you is weak: give help!
He walked on the water
and yet a garden saw *Him* weep.

> *This image of Jesus with His superhuman capac-*
> *ities and His very human tears in the garden of*
> *Gethsemani touches me deeply. We are sitting*
> *around a square table and without our having*
> *noticed it, our hands form the shape of a cross.*

Behold: the sign of the cross filled with force!
The cross no longer stands: it is at rest.
The task is no longer death: the task is life.

> *Silence.*

Let us now sing a song:

LORD OF ALL!
YOU ARE ONE WITH US!
THIS SONG IS OUR LIFE:
YOU ARE ONE WITH US.
WE SEEK NOTHING MORE.
WITH OUR EYES: BEHOLD!
WITH OUR HANDS: ACT!
IN OUR HEARTS: BE!
FOUR SERVANTS ADORE YOU.

YOUR EYE SEES US:
FORGIVE OUR TRANSGRESSIONS!
HEAR OUR SONG!
WE PRAY NO MORE,
WE ASK NO MORE;
YOU AND WE ARE ONE.

LORD! THROUGH US BE BORN!

Friday, May 12, 1944

51. DIALOGUE

*Budapest is bombed for the first time. The house
just across the street lies in ruin. Day after day, the
curious flock by to stare at this sinister sight. Even
farmers from the countryside travel into the city just
to stare ...*

The *Four,* the level of reality, is still empty.
Why do the people stare at what is below?
Why is the ruin beautiful to them,
and not the whole?
Why does the foot trample rather than stride?
To the many 'whys' there is just one answer:
Decide!
and the dividing wall will crumble.
The old decays, the new bud opens.

The force acting in you is
united with the *Whole:*
the Seven Souls of the Divine
and your souls are ONE.
'The one who helps' is the *Two.*
'The one who speaks' is the *Four.*
'The one who builds' is the *Five.*
'The one who shines' is the *Six.*
The *One,* the *Three* and the *Seven* still linger,
but they will come;
and what comes, shall be accomplished.

> *I wonder when these additional companions will*
> *appear to complete our circle.*

EACH LEVEL OF LIFE IS A SOUL,
AND THE SEVEN SOULS UNITED COMPRISE:
THE HUMAN BEING.

The Seven Souls are seven limbs;
their union is the *seed.*
Each of the Seven Souls acts;
THE ETERNAL IS ONE.

To me:
Do you accept the *Six?*
Know that it is pure Joy.
G. Yes, I accept the *Six.*

To Joseph:
Peace and Silence – the *Five* –
descend to earth through you;
but only if you hold tight to the earth.
Take the hand of the *Four,*
that Joy and Peace may find their place,
for they are held by the middle, by the Human essence:
Light-Awareness.

To Lili:
Love blossoms: the *Two.*

Miracle! The Seven Souls stride not in a line,
but in the round.
They form the rim of a cone whose apex is one.
There is no hierarchy,
the circle is unbroken.
Every cone has its apex: Ő.
The cone is the Way.
We sing in the circle, our place,
and our eyes converge at the peak: Ő.
We sing
since the time of no time,
and Ő is the time of no time:
the old, the ancient
and the eternal Infant.
Wondrous is the Divine plan
and thus our song is joyous:

THE CREATOR CREATES THE DIVINE PLAN
ETERNALLY THROUGH US.
BUT WITHOUT YOU, NOTHING CAN BE.
Sing with us!
The name of your song is still a secret,
but what I can say is this:
all of creation will sing with you!
The song that draws your soul from the earth
is neither sad nor serene, long nor short: it is *whole*.
All of Heaven, all of the earth: the Seven, united.

Listen well!
Wonder walks among you,
it walks in the circle: Join it!
The circle narrows, it does not break.
Eternity draws near.
Faith is no longer needed.
Faith is a bridge and the bridge is space.
But:

THE POINT CONTAINS ALL.

Heaven speaks:
The earth will receive wings
through us and through you.
If you speak through us:

WE STAND ON THE EARTH.

If we act through you:

YOU RECEIVE WINGS.

Thus our serving together endures eternally..

*After the dialogue, Hanna attempts to transmit her
inner perception in a symbolic form: to illustrate,*

301

she draws a cone (shown on previous page). How-
ever, she warns us that every diagram can at best
only convey a fragment of the experience. Never-
theless, it helps me to understand that each of us
has his or her own place within the sevenfold levels
of being, and not as a part of any kind of hierarchy.

Friday, May 19, 1944

52. DIALOGUE

The center of the sphere is the point.
From there, Ő radiates;
from there, Ő brings flowers to blossom.

Outside, the earth becomes cold,
and warmth – love – wanders homelessly.
The sphere is matter and Ő is its center:
Ő, Who lives in all, just as we live in you.
Measure deceives.
Outside, everything becomes cold.
Even the warmth of the sun is but reflected Light.
If your eye *looks* outward, there is only decay.
Everything rots; what is finished is dead.

Let your only act be eternal becoming;
and that is not *outside.*
If your eye *sees,* then every obstacle vanishes.
The Seven Rays wait only for this.
The world – stone, branch and horse –
all await your becoming one:

THE NEW HUMAN.

Outside, everything crumbles;
but *inside,* the new is formed.
Everything waits; the price is great.
But only matter is great. The kernel is tiny.
The tiniest of all in us is Ő.

Your eyes look *outward,* and that is not your task:
neither sorrow, nor evil, nor noise.
Do not be shaken!
The *outside* is not your task!
Listen only *within!* Be filled with Ő!
The space *within* is easily filled –
it is so *small.*
What has no weight cannot be measured;
what occupies no space cannot be grasped –
it dwells in the tiniest place: Infinity.

> *Today I feel as if I am under a shower alternating between hot and cold, as I am thrown from one contrast to the next: from* outside *to* inside, *from* great *to* small. *Curiously, I feel enlivened, and eager to encounter new possibilities.*

The Holy Spirit leads you.
The Seven Souls spring from the Divine.
Seven Sounds, still mystery.

THROUGH YOU, Ő WILL SPEAK A NEW LANGUAGE.
THE NEW LANGUAGE GIVES BIRTH TO NEW EARS.

You are the sound: you set the pitch.
No ears can yet hear the new Sound.
It begins to vibrate, and matter

– the original clay – is shaken.
Thus, new Ears are born.
The clay waits; it is inert
but it will come to life, for Ő breathes upon it.
Ő breathes upon it through you.
All shall be born. The earth waits.

All beings bow before the SMALLEST.
In the past, the *great* has been victorious;
but from now on, it shall be the *small*.
Choose! One or the other!
Never-ending is the fall of those
who strive for greatness.
The *too much* will be taken away
and the *great* will be cut down;
the *small* will be kept.

You stand on a *small* circle and that is our joy.
Our circle is still *smaller*
and Ő in us is the *smallest* of all.

Your place is now *small* and that is good.
Evil surrounds you, but its circle is *great*.
It waits for you in vain.
The *great* circle imprisons everything.
The tiny point in the middle opens the gate of Heaven.
Ő waits.

> *Joseph and Hanna leave the apartment only when*
> *absolutely necessary. All Jews are now required to*
> *wear the 'yellow star,' which often elicits brutality.*
> *For safety's sake, I escort Lili to the dialogues and*
> *take her home again afterwards.*

Friday, May 26, 1944

53. DIALOGUE – three days before Pentecost

Consoling, the Seventh Word,
Bringer of the Message of Joy, comes to you.
Await Him on that day!
As He spoke to the ancients,
flames ignited in his wake.
Be united on that day
and Fire will ignite on your foreheads:
the eternal Flame.

Our mouth is too weak,
our essence too subtle;
only the Seventh brings consolation.
Not what was brought to the ancients:
a new Flame will be given to you
and your burdened soul will be renewed.
The tomb where lay the body of the Lord
disappears.

The human, fragile being:
but on the forehead, Light.
Long empty, the vessel will now be filled,
for readiness and not despair
dwells in your heart.
Only to the ready is given.
Here, asking is of no avail.

This week, I measured your emptiness
in order to know when you will be filled.
Each of you will be given exactly what is needed.

What is given to you is LIGHT –
the tiniest ray,
and yet the great vessel is filled.
The Divine Wish is fulfilled.

Weakness is strength;
strength is weakness.
How hard is the rock!
The flame, though, is poured
into the most fragile vessel.
The human receives the task.
Rejoice at being human:
you will become Human!
Your task is to reach this degree of being.
The Holy Spirit comes over you,
becomes your drink.
Take heed! It burns,
but only where you take support.
You have no need for support.
Behold: the Divine lifts you up.

Ő breathes on the fire
and we sing in chorus:

THE ANCIENTS NO LONGER CONFER IN THE ROUND.
NEW BEINGS, ETERNALLY YOUNG,
JUDGE OVER ALL.
UPON THEIR HEAD, THE TIARA,
THE HEAVENLY CROWN,
FIRST RAY OF THE NEW SUN.
THE SUN IS ALREADY RISING,
THE NEW EARTH STILL REPOSES.

WE, ABOVE, CAN SEE THE NEW SUN,

YOU, BELOW, CANNOT YET SEE IT.
IN THE DEPTH OF THE HEART, IT BEGINS TO DAWN.

WITHIN, WE ALREADY SEE THE NEW SUN.
WITHOUT, YOU SEE ONLY EARTHLY PAIN.
THERE IS BUT ONE PAIN: TO BE *WITHOUT*.

ONLY WITHOUT IS DARKNESS;
WITHIN, IS LIGHT.

ONLY WITHOUT IS THERE NOISE;
WITHIN, SILENCE IS BORN.

ONLY WITHOUT IS THERE TIME;
WITHIN, TIME STANDS STILL.

ONLY WITHOUT IS THERE DEATH;
WITHIN, THERE IS LIFE.
ONLY WITHOUT DOES THE SOUL WANDER.

WITHIN, IT FINDS ITS EVERLASTING HOME.

THE CHALICE IS STILL DARK.
WHEN THE SEVEN WITHIN GLOW WHITE,
IT WILL BECOME TRANSPARENT.
DIVINE GLORY PENETRATES THE CHALICE,
AND IT RADIATES.
THERE IS NO MORE DEATH,
NOR NOISE, NOR PAIN.
TIME REMAINS WITHOUT;
AND TIME STANDS STILL.

Ó GIVES THE SIGNAL:
ALL OF CREATION BEGINS TO SING –
TO SING THROUGH YOU.
BE JOYFUL!

The words, "Be united on that day" and "A new Flame will be given to you" fill us with such joy that all the misery around us fades away. How I have longed for this Pentecostal Fire!

Sunday, May 28, 1944

54. DIALOGUE – on the Sunday of Pentecost

No more thundering sound!
No more language of tongues!
No more visible flames!
I AM Ő.

> *These words seem to come from infinitely far away, as from the beginning of time itself, and they awaken in me an unknown feeling of fearsome dimension: awe before the Divine.*

Ő cannot be seen,
Ő cannot be heard.
What you hear is but a faint echo.
The miracle is already below,
there beneath your feet.
The new World knows no miracle.
What comes is the incomprehensible
Source of Sources.
The old miracle is but a footrest for the new,
and the small hide beneath it.

Your force causes glowing.

To you is given the Spirit.
Unseen, you shall become.
Unheard, you shall act.
Unknown to anyone.
Unforeseen, beyond the miracle,
something begins, something moves.
And the blind shall *see*.
and the deaf shall *hear*.
To you shall be given the new Sound, the new Flame.

FORGIVE!
AND Ő, TOO, WILL FORGIVE ALL TRANSGRESSION.
IF YOU DESIRE GOOD,
THEN GOOD SHALL BE.

This is the new Force,
foreseen by no one.
All good comes through you:
invisible, like Ő.
Infinitely great is Ő;
infinitely small are you.
Infinitely great are you;
infinitely small is Ő.

THERE IS BUT ONE.

You do not see the flame,
you do not feel the flame.
You do not speak in tongues.
The many words come to an end.
Does the new already burn?
Heaven has descended.
The end is completed.
Wordless messengers, flameless flames

are the new messengers;
even with hands bound, they *act*.
Speaking is childish babble:
the apostles were *children*.
You are now *adolescents*.

You need not act; you need not speak;
you need not take; you need not give.
And yet the new shall come to be:
Be filled with the Divine –
thus the Word becomes flesh!

All that you conceive ... SHALL BE.
From dawn until dusk: call the new!
Always call!
The level of the *Four* is empty,
but it will be filled.
From morning until evening, call the new!

AND WHAT YOU CALL SHALL BE,
AND SHALL NEVER PASS AWAY.

From eternity to eternity, every moment acts.
A hundred thousand years are not enough
to fill the abyss your heart is ready to fill.
But make no mistake!
You need do nothing more:
the Act is born.
Your Act is conception,
and only in secret.
The heart is the dwelling place
where the wedding takes place.
Spirit and matter are two half-seeds.

The Fire received today fuses the two halves
and they become ONE.
Fulfilled is the ancient promise:

MATTER AND SPIRIT, DEATH AND LIFE
BECOME ONE.
The one who has conceived shall give birth.

TO BE SECRET APOSTLES WAS YOUR WISH.
IT IS FULFILLED.

Your mouth as it speaks,
your hand as it acts
shall be pure.

That is our word.
We are angels and we speak.

The Seventh Voice thunders,
The Seventh Flame blinds.
The Divine is silent,
yet always with you.
Silent, also the message.
Silence cannot be distorted.
Thus, the one who hides behind lies
is unable to hide there.
The invisible cannot be represented.
Thus, the Divine cannot be mis-represented.

The time of the new comes
and the new sprouts.
The new Act is more difficult than the old,
but heavenly force dwells in all of you,
wherever you are.

Friday, June 2, 1944

55. DIALOGUE

It is the evening before Joseph's deportation. What is his destination? No one knows. He prepares in silence and without complaint, in spite of his fore-boding that these are his last moments together with his wife. Hanna suffers deeply but does her best not to show it. She feels a sharp, continuous pain in her heart, as if it were pierced with knives. I am surprised she is able to summon the strength to transmit today's dialogue.

'The one who measures' speaks:
Blessings and peace!
The end of the trial approaches.
Outer existence rushes into the depths,
into eternal night.
You live above in the Light, blessed.
The promise is fulfilled.

The 'Gardener' speaks:
In my hand, the knife,
the sharp knife, the grafting knife.
Now the cut opens a painful wound;
but I insert the new twig.
Already it is possible.
Small and frail is the holy twig,
and unspeakably tender;
yet filled with the force of the Divine.

I dress the wound with heavenly wax,

with wondrous consolation.
The wound cut by the knife is filled:
and the wound is no more.
Still tight is the bandage,
it still covers the cut;
but it, too, I will soon remove.
Seven Worlds pay homage to you,
my little sprig!

The new marriage is consummated
between silence and the word.
The Divine Realm is there,
where silence and word
are eternally wed,
and the new Word is conceived in silence.

> *Only now do I see what a fateful bond connects
> Hanna, the Word (IV) and Joseph, Silence (V).*

'The one who shines' speaks:
I speak of shining love.
There is love and there is shining force:
May they act together!
Give your hands to one another,
love and shining force,
only united are you effective!

> *These words put my deep friendship with Lili in a
> new light: Lili's task is love (II), mine is shining
> force (VI). The diagram of the levels of life shows
> that they are complementary.*

Thus there will be shining silence here below.
If Light Awareness is the bond,

there is no more abyss, no wound, to be bridged.

Our tasks become ever more clear: mine is to shine,
Joseph's is Silence and Hanna's is the middle,
Light-Awareness.

'The one who helps' speaks:
The consoling, loving word hovers over you.
Without love, nothing can be:
Not Light-Awareness, not silence and peace,
not shining force and joy.
The shining ray – joy! – brings glowing;
Peace and Silence fulfill.
Awareness enlightens.
But only love unites.
Love is above everything
and love is in everything.

Its sign is the lily, the snow-white lily
whose scent rises up to the Seventh Heaven,
permeating everything, everywhere;
and yet its stem is green, and rooted in the earth.

'The one who builds' speaks:
The silence that builds,
builds not only above.
Now it builds below, this is already possible.
The old caves in, its stones will no longer be used.
Salt is strewn where the old stood.
Only the jackal howls in the ruins.
Nothing green grows where Babylon was.

But beyond the graspable
a new Homeland already greens.

314

55. DIALOGUE

The plan begins to vibrate in the heart
of 'the one who builds,'
desire to act is born.
The new Building welcomes the homeless.
Those covered by the old,
those restricted by matter, are rejected.
Received are those who make the Divine
their only abode.
I do not fear for you.

Now our angels speak in unison:

Silence is the house of the shining Word
in which love burns.

> *In these words, each of our tasks is related to the others: "Silence is the house" is Joseph (V), "of the shining" is Gitta (VI), "Word" is Hanna (IV), "in which love burns" is Lili (II).*

Thus, four voices become song: new Song,
new vibration here below,
creating new forms,
new hearts,
new ears,
new hands
and *seeing* eyes.

We teach you to sing.

THE OLD SONG DIES –
IT NO LONGER CREATES.

Its essence, grace, has left it;
laws have killed it.
But above grace is ONE, the ONLY ONE.

Sing always! In song, you are united,
even if your hands can no longer touch one another.
Your song rises to a place where new Blood,
new Vessels, new Space and new Matter pulse.
Slowly your voices join the new heartbeat,
slowly you begin to understand this beating.

WATCH OVER THE DIVINE,
AND THE DIVINE WILL WATCH OVER YOU.

   Silence.

The One who bears the new Name approaches.
Prepare His path!
Spread out your garments before Him!
Your only garment: the I, yourself.
Only the naked can receive a garment of Light.
No longer astride an ass,
the Light approaches: resplendent LIGHT.
Blessed be *His name!*

THE NEW LIGHT CASTS NO SHADOW;
FOR NEW MATTER IS TRANSPARENT,
FROM ETERNITY TO ETERNITY.

*Now Joseph must leave us. Hanna is so exhausted
that we do not allow her to accompany her husband
to the* Keleti *railroad station. Thus it is I who
accompany him during this ominous departure. He
is wearing the required yellow star. We speak little.
Both of us know that these are our final words and
moments together. The men are packed into cattle
cars, the doors are sealed and the train slowly
moves off towards its unknown destination.*

Friday, June 9, 1944

56. DIALOGUE

This week weighs heavily upon us. Now that Joseph has gone, Hanna is overwhelmed by sorrow. I am with her almost all of the time. The political situation becomes ever more perilous. The problem of how to save Hanna and Lili from the ghetto is foremost in my mind. Already now, it is too risky for Lili to come to the dialogues. I am uninterruptedly asking myself how it might be possible to save the lives of my friends.

Heavy is the chalice,
but light as a feather is the body: the Host.
Even the weight of the Host is but husk.
The new Body is: sacrifice.
Wherever the chalice is – the full chalice –
there is the altar.

The Host contains little flour.
Its service is no longer to be eaten.
Its service is to be sacrificed.
The one who sacrifices, glorifies matter.
The sacrifice is not the altar,
nor the chalice, nor even the Host.

His body was sacrificed.
He asks a new sacrifice of you.
His blood was shed for the many.
What *He* asks is no longer blood,
but time and space.

317

FOR THE DIVINE DWELLS BEYOND TIME AND SPACE.
DO NOT BE WITH HIM: *BE HIM!*
DO NOT TAKE THE HOST INTO YOUR MOUTH:
BE THE HOST YOURSELF!

> *I am filled with wonder that the angels introduce a*
> *new meaning into the Christian communion, into*
> *the union with Jesus.*

Let the unjust, the weeds, eat you:
they will become wheat!
And also the just. Do not differentiate!
The mouth of the just welcomes you,
and sweet will be the Host.
In the mouth of the unjust,
it will become terrible fire,
devouring all falsehood.

GIVE YOURSELVES!
AND THIS SACRIFICE, THE HOST,
WILL ACT JUSTLY.

How do weeds become wheat?
By burning and turning to dust
and to earth, throughout the ages.
Into this earth falls the seed,
and it becomes new wheat.
The weed does not feel the fire.
But only through fire can it become wheat.

We teach you:
Only in the wheatfield is there weed;
for on the meadow, the weed is a flower.
Life delivered: no more weeds,

only wheatfields and flower-covered meadows.
The roots of the weed cannot be destroyed:
the just and the unjust are threshed together,
as are the wheat and the weed.
But the seedcorn is chosen.
Straw and chaff are cast away –
but never the seed!

Sow the seeds that you, yourself are!
Do not hold them back,
not even the measure of a single Host!
The seed will bring forth new Bodies
on the fourth level,
the not yet completed level of being.

SOW THE SEEDS!
YOU ARE THE SOWERS AND YOU ARE THE SEEDS.
A SOWER SOWS ONESELF.

Sunday, June 11, 1944

57. DIALOGUE

Airless air is Heaven:
Spaceless space,
where everything has its place.
Timeless time,
no beginning, no end: eternity.

The Four:
Airless air, the lungs gasp: not enough air.

319

Yet the new grows.

Spaceless space:
The body is cramped:
the blood throbs and has no place.
'The one who measures' measures:
The new has place and space.

Timeless time:
The head throbs;
thought is blocked.
The heart breaks.
All is cold.
Nerves freeze.

The Eternal gives the sign and
new seeds are sown:
new air,
new space and
new time are born.
The judgment is not end: it is *beginning*.

It was said in days of old:
The earth will be renewed,
Heaven will be renewed.
Light will shine forth and
darkness will flee.

The Seven Flames blaze in glory.
But a new Eye is born,
through which all will See,
as much as each can bear.

We announce this message:
The one who dares to step forward

will See the face of the Seventh,
and nothing else will ever be desired.

The new Eye has already been formed,
but it is still closed:
it is not yet accustomed to the LIGHT.
It opens slowly, but it does not see.
Its task is not to see:

IT MAKES *SEEING* POSSIBLE,
FOR IT IS LIGHT ITSELF:

Terrible, flashing fire!
But only the empty husk
falls to dust.

IF YOU SEE SOMETHING CRUMBLING TO DUST –
BELIEVE ME – THE LIGHT IS APPROACHING.

The earth trembles at its heralding
and everything not filled with the *Eternal Word*
crumbles to dust.

June 14, 1944

*All Jewish men in the city under 40 years of age have
been deported to work camps; the women and children
are forced to live in the ghetto.*
*About the time that this is all taking place, a politically
influential friend of mine seeks me out and tells me of a
secret plan that has been devised by a certain Father*

*Klinda, a courageous and compassionate Catholic
priest in Budapest.*

*As a means of rescuing about a hundred women and
children from the ghetto, a military sewing factory is to
be set up in a small, unoccupied cloister.*

*This operation is to take place under the protection of
the Apostolic Nunciature and certain high-ranking officers in the War Ministry, whose names are, of course,
to be kept absolutely confidential.*

*The women working there would thus be under the
double patronage of the nunciature and the War
Ministry, which is responsible for the uninterrupted
production of war materials.*

*If the plan is to work, a volunteer commander will have
to be found who is capable both of organizing the work
of the factory in a productive manner, and also demon-
strating military discipline to the outside. My friend has
come to ask me to take on this task. Just as I am
replying to him that I don't have the slightest clue of
how an industrial production line should function, and
even less of an idea of military discipline, it suddenly
strikes me that this scheme might be just the way to
save Hanna and Lili from the ghetto. And so I declare
myself ready to take on the role of commander of this
secret operation on the condition that Hanna and Lili be
added to the already-completed list of women who are
to participate.*

A short time later, I find myself inspecting the Cloister
Katalin *in the villa quarter of Buda. It stands in the
center of a large garden not far from the* Jánoshegy
Forest. *However, the house itself, a former villa, is
rather small and already bursting at the seams with*

women and children. Mattresses, cots and whatever the inhabitants have been able to save of their possessions are piled everywhere, from the cellar to the attic. As if that weren't enough, more and more new refugees are arriving to squeeze themselves into the last tiny cracks of space.

This tragic, totally disorganized mass accumulation threatens to endanger the entire operation, whose key to success will be keeping secret the fact that these women are of Jewish origin. The vital importance of providing at least the appearance of a well-organized military sewing factory is obvious to me. During my inspection rounds, the women observe me with fear and mistrust because, as I later learn, a rumor has been circulating that a strict and uncompromising commander has been appointed by the War Ministry. I have to seriously ask myself if there is even a possiblity of bringing any semblance of order and discipline to this unbelievable chaos, and to make assembly-line workers of these women, most of whom have never worked in an organized fashion.

I decide to take advantage of their fear of the evil commander and to introduce at least a provisional structure of order. A wooden shed stands in the garden, and I select this to be my office. I notify the War Ministry of my acceptance of the post and, as the daughter of a former high-ranking military officer, I am judged to be trustworthy: my official 'appointment' as voluntary commander follows almost immediately.

Sunday, June 16, 1944

58. DIALOGUE

This is the last dialogue in the apartment of Hanna's parents. In a few days, Hanna and Lili will begin working in the military sewing factory.
In Budaliget we had celebrated the 'June Festival,' the period between Hanna's birthday, the 14th of June, and mine on the 21st. This year, there is no question of such a 'Sun festival'; this year, it is the angel who solemnly announces the new Sun.

The sun rises
and climbs to midday;
then it sinks and dies.
Appearances are deceptive.
Motionless is the sun
and motionless is the *Giver*.
The Giver only appears to move,
its rays are all-penetrating.
Why should the sun rise? To what end?
Its rays have penetrated where there was lack.

MOTIONLESS IS THE GIVER;
GIVING IS THE GIVER.

The sun is master of a universe.
This universe and the sun in its center
are but images.
They move in a still greater circle.
But, in truth, there is neither great nor small,

FOR THE SMALLEST *GIVER* IS AS GREAT AS THE SUN
AND AS GREAT AS THE *ETERNAL GIVER:*
THROUGH *GIVING.*

All else is illusion, deception: perishable matter.

> *I feel that the angel is destroying all outer appear-*
> *ances so as to make us aware of what is really*
> *essential:* GIVING. *I am amazed to see that every*
> *human is Divine in the moment of* GIVING; *for then*
> *a Divine function is practiced.*
> *Silence.*

If you ask for our word, we can give it.
That is *our* deliverance.
When we ask for your hand, you, too, can *give* it:
that is *your* deliverance.
So it is: you ask and you *give,* we ask and we *give.*
If our song and your hand are joined,
even asking disappears:

WE ARE ONE.

Our word is yours; your hand is ours.
The abyss is filled.
Thus the living God, without flaw, without lack,
is born in you: the one vibrates.

Asking and giving
are already but vibration.

IT IS THE NEW FORCE.

Your asking never ceases; ours, too, is eternal.
Vibration, Wonder: never-ending wonder!
In the union of *asking and giving* for a single instant,

THE SEVEN FORCES ACT AS ONE.

The diagram shows how light-energy emerges from the Divine Source, diminishing gradually in intensity. The three dots in the middle indicate the not-yet-bridged lack between the lowest vibration of the angel and the highest vibration of the human. Mutual asking and giving can fill this gap.

Eternal life is spaceless space;
not emptiness, not void,
but life, intense vibration, fulfillment.

Somewhere the Divine Heart beats,
and we all beat with it.
*If the finest vibration reaches the densest,
then the connection remains unbroken,
and death ceases to be.*

The Divine Heart beats,
and we pass on the rhythm.
Pass it on, you too: further, always further!
This is the only task.
Serve in joy, for death is already dead!

If your heart is weak, its vibration is still untuned.

It is not in harmony with ours.
Only the vibration is at fault,
there is no other possibility.
The rhythm, the shining force
does not break through: it permeates everything.
One of its names is LOVE.
But it has many names,
all of which reveal the ONE truth:

THE DIVINE IS LOVE,
AND THE DIVINE IS *ALL* THAT *IS*.

The new Love is already born.
Its name is still secret,
but even while nameless, it acts:
through you, it acts.
Thus you, too, are nameless.

See! The ray vibrates:
Joy and Force ...
Silence and Peace ...
Light-Awareness ...
Rhythm ...
Love
and at the base: Truth.
The ray descends.
The planet revolves, the sun is motionless.

We bless you.
And our blessing vibrates on and on,
ever further ... and it creates.
The tiny crack between us
is but a slight difference in rhythm;
it is no longer separation.

We are ONE.
Our word is the word of angels
and we are angels through the Divine.
You are with us, and

OUR LIFE IS ONE.

> *Two urgent problems are facing me: I will have to
> introduce a para-military system of order into a
> sewing factory of unskilled workers that must be
> organized without financial means! We have been
> given only the empty cloister – everything else is up
> to us. Soon the balls of textile will be arriving and,
> all too soon, we will be expected to deliver finished
> soldiers' shirts. Only then will we be authorized to
> have military protection.*

> *I receive instructions in military discipline at the
> War Ministry. A few days later, when Hanna and
> Lili arrive at the sewing factory, they are more than
> a little amazed to see me standing at the top of the
> large main entrance stairway giving orders of the
> day to the assembled workers, who are standing in
> rows before me.*

> *At first, it requires my full concentration to keep
> from laughing at myself in this strange and
> unfamiliar role. However, the gravity of the
> situation quickly silences my urge to laugh. I order
> every worker to procure her own sewing machine,
> by whatever means; further orders concern the
> sewing courses which will be starting immediately.*

Wednesday, June 21, 1944

59. DIALOGUE

Today is the summer solstice, my birthday.
The three of us meet at noon in the wooden bar-
racks of the 'commanding officer' in the garden; no
one else dares to approach my 'headquarters.'

The asking of those who no longer ask for themselves
reaches Heaven and calls Heaven to descend.
Thus the new Earth – Heaven – is able to come.
And the earth is elevated, raised ever so slightly.
This 'slightly' is enough:
the earth leaves its course and enters a new orbit.
The seven outstretched arms of Seven Forces
are rays embracing the new Circle.

THOSE WHO ASK FOR THEMSELVES
SWALLOW THE RAYS.
THOSE WHO NO LONGER ASK FOR THEMSELVES *ACT*.

The new Force is the point
from which the earth can be raised up.
This change cannot be perceived.
Perceiving is a child of the earth.
This change cannot be felt.
Feeling is a child of water.
But you can intuit that in spaceless space,
the earth's orbit does not increase: it decreases.

I wonder if this means that the earth is approaching
the center of all centers: the Divine.

The wings of angels and the shadows of devils
become unnecessary.
The angel no longer hovers. The wings of angels and
the shadows of devils
become unnecessary.
The angel no longer hovers.
The angel *acts*.
The human no longer tarries:
the human *gives*.
The animal no longer flees:
the animal lives, without fear.
The seed is no longer blind:
the seed sprouts.
And radiant is the stone.
The new – long since proclaimed – is born!

But you: ask! Always ask!
Your asking creates,
both here above and there below.
Now the new Sound vibrates,
now the new Sun rises.
Just now, when the old sun is at its zenith.

NOW EVERYTHING BEGINS.

The sun is motionless.
But the earth flies and finds its new Sun.
Thus it is.
The turning point is now.
From eternity to eternity.
Amen.

> *These last words are uttered with such intensity that
> I have the overpowering feeling we human beings
> are entering into a new epoch: I sense that a new
> phase of human evolution is beginning.*

Wednesday, June 21, 1944

60. DIALOGUE FRAGMENT

Later the same night, we are all in the wooden shed, headquarters of the 'commander,' unable to sleep. Suddenly Hanna feels the presence of the angels. Taken completely by surprise, I am unfortunately unable to record most of the dialogue.

… The time of the deceiver has expired.
The power sought after,
the power which was given,
is now taken away.
The deceiver used it selfishly
and covered everything with lies.
But now: all that was kept secret
is loudly proclaimed,
and the power is taken away.
Deception is dead.
Its days are numbered.
The Divine says: ENOUGH!

The end is also a beginning:

FROM DEVILS THERE WILL AGAIN BE ANGELS.

Take heed! All that was proclaimed
occurs inside of you. *Within!*
Ask always – give always!
And then no harm will occur.

Everything is completed,
and everything begins anew:

THE ACT IS BORN.

The sewing machines arrive and the sewing courses begin. With her exceptional talent for organizing, Hanna trains some of the more skilled women to be supervisors, and they, in turn, inaugurate the others into the ways and means of industrial production. The team of supervisors later come to be known as 'the jolly jokers.'

After work, Hanna, Lili and I meet in my 'headquarters' in the garden. The fear and respect which everyone else has before the 'commander' allows us to meet with the angels undisturbed, in the peaceful tranquility of the night.

Friday, June 23, 1944

61. DIALOGUE

The Divine heart draws you near.
Ő calls … and you approach.
Behold, you may go no closer,
for already the Divine heart embraces you.

BEWARE: YOU MAY NOT DWELL
WITHIN THE DIVINE HEART!

The new Love, the new Heartbeat is different,
completely different from what has been.
It is continuous giving,
continuous pulsing: Dissemination.
One Divine heartbeat is an instant;
one Divine heartbeat is an aeon of time:

332

each heartbeat is a turning point in eternity.
The new Love is blood red,
it is a wondrous force,
milk for the new Child.

ONLY THOSE COMING FROM THE DIVINE HEART
ARE ABLE TO GIVE.

A new Rhythm creates new Worlds.
New Organs grow according to new Plans.
The world is renewed; it brightens, it widens.

THE GREATEST GIFT
GIVEN US BY THE DIVINE
IS THAT WE MAY GIVE.

In this way, we become – indeed,
we *are* – a part of Ő.
The great Law there below is: to *give*.
Every grass gives fruit.
Every creature gives; this is the law.
They are all compelled to give,
but we are free: *we give freely*.

The ACT is free;
not, however, the will!
The moment of deliverance draws near:

ABOVE THE WILL: FREELY GIVING.

No longer action and reaction;
no longer reward and punishment;
no longer knife and caressing.
Different, completely different
from all that has been before:

GIVING FREELY.

It is new; completely new and different.

The Divine Heart beats.
Arteries lead to the Heart,
wherein all the Divine blood finds place:
for it is given on.

The Divine Heart beats, and you beat with it.
The Seven Arteries are filled, filled with red joy.
Give it on! Give it on, ever further!
When the blood becomes tired,
it returns to the heart, where it is renewed.
But if it is not given on, it coagulates: it clots.

THAT IS THE SECOND DEATH.

Take heed! Be whole! Give!
Always give freely! Always give with joy!
The new Joy, the new Element,
is different from all that was before:
it is the new Heartbeat, it is deliverance, it is creation.
The one who lives this: LIVES.
You: LIVE!
Then we can live *ONE* LIFE.
Fear nothing! The one who truly Lives: ACTS.

> *It is practically impossible to establish a somewhat*
> *'normal' system of production in the sewing factory.*
> *Far too many of the women are simply useless as*
> *seamstresses, and even more are just plain irrespon-*
> *sible. But every one of us is highly aware that,*
> *without the production of uniforms, our justification*
> *for 'military factory' status would be gone.*
>
> *To our utter horror, an inspection is announced for*

the near future. The piles of ruined army shirts multiply by the day. The 'jolly jokers,' those women capable of jumping in at any point, are forced to work feverishly day and night repairing the damage done by their less-skilled colleagues.

I apply for an extension of the delivery date for the uniforms, and I appeal to an officer in the War Ministry who is aware of the true reason for our existence. Very few officers are actually 'in the know' about us: to be caught assisting in the protection of Jews would result in the immediate end of a military career. Although I do not know any of these higher officers personally, with a great deal of luck, I succeed in obtaining a postponement of the delivery date.

Thursday, June 29, 1944

62. DIALOGUE

Only what is *more* than the old is Act.
Your *love* is still an inclination,
still a form of separation between us.
The new Being no longer *loves* in the old way.
The new Being is capable of *more*.
Without taking and without giving: it acts.
It is already possible.

To be active is not to act.

The animal feels, it wants and it is active.
Humans, imagining themselves to already be Human,
fancy themselves no longer being blind;
after all, knowledge enables discrimination
between good and evil.
But knowledge is the unripe fruit of the old tree!
The child plucked it before its time.
Now the fruit has ripened.
Now you may eat it.

FOR THE WISE,
KNOWLEDGE IS BUT A MEANS.
NOTHING ELSE.

Feeling, willing and doing are not free.
Only the Act is free!
The free Act penetrates everywhere;
for the free Act, there is no dam and no wall.
The free Act permeates everywhere.

The living gains new Life
and the lifeless crumbles to dust,
for the Act *acts*.
The Act does not destroy, nor build,
the Act does not make ugly, nor beautiful.
The Act *is*.

> *At first, I am confused by this apparent contra-diction between acting and non-acting. Then I grasp that the Act* originates *beyond time and space, while* acting *in time and space.*

All is revealed.
All becomes what it is meant to be,

and not what it pretends to be.
The façade of the lie disintegrates,
for the new vibration *acts*:

DIVINE GIFT!

The old worm-eaten cross decays
and with it decays the crucified body.
But a new Body is born, and It grows.

Light streams everywhere.
The new Being, the Being of Light,
spreads its arms open wide,
and the cross, too, becomes Light.
Its four arms are the holy FOUR
with the Heart of Light in the Middle: Fulfillment!

> *The angels told us that Life can be redeemed only*
> *through the new ACT: by uniting the seven levels of*
> *Life in the MIDDLE, in the HOLY FOUR. Now all of*
> *the symbols and images seem to point to this same*
> *goal, each in a different way.*

No need for nails or the crown of thorns,
no need for torments or the horrors of war!
None of these are needed anymore!
The Light opens its arms and waits;
it closes into its Heart, and yet all are free.
In the Heart of Light there is no lock,
no binding sentiment,
no sluggish passivity,
and no ambitious striving.
There is not even a way or an abyss.
The Heart of Light embraces everything

and radiates everywhere.
It Acts, for the Divine gives power:
over the living and the dead,
that the chosen may ACT: ACT FREELY.

We cannot act.
We can only be the wordless word.
But if the *word* and the *hand* are one,
then everything is possible
and the heralded Realm can become reality:
the Realm whose foundations have been laid
since the beginning of time.

The connecting link between the nunciature and our factory is Father Klinda, who is well known to us as a kindly, benevolent man. One day, in his concern with the fate of our refugees, he suggests that he baptize them. Because the Christian certificate of baptism provides a certain protection from the Nazis, practically everyone is prepared to take this step. Only Lili and Hanna, considering this to be opportunism, are against it and refuse to participate. I disagree. For me, the sacraments are symbols of an inner process. I think back on the 13th dialogue and the overwhelming experience of my baptism with the Blue Water. I wish so strongly that my friends might receive the same Grace. I argue to them that a spiritual reality might act through a corresponding symbolic form. This corresponds to the union of heaven and earth, and is a part of our task. After some days of deliberation, they finally declare themselves ready to be baptized. How completely independent of any so-called opportunism their decision truly was became evident later: Hanna could have saved her life in the Nazi camp by claiming to be Christian; instead, in the face of death, she testified that she was, indeed, Jewish by birth.

Sunday, July 2, 1944

63. DIALOGUE MORNING

The Seventh Word is neither sound, nor light,
it has not been, nor shall it ever be.
The Seventh Word is the voice of all.
Everything and nothing,
it is the unutterable:
yet the Seventh Word ACTS.
Only the unutterable IS.

The pillar of creation is shaken:
already it is overgrown with moss.
But Ő builds the new.
The old pillar crumbles –
and see! – within, it is hollow.
Only the seed is full.
The old pillar of creation crumbles,
but the pillar of Light will never crumble.
Nausea at the *too much* causes matter to explode.
Let the *more* come!
He does not come. He IS ... He IS, the Seventh.
Everything is filled with blinding Light.
It is impossible for you to hide from it,
for the new Light permeates everywhere.
There is no place to hide,
but there is also no reason to hide.
Purify yourselves while it is still possible.
The souls of those who do not
are paralyzed by the cold.
Choose!

The 'blue Light' dawns –
and then, the 'white' appears.

> *I am immediately reminded of my question about
> the fascinating 'Blue Light,' which remained un-
> answered in the 12th dialogue.*

The 'Blue Light' is already the Sixth.
The yellow sun beside it
is but a flickering tallow candle by comparison.
In the 'White Light,' the seven Colors
flow together and space comes to an end.

We will teach you again later today,
but this is enough for the moment.
Peace be with you!

> *Hanna and Lili are baptized at noon. Late in the
> afternoon, we wait in the wooden shed for the con-
> tinuation of our dialogue with the angels.*

Nothing may be left out!
Only the *more* Acts.
Fire *absorbs* water;
baptism by water releases.
But it delivers through the baptism of fire
that links to the Divine.
Nothing may be left out.

There are seven baptisms,* seven solutions,
seven deliverances.
They are not form: they are essence.

---

* In Hungarian, the word *keresztség* means 'baptism' as well as
'crossing' and 'crossroads.'

Listen carefully!
The Son of God on the wooden cross:
beginning and end, earth and Heaven ...
the first baptism.   (Connection of I. and VII.)

The second is water baptism:
union of water and Joy. "   (Connection of II. and VI.)

The third is baptism by fire:
Harmony united with silence,
movement with peace.   (Connection of III. and V.)

Thus the Six become Three.
The Fourth is the middle:
Heaven and Earth, Creator and creation united.
No longer seven, but ONE.

CREATED WORLD   CREATING WORLD

I   II   III   IV   V   VI   VII

THIRD BAPTISM

SECOND BAPTISM

FIRST BAPTISM

The small circle now closes;
from here and from the beyond,
the two hands already reach one another
and there is no longer space between them.
Spirit and matter are united.

   Silence.

He, too, chose baptism.
He knew that to go on
would be possible only in this way,
and He knew that all would follow in His footsteps.

Churches are mortal – baptism by water is immortal.
Matter is delivered by water.
Water is delivered by fire.
The seed of Light delivers the Six.

Churches live or die: form.
But the *House* of the Divine is all: the *Whole*.
Churches are only a small part of the Whole.
The Good Shepherd has many flocks:
in *one house,** the blind dwell contentedly,
in *another house,* those who seek are weeping.
In a *third house* dwell those who have ears
but do not hear.
One Shepherd and many flocks.

Time destroys old houses and builds up new ones.
The only house for you to live in
is no longer a house, no longer a whitewashed façade,
Ready to welcome all since eternity is the Divine Heart,

---

* Literally translated from Hungarian 'church' is 'one house': *egy-ház.*

the Heart of Light, the Middle, the Seed:
the only Dwelling.
My dear ones, from now on you may dwell only there.
Thus Ő can Act, for your hand is ready.
It is no longer a part; it is *whole*.

Friday, July 7, 1944

64. DIALOGUE

Early this morning, many of the newly-baptized take first communion. The tiny chapel is filled. Father Klinda joyfully celebrates the mass. I had assumed that most of the women had accepted baptism only as a means of obtaining the protective baptismal certificate, but I now see how wrong I was! These unhappy women, whose lives hang by a thin thread, pray with complete devotion. The host which they take today for the first time in their lives provides many with hope of protection from a higher dimension.

The one who is not hungry will be satiated and
the one who does not thirst will be given drink:
that they *give it on*.

Bread is the first sacrament,
wine the second,
fire the third; they are
given to the one who no longer asks.

Your body and His are already one.
The cup in which His blood glows
is already yours.
No gift, no alms: but *unity*.
Bread can be broken in half
and wine can be spilled;
but Light – the new Light –
is indivisible.
We watch over the altar,
so that your heads are never raised:
for now you have been given everything!

> *In accordance with our inner change, the teaching*
> *of the angels also changes. How often we have*
> *been told: "Always ask!" Now the message is just*
> *the opposite: "… you have been given everything."*

In the church, everyone pleads and begs.
But this is not your way:
Your heart and His are ONE.
This is not a gift: it is your task.
Never again raise your head to ask for yourself.
You are being begged for deliverance.
Open your arms wide!
Give: always give! Act: always act!

Believe me, if your heart is dry,
it will be filled anew without your asking.
Do not ask!
The new Body, the new Blood and the new Spirit
will be given only to those who *no longer ask*.
If you give, then the small one,
the old one, the earthly one

that lives within you, will also be given.
To the Heavenly One in you, nothing is given,
for the new is ONE with the Divine.

WE WATCH OVER THE ALTAR.
THE ALTAR IS THE EARTH: THE WHOLE EARTH.

The *too much,* called forth by the blind,
will be cut off.
Blindness sacrificed and poured out the blood.
But when the Light comes,
blind tyranny can no longer reign.

The new Light does not flicker in the sanctuary lamp.
The new Light flows everywhere.
Blindness is no longer possible.
Either you are burned ... or you SEE.
This is not the end: it is the beginning.

Without the new, even the greatest earthly joy
would be like the fire of damnation:
the sun shines ... the bird sings ...
the red heart beats;
but without the new, all is but damnation.

Beyond the old circle shines the new Light,
still unknown to you.
The core of the Light, the new Host
will be raised above all.
Where the Heart of Light beats,
the sanctuary lamp does not flicker,
for wind is a child of space:
there is no place for space, there,
for space is transcended.

Light streams everywhere:
above is below and below is above.
There is no separation:
Heaven and earth are one.

May your hand redeem matter!
May your mouth announce the message!
May your heart sow the seed!
May your whole being give the Six,
so that the Seventh may come!
The only way for light to descend is by way of *Giving*.

GIVE WHAT IS YOUR OWN: GIVE YOURSELVES.

For you, 'Communion' is not receiving,
but giving.

Thus the Seventh will come: believe it!

We watch over the altar.
The altar is the earth: the whole earth.
Blood runs down from the altar: His blood.
The lamb was slaughtered
at the hands of false prophets.
But the blood that was shed returns.
The body loses only what no longer lives.
Behold! The Divine sows the new Seed
and It *grows*.
The bodily, having conceived of the Divine Seed,
is delivered.

THIS IS THE NEW IMMACULATE CONCEPTION.

The bell of the small chapel rings.

The bell calls to the ancient mass.

346

But the new Sound penetrates everywhere.
The Earth cries out with joy:
it is One with Heaven

AND YOU ARE ONE WITH THE DIVINE.

Friday, July 14, 1944

FRAGMENT

> *Late this evening, the angels unexpectedly speak to us again. I am able to note only a small fragment.*

The goal is not above; the goal is not below;
for the Divine dwells neither above nor below.
Above and below are but parts:
the Divine dwells in the WHOLE.
To unite: that is the goal.
Without union, nothing lives.
The chosen strives not upwards,
the chosen strives not downwards;
the chosen lives *both:*
the 'up' *and* the 'down.'
The chosen *unites.*
Matter calls for Spirit.
Spirit kneads and forms matter.
The song of the chosen is union:
Spiritual matter and material spirit.

To sink into matter is death.
To vanish into spirit belongs to the past.

Now the *bridge* is formed.
What was – is dead.
The old God is also dead,
but the new One will be born.

> *The 'old God' seems to refer to our old image of a*
> *God high up in the heavens, far away from creation*
> *and matter. To find God, it was believed necessary*
> *to go ever higher, to 'vanish into spirit.' Now,*
> *however, we learn that this is not so, for God is to*
> *be found in the* union *of matter* and *spirit.*

If the birth is delayed and strength is lacking,
the womb kills.
Mere force is blind, but it strives
to connect light and matter.
The womb is dark,
but it radiates the Seven: LIGHT.
Matter protects, but it also restrains.
Now the old bond
between matter and matter is torn.
It is not Light that is born,
but the new: LIGHT-MATTER.
LIGHT always was, and forever shall it be.

Planned since the very beginning of time
was the UNION.
The song of the Chosen is unity.
We bless the earth, we bless Heaven,
and we bless the Divine,
uniting all: Heaven and earth.

Hanna again sketches a small diagram for us (see p. 326), illustrating the deep meaning of this dialogue unforgettably:

The entire Creation consists of nothing but LIGHT. It appears to me as though in reality there is no matter and no spirit: only different degrees of vibration of the one and only LIGHT. Hanna illustrates this vibration by showing LIGHT emanating from one point: the Divine Source. It springs forth with unfathomable intensity, from the most subtle tremblings to ever denser frequencies. The densest of the frequencies is known to us as 'stone.'

In the middle of the diagram is an interruption indicating something very meaningful: the stream of light is not yet closed; there is a break in the vibration.This indicates that the human being and the angel, that member of the spiritual world able to descend the furthest, are not yet united. But the most intense and highest vibration of which the human is capable could reach the deepest vibration of the angel. The new being which is to live in the completed vibration is the new HUMAN, whose nature is Light and Matter: LIGHT-MATTER. At the moment, however, the break still exists; it is also known as death. The birth of the new HUMAN is the death of death. I perceive that the teaching of the angels has as its goal our becoming capable of bearing Light that is ever more intense: I think that the final goal is not just to be able to reach the lowest vibration of the angels now and then, but to reach and live *it consciously – and always.*

Sunday, July 16, 1944

65. DIALOGUE

Be aware that every movement acts:
the half-hearted, the solemn, the careless.
Each of them acts.
The scornful, the wild, the weak, the gentle.
Each of them acts.
Take heed: Ő will speak to you.
Begin to move then – only then!

A HALF-HEARTED SMILE
SHATTERS THE SEVEN SOULS.

May each of your movements be a movement
of deliverance, release.
Deliverance is the goal;
you have no other task.

It is no longer your task to act: only Ő acts.

Take only when Ő takes.
Give only when Ő gives.

Thus matter will serve.
For the only source of every act
is Divine Design.
If you act without the Divine,
you agitate matter.
You may choose: Do *you* want to act?
Or the Divine through you?

65. DIALOGUE

Addressed to me:

— Do *you* want to act?

G. Only through the Divine.

To Lili:

— Do *you* want to act?

L. Also only through the Divine.

— THE WORD CREATES.

Withdrawal is no longer possible.
It is done: you have chosen freely.
There is no more halfway.
Even the smallest thought, the shortest word,
is a movement that acts.
The lie will be vomited from the world.

> *The cooing of a pigeon can be heard from the*
> *garden.*

The pigeon speaks and that is truth.
But from the mouth of the human
comes idle chatter, complaining
and half-hearted consoling.

Sacrifice no more on old altars!
The idol has fallen, the pedestal is cold.
The new sacrifice is union:
FREE UNION!

May your act be done well!

Friday, July 21, 1944

FRAGMENT

The task comes to an end.
The task is still matter, still burden.
Your feeble strength worries you.
But dense matter was elevated,
as high as it could be,
and thus the task comes to an end.
The task was preparation.
Now comes free new Matter.
This new Matter forms itself.
The old fades and recedes.
Ő spoke: MAY IT BE!
May the new act in you!
The new Name forms itself,
without word it forms itself.
The new Name already lives:
force that was never before known
is sprouting.
Just two letters: AD.

> *I am baffled: the letters A and D in Hungarian form*
> *the words: 'she/he GIVES.' I ask myself what it*
> *could be in other languages, for instance, German?*
> *The answer comes immediately.*

Im Anfang
war das Wort:
DEIN.
Es war bei Gott –
es ist bei uns.

In the beginning
was the Word:
THINE.
It was with God –
it is with us.

Ő hat ... Ő gibt.   Ő has ... Ő gives.
Ő ... wir.   Ő ... we.
AGNUS DEI ... AD.   AGNUS DEI ... AD.

Now I feel how rich with meaning the two letters A and D are. They are the first and the fourth letters of the alphabet. The angel spoke of the created world as 'matter' – and of the creating world as 'glory.'

In Hungarian, 'matter' is Anyag – A! – and 'glory' is Dicsöség – D! AD, then, signifies the Created World and the Creating World united. Now I realize how powerful this symbolic word is. It contains unifying force, and it acts accordingly. Hanna later tells us: "As I heard 'AD,' I saw two triangles in space approaching each other in irresistible mutual attraction. Bright sparks flashed between them and the two triangles became one: one *united whole. The two triangles symbolize the Creating and the Created World.*

First: the task.
Second: the union.
Third: GIVING, THINE, AD.
Divine Mystery.

*The angels are in the Creating World; they clearly
foresee the coming union of the two worlds.
We humans live in the Created World and feel only
the task not yet accomplished: the union. We are
helped in our task by the power and immense joy of
the angels, but above all by the creative rhythm of
their song:*

There is only one prayer:
GIVING, THINE, AD.

There is only one act:
GIVING, THINE, AD.
There is only one creating name:
GIVING, THINE, AD.
Rhythm, song.
Your ear is not yet able to hear.
Your mouth is not yet able to testify,
but it shall.
Your hands no longer grasp:
your hands GIVE.
The new fig tree bears no fruit: it creates.
The new fig tree is wild,
it bears no fruit: yet it GIVES.
The new fig is the Word:
GIVING, THINE, AD.
Four cherubs guard the tree
to which no way leads.
Every way leads to nothingness.
The Light attracts,
but the four cherubs strike down.
The fruit of the new tree is holy;

as above, so below.
The new fruit is unattainable.
The four cherubs defend it
and the Seven guard it.
You cannot take the fruit,
and you cannot eat it,
for the sword splits you
and the fire blinds you.

But behold! You yourself are:

GIVING, THINE, AD.
The new sacrifice
is Silence;
Mystery,
Source:
GIVING, THINE, AD.
Every sacrifice made for personal benefit
comes from Cain.
Its smoke remains below,
and anything living suffocates.
But Abel GIVES.
Sacrifice is not renouncement,
or pain,
for pain is not necessary.
The one who sacrifices is not blessed,
for sacrificer and sacrifice are one:
GIVING, THINE, AD.

Friday, July 28, 1944

66. DIALOGUE

The first body is inert: matter.
Its Word is: *the Law;*
its essence: ORDER.   (I)

The second body is still bound, and yet it grows.
Its Word is: *the possible;*
its essence: REACTION.   (II)

The third body is unbound, but still it adheres.
Its Word is: *the will;*
its essence: CAPABILITY.   (III)

The Word of the new body is: *the free.*
Its essence: GIVING.
The new body is the fourth,
containing the three: it is ONE.   (IV)

'The law' *is.*
'The possible' *grows.*
'The will' *moves.*
'The free' *acts.*

Every body is a radiated image
whose source is the Seven Vibrations.
Every existence is but projection.
But the new Vibration already acts.
New matter is unbound and free.
In new Matter, Heaven and Earth are one.

> *I dearly wish to see in what way this* oneness, *this union takes place! The angel continues:*

356

Matter is motionless and it is blind.
The Seventh is also motionless;
but the Seventh acts. (I and VII)

The plant grows as it strives toward light.
The seraph strives toward the LIGHT. (II and VI)

The animal wills, rejoices and fears.
The angel lives, acting through song. (III and V)

Just where all converge to one point,
exactly there the new Being is born: GIVING.
Its new Vibration uplifts all others.

TRUTH becomes blinding LIGHT.
POSSIBILITY becomes CAPABILITY.
WANTING becomes FREEDOM.
The new Vibration uplifts all others.
All move on until they become GIVING,
radiating, motionless sun.
GIVING: it is the nest where the soul dwells.
Eternal home: Heaven and earth united.
Glowing force, tremendous lightning:
Seven infinites in one instant: GIVING.

Neither matter nor life nor death remain.
Then comes the great transformation:
Resurrection.
All secrets are unsealed,
lies and betrayal are no more.
The tremendous Light penetrates everywhere;
and GIVES.
One and only Primordial Source.

The Seven assume no new form:
they are ONE.

The sword of the four cherubs is lowered:
THE TREE IS NOW FREE.

Sunday, July 30, 1944

67. DIALOGUE FRAGMENT

*Unfortunately, only a small part of this dialogue
has been preserved.*

The tree was uprooted.
Without its roots, the tree hovers;
but it shall receive new roots.
Its fruit is GIVING.
To be chopped down is pain;
to be uprooted is horror;
but the inner force grows.

This is the secret of 'original sin':
cutting down and uprooting are but illusions
in space and time.
This is only one half of deliverance.

When you hammer a nail,
you first raise your hand:
though the hammer moves away from its target,
force is increasing as a result of this retreat
and the blow will thus be greater.

Retreating from God
gives a wonderful strength.

The last wall of separation is still in place,
but it will crumble if the aggressor retreats
rather than rushing blindly forward.
First a gathering of force,
then the rush forward,
and force and matter clash:
they cease to exist.
GIVING lives and GIVING acts forever.

Adam retreated.
Jesus rushed forward.
But GIVING is motionless.
Be aware!
The one who retreats creates distance.
The one who rushes forward creates distance.
The one who is motionless,
the one who lives and acts without fear,
GIVES.

> *At last, the long-feared inspection takes place. The*
> *inspecting officer is stern and unapproachable.*
> *However, I soon become aware that, behind his*
> *strict façade, he has no idea of the workings of a*
> *clothing factory. All of our failings go unnoticed!*
> *The number of completed shirts corresponds to our*
> *quota, and that satisfies him. We all breathe a sigh*
> *of relief. Finally the jolly jokers can have their well-*
> *deserved sleep.*

Friday, August 4, 1944

68. DIALOGUE

Matter and force,
bones and marrow,
skin and tendons:
searing pain,
time and space.

We sat before the rock,
and He was behind.
Tomb hewn in the rock.
Without: nothing grew.
Within: He.
The corpse concealed from human view.
Mysterium.
The time: three days.
Past, present and future
are gone, they are fulfilled.
Beyond the future: He comes.
The body does not decay to dust;
a New Body comes.
Only the shroud, only the husk remains.
Death is gone.
TRANSFORMATION.
Only the vibration is different.
The empty husk bursts – but the kernel lives:
GIVING.

In the vaults of great cathedrals,
every thread of the shroud is preserved.
But every cathedral will fall.

360

The stone was raised to heaven
and the living was stoned.

That is not the faith He taught.
Stones will fall down
and the living raised up.

Every cathedral in which the WORD,
the Good News,
is merely a word, is a *tomb*.
May words become acts! Realized!
Would they not, then the Proclaimer of the *Word*
would be a deceiver.
The voice crying in the wilderness ... was.
What was, what is and what shall be:
is in time.
But that which TRANSFORMS, the new,
is out of time: eternal.
The one who awakens, who sees beyond,
who grows beyond,
who lives beyond the future,
is one with Him.

The stone is rolled aside
and matter is TRANSFORMED.
A new Body is given; a hovering Body.
There is no more death, no more fault;
only TRANSFORMATION.
We were the witnesses,
our word is true.
The body transformed, delivered.

The stone, the keystone found its place
in the middle, in the Fourth,

361

and supports the arch.
The living lives, the dead is dead.
He reigns.

At last, the human eye gazes to Heaven
no more, for Heaven is now here below.
Heaven is but space
and the infinite finds no place there.
But within, in the depths of the heart,
it finds place in the smallest place.
There the new Rhythm is born.
There dwells dazzling Light, oh holy mystery!
The seed which grows only through Him:
GIVE.
Eternal instant, creative and free!

Long silence.

Parting of the ways:
The fool rushes toward the light
and perishes, like a moth.
The wise one neither advances
nor hurries nor flies;
the wise one remains in the dark
and is found by the Light.
With ear unhearing,
with eye unseeing:
yet through *this* eye, the ray of Light shines.
With unexpectant heart,
for there is nothing to expect;
with unbidding hand,
for there is nothing to ask for.
No faith and no more space!

But He acts because He GIVES:
HIS BODY BECAME THE WORD.

I have observed that the angels seldom pronounce the word, 'God.' It seems to me that this is a result of humankind having soiled this holy word with their 'Holy Wars' and 'Holy Inquisitions' in the name of 'God.' Similarly, the name 'Jesus' is seldom used. In its place, the angels generally choose the pronoun 'He.'

One evening, we receive a teaching which only a film could demonstrate, for, through movement, it shows how spirit and matter unite in the human body. I am able to record only the static part concerning the human face. The lower part of the face is related to matter, whose nature is subject to gravity. The upper part is related to the spirit, whose nature is smiling. Spirit strives downward and the mouth is flooded over with an angelic smile. Matter strives upward and the eyes become true. This is the union of spirit and matter in the human face.

Friday, August 18, 1944

69. DIALOGUE FRAGMENT

May you be filled with LIGHT-AWARENESS!

The five senses are five stages or degrees:
Matter, the *touching* hand;
water, which dissolves: *taste;*
air, subtle matter: *smell;*
still subtler vibration transmitted by the ear: *hearing;*
through the fifth sense, *the eye,* light radiates: *sight;*
the sixth sense is the *union* of the five;
the seventh is the seed of AWARENESS.

When these Seven no longer take, but GIVE,
the instant is creative.
This Act creates above as below.
"Thy will be done" above as below!
Your task links above and below.
Your task is the creative human element:
LIGHT-AWARENESS.

May you be filled with LIGHT-AWARENESS!

Awareness is not knowledge.
Awareness is Light:
acting Light, giving Light.

Your eyes are still blind.
The Light still disturbs you, pains;
it is still cold.
The new Light sweeps away every belief.
The one who *believes* in the Divine is mistaken.

69. DIALOGUE

DO NOT BELIEVE IN THE DIVINE!
LIVE THE DIVINE!

May your third eye begin to open!
To become one with the Divine
is still but a possibility.
The vibrations are not yet tuned, united.
Neither you nor the Divine is the cause of this.
The cause is *time*.
To perceive is time;
to hear is time;
to see is time.

But there is a time beyond time,
a space beyond space,
where you may act,
where you may unite,
where you may live the Human Essence:
LIGHT-AWARENESS.*
LIGHT-AWARENESS IS, IN TRUTH: LOVE.
Only LOVE acts.

Creative instant, flood of Light,
streaming through the new Eye!

---

* Hanna is unable to find an appropriate word for the attraction and union of spirit and matter, for the new unifying element. For lack of anything better, she chooses the Hungarian expression *értelem* (intelligence, mind, meaning). The angel then goes beyond the one-sidedness of this term in adding: "Light-Awareness is, in truth: Love." For this English edition, we chose the expression *Light-Awareness;* the German uses *Erkennen,* whose original meaning includes uniting as well as becoming conscious. For the French translation, the expression *co-naissance* was used, and for the Italian and Spanish translations, corresponding neologisms. All of these are unfortunately but approaches to a state of being which we are not able to name.

There is no more below, no more above,
there is no more father and no more mother.
Creative instant: GIVING.

The Light flows.
Chalice of gold, of translucent gold;
not to be seen,
not to be touched.
Only to be GIVEN.

THE CURSE HAS COME TO AN END.

> *The political situation worsens by the hour. The*
> *Hungarian Nazis – the* Nyilas – *are gaining power.*
> *The general apocalyptic atmosphere is undermining*
> *the hard-won discipline in our sewing factory. The*
> *compulsory work situation, being completely*
> *closed in and the imminent outer danger all weigh*
> *heavily on the women. They often react during*
> *break-time with uncontrolled shouting and hyster-*
> *ical laughter.*

Sunday, August 20, 1944

70. DIALOGUE

The crowd laughs.
They do not foresee the Name of the new.
New existence is immaculate matter;
the Light in its womb, transparent and free.

There the stone is TRUTH, the One;

there LOVE grows, the Two;
there the ANIMAL is harmony, the Three.
The Five is PEACE,
the Six is JOY
and the Seven is WHOLENESS.
The heart, LIGHT-AWARENESS, the Four,
unites them all.

The human rejoices when the seven senses,
the seven souls, act in unison.
That is the key.
May the new Being be born in you!
Before birth, there is love.
Love, the most secret rhythm,
the new Rhythm: LIGHT-AWARENESS.
It is half matter, half Glory.

> *The screeching, uncontrolled laughter in the garden*
> *seems to go on endlessly.*

The crowd laughs …
and wastes everything that belong to the Human.
They do not foresee the Name of the new,
the new Name which alone
makes the human HUMAN.
MAY LIGHT-AWARENESS PENETRATE YOU.

May your ears not hear,
may your eyes not see;
rather may they *penetrate* – everywhere!
The new penetrates everywhere.

Away with you, deceit!
The new Ray is all-seeing.

Eternal joy is your inheritance.
Pass it on!

ONLY THE ONE WHO GIVES IS WITH ME: DIVINE.

*These last mysterious and powerful words touch
me deeply:* Giving is a Divine attribute.

*One day we are informed that the Papal Nuncio,
Mgr. Angelo Rotta, will be paying us a call as a
demonstrative gesture of papal protection. In the
Nuncio and in Father Klinda, I for the first time
encounter priests who give testimony of their faith
not with beautiful words, but with courageous acts.
Their visit raises our status in the neighborhood
tremendously. The morale of the workers themselves also noticeably improves.*

Friday, August 25, 1944

71. DIALOGUE

Be aware!
The trust placed in you
is like the humus, good earth.
The seed sown in you is the Word, Giving.
Already the ever growing force swells,
causing the husk to stretch
until finally it bursts.
Fear not! Live!

Have no fear at the bursting of the husk!
That which no longer serves disintegrates.
Shedding is not painful.
Do not regret it,
for see: the sprout lives!

Water the seed! Unnourished, it will die.
Water it with what is lacking in you,
and there will be no more uncertainty.

'The one who speaks' nourished the seed
with the water of humility: and the seed grows.
Do likewise!
But watering wet soil causes the seed to rot,
and only mud remains.

To Lili:

Seek the lack in yourself
and you will become whole!
Everything you do for the Divine is blessed.

To me:

You, too: be aware!
There is only *one* lack.
If you find many, you are wrong.
But if you find the *one* lack,
then ask that it be filled
and heavenly Grace will fill it,
for you have asked for only *one*.

Thus, the sacrifice is completed;
the holy seed grows, it swells.
The husk bursts of its own accord.

What makes the seed swell?
Discovery of the lack!

Do not talk about the lack!
May this be kept a secret,
even among yourselves!
But reveal it to the Divine.
For see: The Divine heart is always filled
and always gives freely.

*I immediately perceive a great opportunity in the
conscious lack: a void attracts fulfilling forces, and
this is intensified by asking.*

*Lili organizes relaxation courses during breaktime
for the women, who are under constant nervous
pressure and completely exhausted. There is
enormous interest in these courses, with the result
that now Lili is exhausted. She never has a free
moment for herself. Hanna is burdened with a
feeling of responsibility for production in the
factory. In addition, she has not had a word from
Joseph, and she asks me daily if any mail has
arrived.I call all of my acquaintances whose friends
and relatives were taken away at the same time, but
no one has heard anything. Hanna is deeply
worried and I, too, have been lacking in inner
vitality for quite some time. Meanwhile, the political
news becomes ever more terrifying.*

Friday, September 1, 1944

72. DIALOGUE FRAGMENT

Somewhere in the vicinity, political propaganda speeches blare from a radio.

The word has become a hollow senseless din, confused noise.

Ear-splitting shrill cries can be heard from the garden. It is lunch-break.

Uproar! Pandemonium!
Blood and marrow become dry.
The husk is merely a covering.
Yet every word conceals the WORD.
The Divine Heart longs to reveal itself
and fills the word with Divine Force.
When the Seven Forces blaze within,
the word is eternal Fire.

'The one who measures' speaks:
No lukewarm 'maybes' on the Divine table!
No more indulgence!
Self-pity is the air of the weak.
The one in whom the Divine Word dwells
has but one wayless way: *Wholeness*.
Be whole!

Only the pure sound is worthy.
THE MASTER TUNES YOU.

Listen carefully: you are no longer incapable.
Mouth, sound, harmony: sequence of laws.

The song is new; the song is free.
Day breaks: sing!
But if need be: be God's whip,
for dawn is the wake of darkness.

No more pity! Especially for yourselves!
No more lukewarm mud puddles!
Away with every false breath in you!
Raise your hand and ask for strength;
ask for a sword.
Cut away all that is not filled with the Divine;
cut it away!
Tear out your eyes,
cut off your hands,
if the Divine cannot act through them!
What is the purpose of their existence?
Divine scorn comes down upon perishable matter,
upon mud that does not endure.

But if the spoken word has its origin in the Divine,
then it is the WORD, the GIVING: eternal.
Every weakness disappears
if you truly acknowledge faith
that is not word, but strength.
Do not be weak!
May your mouth remain closed
if not speaking the truth.
May your hands be petrified
if not acting for the Divine.
Fear no one! There is nothing to fear.
And NEVER FLEE FROM YOURSELVES!

72. DIALOGUE

IN YOU DWELLS THE HOLY, ALL-POWERFUL WORD:
THE POSSIBLE.

Everything is possible!
Everything is possible
if your faith is as great as a mustard seed.
Half-heartedness is repulsive to the Divine.

The Seven Sounds have always existed.
In the Master's Hand is the lute,
in the Master's Ear, the sound.
Each string of the lute is a sound;
but the string is still loose.
Listen! If a string is tightened,
it vibrates and gives birth to pure sound.

The lute is not yet vibrating
in the Master's Hand.
The tone is still false,
the string is still loose,
but the world yearns for the Holy Song.
Stretch yourself! Not too much and not too little!
The flame ignites neither before nor beyond,
but *at the focal point.*

My task is to measure.
I do not frighten you; I do not entice you.
Only in this way is measuring possible.
No more self-pity!
Strew ash upon the dead and live a new Life!
It is possible now: POSSIBLE!

Answer our word once more:
"MY GOD, THY WILL BE DONE!"

My hand does not admonish,
my hand does not bless,
my hand does not measure;
for the measure is full,
within as without, below as above.

THE ONLY MEASURE: BEING WHOLE.

> *The underground news in Budapest spreads rapidly. We hear of a new sport called: 'Jew-hunting'... We hear of hundreds and hundreds of Jews being driven to the banks of the Danube, lined up and shot: the great river makes the digging of graves superfluous. We hear of torture-chambers ... But we do not hear of Joseph. We will never hear of him.*

> *Nevertheless, when the 'measuring angel' speaks to us – pitiless as it might seem to be – we are nourished with the force of a new Life.*

Friday, September 8, 1944

73. DIALOGUE

The Message speaks of the sin of the chosen ones;
it is no longer the old sin.
The wild tree sprouts branches
and leaves aplenty: too many.
But excess foliage is detrimental to the fruit,
for it diverts the strength.

374

WHEN LIVING FORCE DOES NOT BEAR FRUIT,
IT IS SIN.

The chosen tree was pruned
and thus the old sin could disappear.
A new Eye was placed in it by the Divine Hand,
a holy noble sprout, that it may bear fruit
and serve the Holy Plan.
The new Eye, the new Bud, is already opening.
But the dead stump of the old branch
hinders the new.
A sharp sword cuts
and the dead stump falls away;
the wound heals.
Worms can hide beneath the dead bark.
But when your hand brings the cutting sword down,
new bark can grow
that will protect the new streaming Force.
The sprout placed in you is Divine.

ONLY WHERE THE TREE IS DEAD
IS THERE SIN.

The message speaks of the sin of the chosen one.
There can be no more error.
The knife is in your hand: do not hesitate!
Cut away the dead! That is *your* task!
The chosen is not cut;
the chosen cuts and, if need be, is even self-cutting.
Now Ó waits no longer!

    Long silence.

The feminine, virgin matter, conceives in its womb.

If there is no conception,
the new does not grow
and the half-seed is pushed out,
pushed out with all the blood, strength and matter
that was given for its growth.
Reject dead matter!
Detach yourself from it!
From it, too, new life can grow,
and thus the dead can be released.

Do not bind yourself to anything.
Do not fear cutting away the dead.
This does not cause any lack.
Behold!
The new has been grafted into you,
and it sprouts.
Secret of *The Last Judgment:*
nothing in the Divine Hand goes astray.
The new Bud swells and bears fruit.
The old branch decays,
is swallowed by the earth,
and becomes nourishment there below.
Not death, but transformation.
Not waste, not garbage, but new earth:
new nourishment for the green tree.

What is without is buried in the earth.
What is within is fulfilled.

WE TRANSMIT THE DIVINE WORD;
YOU LIVE IT!

  Long silence.

The new Element joining heaven and earth is:
LIGHT-AWARENESS.

Below, graves and 'hell.'
Above, a Heaven where God is supposed to dwell.
Between them lies the New-Born,
the one who unites.
No more death, no more graves and no more hell,
no more unattainable Heaven 'somewhere up there,'
where the 'ever so glorious souls dwell,'
and songs of angels resound!
No more right and left!
No more freedom and no more walls.

The new Child is Divine.
Its Body is glorified Matter, transparent, subtle.
Its Soul is a growing, fruitbearing Ray.
Everything which previously grew
on the fallow land is wild,
is but the straw on which *the Child* rests.
Your child!
The choir of angels hovers over *the Child*
and adores it.
All of our songs are sung for *the Child*.
Each of our words is food for *the Child*.
Our adoration embraces *the Child*.
It is a small *Child,*
but It has immeasurable Force
and an immeasurably infinite future.
It is the Soul of 'the one who measures.'
It is 'the one who helps.'
Its voice is 'Silence.'
And it is the 'Eternal Ray.'

Friday, September 15, 1944

74. DIALOGUE

The persecution of Jews becomes ever more ruthless. Many of the women in our group have had no news at all of their loved ones. In their desperation and fear, they frequently make their way to vespers in the tiny chapel.

As we wait in the shed for our angels, the chapel bell tolls.

The bell tolls.
The old sound calls to the church.
The knees of the believers tremble,
they throw themselves to the ground,
hearts in anguish, tears flowing.
Outside, indifference reigns –
the masses stare: indifference.
Beyond the church, beyond the altar:
only there is the new to be found.
The church is the ancient hearth,
protection for old feelings.

The new Law, the new Grace:
LIGHT-AWARENESS is all-filling:
every emptiness,
every crevice hidden in the earth,
be it a grave or an empty heart,
be it a mouth in search of bread,
or a murderous hand.
The empty shall be filled.

The one who seeks shall find.
Everything is filled through the Divine,
Who never takes and always gives.

Long silence.

I will teach you what dwells
beyond the *Black Rainbow.*
Above the flood arches the *rainbow,*
joining Heaven and earth: promise.
What is more than its seven colors?

THE ONE, GLOWING WHITE.

A black rainbow embraces Heaven.
What is behind the blackness?
The black abyss.
The seven colors are erased.
Above the borders of earth
a black void in the heavens,
and the Lord said: "I WAIT."
But now has come the time
when Ő no longer waits.
The black emptiness between Heaven and earth
glows white, incandescent white.

> *I feel immersed in a world of powerful forces, a*
> *world of timeless happening which nevertheless*
> *influences happening in time. I am touched to the*
> *core.*

The black grave swallows up only the dead.
The Light, glowing white,
shoots glowing white flames
and all is burned that lives and breathes,

all that is lifeless and all that is dead,
all that was and all that shall be,
all that is soiled and all that is immaculate.

HORRIBLE FIRE OF HEAVEN.
EVERYTHING PERISHES
AND EVERYTHING IS REBORN.

The innocent virgin creation does not die:
it lives anew.
The Light dazzles, eternal Light:
all creatures are delivered.

To Hanna:
Black rainbow; black hole, the heart;
black sorrow, black torment.

To me:
Black pit, the eye.

To us all:
But within vibrates, grows and is born:
eternal Love, the Seven united, the white Glow.
Between two infinites, spaceless space:
LIGHT-AWARENESS.

At this moment, a shooting star crosses the horizon.

A star falls.
Glowing white light, drowned in the black.
Dust of the old creation heralds the new creation.
Gather in the old stars
and sow new ones across the sky!
Many, an infinite number.
Thus, out of the night, grows the day,

eternal Light, always GIVING.
Between the heavenly chorus and the soil of earth
is eternal Light,
eternal love,
eternal adoration,
eternal GIVING.

The Seven vanished,
the old bridge disappeared.
Gone is the black abyss,
the *and* joining Heaven *and* earth.

Now the new can come,
now the eternal can come:
not to replace the black,
not instead of the Seven,
but beyond all:
THE SEVEN UNITED.

Beyond *perhaps:* the possibility of BEING.
Beyond *burden:* the ability to ACT.
Beyond space and time,
where fantasy spins its web:
ETERNAL REALITY.

Beyond the multitude of religions:
the ETERNAL SOURCE and the ACT,
which can become one
only when LIGHT,
the possibility of BEING, *ignites.*

Only Light unites.
The stone once rejected is now the cornerstone.
He returns and He is the LIGHT.

Friday, September 22, 1944

75. DIALOGUE

The chosen one neither rises nor sinks,
but walks on the water.
The only burden is the task,
the freely accepted task.
Grace lifts up above the water.
The magnitude of grace
is equal to the magnitude of the task,
the voluntary, free-willed task.

GRACE IS NOT KIND CHARITY,
GRACE IS NOT RANDOM MERCY.
GRACE IS A FACT:
A RESPONSE: A CROWNING OF THE PURE ACT.

It is done:
you feel the burden no more.
The burden weighs heavy,
but you may sink no more.

THE ONE WHO IS JUST THROUGH CONSTRAINT,
THE ONE WHO ACTS THROUGH CONSTRAINT,
IS A SLAVE.

Do not be slaves!
Breathe only the air of freedom!
Cut there, where you are still slave!
Woe be upon you if you act out of constraint!

EXISTENCE IF IT WEIGHS,
EXISTENCE IF IT PRESSES DOWN,

75. DIALOGUE

IS A BRAND OF SHAME ON YOUR FOREHEAD.

I must is a curse.
I can is deliverance.
The chosen one chooses: the chosen can ACT.
The chosen could go, yet remains.
The chosen could lie, yet harvests.
The chosen could take, yet gives.
Without eyes, the chosen one sees.

The lock has fallen away

and spaceless space is free:
LIGHT-AWARENESS.

There is no more whip or reward.
The curse has ended, the abyss is gone.
There is no more slavery.
'Here' and 'beyond' are not enough.
'Here' and 'beyond' are still slave and master.
Only the fourth dimension can fill the abyss.
The fourth dimension is matter of the spirit,
and the spirit of matter.
The fourth dimension is free: ONE.

The new Body is weightless.
Nothing is injured where its foot steps:
everything blossoms there!
The chosen one walks on the water.
The chosen one is humble,
but upon this humble forehead
dwells the highest: LIGHT.
There is no more 'here' and no more 'beyond'
when the Light appears.

To Lili, whose birthday is approaching:

This message is for you:
Be born, Child, it is already possible!
The womb constricts you now.
Leave it, or it will kill you!
Do not tarry! The opening is narrow, but it yields.
Be born, Child!

L. I would like to be reborn on my birthday.
Please help me!

— 'The one who helps' will not be helped.
The strength which now fills you is enough!
I will not help you!
Come to the world by yourself!

Birth is not only a beginning;
it is also an end.
Between the old existence and the new,
there is a connecting cord.
Tear it apart, Newborn! Free yourself!
Birth is eternal: eternal love
that acts in every instant.
There is no more birthday,
for birth is eternal.
Birth is neither will, nor desire, nor grace:

BIRTH IS THE FREE.
THERE YOU ARE ONE WITH THE *DIVINE*
AND THERE YOU ARE *YOURSELF*.

To me:

And you?

G. How could I free myself from slavery?

— Bound by old bonds, the slave struggles.
But the bonds fall of their own accord
if the good servant and the Master are united.
LIGHT-AWARENESS cuts through the bonds,
through the ancient dragon,
the slithering serpent
with the apple of knowledge in its fangs.
Do not eat it! Behead the serpent!
LIGHT-AWARENESS makes everything possible.
Be free!

Long silence.

The head of the serpent rolls in the dust.
The woman clothed in sunlight
gives birth to the CHILD and is lifted up.
Rushing streams of water roar below,
but the woman is given wings,
wings of eagles soaring to the heavens.

Night approaches and I light a candle in the wooden shed. The door is open wide and we see shooting stars crossing the sky.

Dust of the old creation, rainfall of stars.
The dragon is striking wildly about,
but is unable to reach the new.
All of the old is seized,
but the new cannot be harmed.

Another star crosses the heavens.

The old teaching is a star, decayed to dust.

385

The new LIGHT joins heaven and earth together:
LIGHT, LIGHT, LIGHT!

The star shows the way,
and the wise pilgrim advances.
When the Light comes, the pilgrim stands still
and finds the Newborn.
The old teaching constricts.
The new Light streams over all:
all generations, all peoples and all negations
with an everlasting *YES!*

When the Child is born,
it cannot yet use its limbs,
but the eternal Force it is given
teaches everything.

BROTHER-SISTER OF CHRIST IS BORN.
THE NEW CHRIST IS LIGHT OVER ALL.

The host of angels adores the Child,
adores freely.

An air raid siren suddenly begins to howl.

Sing with us! We act with you!
May Heaven and earth resound with our praise!

As the angels rapturously sang, "Light, Light, Light!" it dawned on me that the whole of creation is but Light. Neither spirit nor matter exists; only the one *Light in different vibrations. I discover a new meaning of this image: Light emanates with incredible intensity from the Divine source, then diminishes to ever coarser frequencies. The densest vibration of all we call 'stone.' The interruption in the middle indicates that the stream of Light is not yet closed; this means that the human (earth, matter) and the angel (heaven, spirit) are not yet united. I now perceive that the teaching of the angels has a goal of making us capable of enduring ever more intense Light. I realize that our final task is to attain and live the lowest vibration of the angels, not just now and then, but* constantly, *and with great awareness.*

Friday, September 29, 1944

76. DIALOGUE – Feast of the Archangel Michaël

On the lips of the angels
swells the song of the host:
"Who is like God."*

The immense love with which you seek God
dies of thirst:

YOU CAN NEVER *REACH* THE DIVINE,
FOR YOU AND THE DIVINE ARE ONE.

The song of angels is praise, is glory,
to which creation replies.

THE HUMAN CAN NEVER *'FIND'* THE DIVINE,
FOR HUMAN AND DIVINE ARE ONE.

* *Michaël* in Hebrew signifies: 'Who is like God.'

THEIR UNION IS THE MIRACLE.

The human being:
beneath is the sea,
beneath is the soil.
Creation has conceived the HUMAN:
above is Heaven,
above is the Light.
May the immense love with which you seek God
turn *inward*.
When the earth serves,
when the host of the angels serves,
they unite within you.

Your body is the earth.
The body of the old serpent has crawled forth.
The old serpent's body is the curse
brought upon earth by all of the Adams.
But the Christ, the New, will come
when earth and angel are united *in you*.
You know what needs to be done.
There is no escape,
for all ways converge at one point.

MICHAËL!
YOUR SCALES WEIGH,
YOUR SWORD CUTS:
THE LIVING FINDS NEW LIFE
AND WHAT IS DEAD – DIES.

If decision is needed,
if cutting is needed
and you are unable,
and you dare not,

then call:
MICHAËL, GIVE STRENGTH!
YOUR FOOT
CRUSHES THE SERPENT'S HEAD
WITH COLD FORCE
THAT YOU ALONE CAN GIVE.
FOR SEE: WHAT YOU CUT IS ALREADY DEAD.

Mystery:
All angels, seraphs, cherubs,
all heavenly forces singing and serving:
they all come to serve the Divine *in you*.
Call, and we come!
We are nearly united now.
Call! Your word creates!
Call the new Fire, the cold Fire, the Light!
Always call!
If we come, then Ő, too, can come.
The way is one.
The host of angels waits behind the *Black Rainbow*.
The angel is still color.
But Ő, the ONE, is Light: white Light.
A mysterious force,
flowing, streaming, living,
responds to your call.
Live with it, for it is half of your Life!

You and your act are one if you call
the leader of the heavenly host: MICHAËL.
Michaël comes and cuts
if your acts do not spring
from purity, harmony, love and truth.

Michaël cuts both the doer and the deed,
for they are one.
Michaël judges and helps.
Call Michaël, who always comes,
and the serpent will be beneath your heels.

May your acts never again spring
from shallow currents,
but from the deepest depths: the source.
The creation and the heavenly hosts
expect this of you.

Ő IS THE LORD OF ALL THE HOSTS.
YOU MAY NEVER *SEE* THE DIVINE,
FOR YOU ARE ONE WITH THE DIVINE.

The host of angels bows in homage before the Plan.

Worship of God and religions are but frames
that delimit space.
The Divine Plan is spaceless space, matterless,
and yet it is all that really IS.
Chalice, temple and church are graspable.
Only Ő, the Ungraspable, IS.
Everything else is but a frame.
Flying is possible only without wings.
Everything else is an attempt to equal God,
and the fall is inevitable.
My wings are incorporeal
and this makes them free.
If you are united with me, I carry you,
lift you above time and space,
until your spirit finds its rest in the One.
May peace come over all who are of good will!

Long silence.

He walked upon the sea and *He* is the way.
He is the well from which the water of life springs.
Drink of it and you will never thirst again.
Behold! This water unites you with Him.
What you drink is eternal water,
the Fire of the Seven Souls.
May your lips call *Him!*
If you call, He remains in your midst forever.

The creation is a frame,
the creation is a chalice.
Fill it, human being!

Blood and bread are no longer enough.
Only the Light – the coming Light –
can fill the Seven.

The black emptiness contained in the chalice,
framed by the frame,
is filled.
Ő, the LIGHT, is born.

After today's dialogue, I open the calendar and am
amazed to discover that September 29 is the
traditional feast of the Archangel Michaël. I also see
that the feast of the Guardian Angels will soon be
celebrated. None of us had ever heard of these
feasts before. I now look forward to the feast of the
angels with great expectation.

In the garden stands a small, empty toolshed with
no glass in the windows. Because the main
'factory' building is hot and overcrowded, Hanna,

Lili and two of the jolly jokers decide to move into the toolshed. The nights are humid and we sleep very little. The presence of the angels can almost always be felt. They seem to use every opportunity for teaching.

Friday, October 2, 1944

77. DIALOGUE – Feastday of the Guardian Angels

Ő is the Lord of the hosts.
The host of angels is a scale of frequencies:
vibrations.
Our deepest note is heavy.
When you have reached it,
the scale of creation is complete.

Matter has a threefold existence.
The Law – the great Law – is strict, and It states:
Everything is contained in what is greater.

Belief is merely preparation.
Cease to believe!
The unattainable is born,
the only ACT, the bond:
union through the Fourth vibration.

If we reach you,
then all the multitudes of Heaven reach you:
those who surround the throne of God,
those who sing and those who serve.

Your body contains matter in its threefold existence.
If your hand moves,
then the levels of inert matter,
of the cold and growing,
and of the warm and moving,
move as well.
This is the key.

If you call us, your eyes will see heavenly Light,
for your eyes *see;*
in your ears will resound the heavenly song,
for your ears *hear*.

If you merely take up the salt of the earth in your hand,
then, in truth, *the salt is not raised up*.
But if the salt dissolves
and circulates in your blood,
then, in truth, *the salt is raised to the Four*.

The taste of the salt is everlasting.
It does not disappear as it dissolves.
The salt is delivered when it becomes blood.
It does not disappear:
it enlivens and fulfills.

THE NEW BLOOD IS THE FOUR:
MATTER DISSOLVED IN LIGHT,
THE NEW LIGHT-MATTER.

Dissolve yourself!
Your 'small I' identity disappears,
it becomes dissolving,
fulfilling blood:
the solution of all.

If you dissolve your 'small I,'
matter will be delivered in you and through you,
and then the spirit can act.

DISSOLVE YOURSELF! GIVE YOURSELF!
THUS THE SALT REACHES THE DIVINE.

Creative Instant!
The lifeless will be filled with life,
and all beings glorify the Creator of the Plan.
Bring the Plan to life …
the impossible, the only possible!

Heaven and hell vanish, for the LIGHT comes.
It does not descend,
for there is no more hell.
It does not ascend,
for there is no more Heaven.
Here the ONE dwells eternally.

Call the HUMAN into Being!
Call the former rebel into existence,
and the split, the abyss and death
will disappear in the wonderful Plan of creation.
'The Bearer of Light,' who stems from our midst,
the serpent, the rebel, the betrayer:
all shall be delivered.
From this moment, there shall be
no more dwellers in 'hell.'

The strength is given to you!
There is no escape: you know what is True
and you know your task.
Do not attempt to evade it.

It is the slithering serpent in you that tries to escape.
But in you also lives the free, the possible.
And what you call for SHALL BE.
No moment of weakness is allowed:
The artery of creation would burst
and the new Blood would fail to attain its goal;
blind matter could not reach God.

Dissolve yourself!
In the wake of the Black Rainbow follows Light.
Let us call for the Light!
The host of angels greets you.
Call the Seven to life!

This feast is over.
Every feast is a Ray descending from eternal Life,
from the everlasting Feast.

Joyous anticipation of today's feast aided me greatly in comprehending it. Never had the teaching seemed so clear and luminous as it did today.

In Budaliget, when we read through our notes after the dialogues, Hanna would often replace some of the words with others that seemed better. She always tried to convey the meaning of the angels' message as clearly as possible. But now the teachings come in rhythmic verse form and Hanna has only to pronounce them to us.

Friday, October 6, 1944

78. DIALOGUE

Our teaching is mysterious.
It is given to you
that you may give it on.
It is given to you
to clothe the teaching in earthly words.

Earth is not salt, nor grass,
nor the horse, not even the one who thinks.
Earth is what clothes Light in matter,
what transforms,
protects and envelopes Light.
In this way, the teaching of LIGHT
can be perceived even by eyes that do not yet see.

   Silence.

THE DIVINE HEART BEATS IN THE HUMAN BODY.

The Divine heart is fire,
the Divine heart is Light.

IF THE HUMAN BLOOD ATTAINS THE LIGHT,
IT IS TRANSFORMED.

The first HUMAN was Jesus, the Master,
the first to master the body.
The body was crucified:
but it was a free act, a free sacrifice,
a triumph over matter and over death.
The body is nailed to the cross,
and the lance of blind force pierces the Divine heart.

From the wound,
from the ungraspable Heavenly Artery,
streams the LIGHT-bearing Blood.
"Drink! This is my Blood
and this is my body, the bread!"
The wound has been open ever since,
for every bleeding wound
cut open by the knife of blind force,
every pain, every suffering,
is in His Heart.

What our lips now proclaim is the greatest mystery:

HEAL THE WOUND!
IT IS ALREADY POSSIBLE!

Divine Blood descends only into the human body.
Divine Blood is Light.
But without the wound,
It could never have reached the human;
without the wound, it could never have become drink,
for between the human and the Divine,
there is an abyss.

But if body and Light,
the human and the Divine, are *united,*
the wound is no longer needed,
for then the Blood circulates
and Heaven and earth are joined.

Until this occurs, the wound pains.
But union is now possible!
Behold, the wound is no longer needed!
May the wound be healed!

That is the secret of deliverance.
It is no longer necessary to pierce His heart
once His heart and yours are united.
Thus inert matter,
the grass that grows,
and the animal that moves,
all reach the Light … through you.

BE ONE WITH JESUS: YOUR BROTHER! *

> *On the rare occasions when the angels pronounce
> the name, 'Jesus,' it is with such veneration that I
> become very aware of how we humans have lost all
> sense of the sacred.*

Blind force, blind tyranny *had* to pierce
the Divine heart, that Light might become ours
through the water of the blood.
But body and blood no longer suffice;
for they are but the foundation of becoming HUMAN.
Heavenly Light is given only
to those who bring fruit,
to those who walk on the water,
to those who are of the mountain peak,
to those whose thirst is never quenched,
to those for whom the Divine Word is salt,
creating thirst ever anew.
Behold! Every tormenting thirst of earthly existence,
every earthly pain burns in you,
on Mount Golgotha.

The reply: Light, new Life, new Easter,

* In Hungarian the word 'brother' is made up of two word-syllables:
'body-blood' *(test-vér)*.

new Resurrection: LIGHT-AWARENESS.
Eternal love: LIGHT-MATTER.

The teaching is the Word.
The Word will glow when it crosses your lips.
May new Words be born!
Simple ones, rooted ones!
Yes, yes – No, no!
There is no 'maybe,' nothing lukewarm.
Words are wings: they uplift and they create.

Long silence.

DO NOT LOVE THE DIVINE ... LOVE EVERYTHING!

That is love of the Divine!
Its lack reopens the wound, again and again.
If your heart is one with the Heart of Light,
then the wound can heal.
It is not difficult, believe me!
Is it difficult to love one another?
No, it is not!
It is even easier to love the small,
the unredeemed, the persecuted and the helpless.
Believe me, nothing is easier
than to love the Divine in everything!
For you, the free, redeeming act is possible!

The first stars appear in the evening sky.

The star guided the wise men from afar.
After that star, a sea of stars,
a sea of tiny lights appeared.
Still, the vault of heaven was dark.
And then, gradually, the stars turn pale,

for dawn approaches.
Every light, every tiny glimmer of light,
disappears on the heavenly arch.
The first still shines; but when the LIGHT comes,
even the first and the last disappear.
The LIGHT grows and absorbs each spark of matter.

ALL OF THE STARS DISAPPEAR
IN THE WOMB OF THE HOLY DAWN.

> *We are no longer able to ask questions and yet we
> receive answers. The angels read our thoughts and
> answer us by means of the topics. Since our move
> to Budapest, the teaching has been transmitted in
> rhythmical verses which have such nourishing force
> that any asking would be utterly superfluous. The
> verses are short and extremely clear.The fact that
> the angels repeat themes again and again, in variable
> forms and very patiently, indicates to me that we are
> still far from really living the teaching.*

Friday, October 13, 1944

79. DIALOGUE

The teaching word sounds forth:
The Four unifies.

The surface of the globe undulates,
flooded over by the water of the seas.
Only the mountain peaks protrude.

The island, the peak, is *Individuality,*
the indivisible 'I' that has become ONE.[*]
The masses remain submerged.

The created world mirrors the creating Plan.

The primordial seed once dwelled
in inert matter, in blind matter.
The seed broke through and transformed.
The waves of the sea embraced it,
and there it remained.
The seed lifted itself above the sea,
for the path leads further, far beyond the water.
Air welcomed it.
The ground of air is the 'I' that has become ONE.
Individuality.
That is not yet the end;
it is not enough.
For after air comes the new,
which has been planned since eternity.
The Divine Force which weaves the Plan
IS ACTING NOW.
Reach the new level!
Without the 'I' that has become One,
the air is empty.
And the striding foot of the angel
seeks the peaks, the islands, in vain.
The 'I' that has become One
IS THE PUREST GROUND:
NOT GOAL, BUT FOUNDATION.

---

[*] In Hungarian, 'individuality' is composed of two words:
'One-I' = *egy-én ... egyén.*

The house on the rock.
He is the rock.
His foot trod upon the rock,
and climbed to the peak
where Heaven opens
and matter becomes glory.
The young, unknowing disciple who had never seen
matter and Light united – oh, miracle! – stammered:
"Here on high let us pitch our tent;
here in the Light, on the mountain!"
He knew not what he was saying.

The new dwelling will not be built:
the new dwelling descends
if it finds the true rock.
The true rock, embraced by Heaven,
is the pure, unbroken 'I'
that has become One.
The rock, too, is only earth:
but earth striving upwards,
wondrous force, towering high above,
gathering and uniting.
Its peak extends above the mist.
Home of eternal joy and serenity!

Stand on the mountain!
Always be at the peak!
May each of your acts be high on the mountain.
Beyond guilt, beyond the mist, beyond the devil.
Be above, always above at the very peak,
beyond even Grace.
For above Grace dwells the ONE:
If you are ONE with the Divine,

then grace streams down through you.
May every movement, every thought, every true act
be in the free air on the mountain peak!

The one who struggles up the mountain
might live there.
But you, you *are* mountain!
You do not *dwell* there,
you do not *struggle*.
You *are* the towering true rock.
The one who is true *is rock*.

We dwell high on the mountain peak –
in the depth of the heart.
The Plan is ready, but the Act still rests.

   Silence.

The serenity of Heaven vibrates.
I teach you:
The great secret – death – is but vibration.

BETWEEN BIRTH AND DEATH,
A VEIL OF MIST DECEIVES YOUR EYES.

Birth and death are but vibrations.
Life is not a gift of charity.

LIFE IS ETERNAL.

Your eye cannot see through the veil.
Rebirth, resurrection, darkness,
death and fall:
that is all different, far different
from what you believe it to be.

From my reading, I am well informed about the concept of reincarnation in Hinduism and thus I listen with great interest.

If you could raise your eyes above the veil,
you would see that there cannot be *many lives*.

LIFE IS ONE AND *INDIVISIBLE*.
LIFE IS ETERNAL.

This is your inheritance; pass it on!

Silence

Beyond the depths of the seas,
beyond the seas themselves,
beyond the peaks of the high mountains,
the Divine Finger traces new Plans in the sand.

THE DIVINE: THE ONE WHO ETERNALLY PLANS.
YOU, THE HUMAN: THE ONE WHO REALIZES.

On the very first day, sun and moon
did not yet appear on the heavens,
although the eternal Plan had been made.

Heaven descends.
We are the walls, you, the foundation.
If you are not at the mountain peak,
our feet step into emptiness
and the new Home drifts.
The only error which your heart can commit
is to not unite the Seven,
to not be at the peak,
for then our feet step into emptiness.
You have long understood it,

but where is your Act?
You do not lack faith:
your Act is lacking.
May your Act equal your faith!
Only thus is balance on the peak possible.
The one who stands high in the mountains
needs a good sense of balance –
otherwise our feet step into emptiness.
Our being is drifting:
beneath our feet we need the truth
and the strength of the rock.

My beloved ones, is it so difficult
to reach the mountain peak?
It is beneath the depths of the seas,
and it is far beyond the seas.
It is above, high above:
in the depths of the heart.

Our teaching Word
now softly departs and fades away.
But its truth remains,
from eternity to eternity.

At the conclusion of today's encounter, Hanna traces a simple sketch: all the forces of the earth are concentrated at the 'mountain peak.' All the forces of Heaven are concentrated at the lowest point of the angel, the 'foot.' The 'mountain peak' is the only point where the two can meet and penetrate each other.

As a result of this lesson about the 'I' that has become One, or Individuality, it becomes clear to me that the teaching of the angels – according to which everyone at the peak of Individuality *can become the material half of his or her angel – is a deeply personal matter, and could never be a collective movement.*

Friday, October 20, 1944

80. DIALOGUE

The Pfeilkreuzler *– the Hungarian Nazis – have taken power and we are deluged with incredible news reports. Their leader in our district is a former priest, the notoriously sadistic 'Father' Kun. In the basement of a building not far from us, he constructed a torture chamber and his followers surpass even the German SS in their cruelty. They go out hunting for Jews, track them to their hide-outs and then torture them to death. So as to be prepared for a possible invasion, I always assign one of our workers to hide in the bushes and keep vigilant watch over our front gate. We also prepare some escape holes through the fence around the garden and cover them with branches and leaves, hoping, of course, that they will never be needed. Today Hanna returns from the main building only very late at night.*

Friday's last hour tolls,
but only outside.

The last circle is the *point*.
The *point* cannot be broken.
Unbroken rhythm is unity.

*The angels show us new symbolic images of the
fourth dimension of life. The mountain peak symbolizes human individuality capable of reaching the
level of the angels. The diagram of three superim-
posed circles of the created world shows the concentration of their force in the* ungraspable *dimension of the 'point.' I suppose that these diagrams
are meant to develop our awareness, for only this
can lead us beyond the* graspable.

The *Seven* is with you
until the end of the world,
until the beginning of the new World.

He is 'the one who helps';   (Lili II)
He is 'the eternal shining force.'   (Gitta VI)
His word is the Word: the only good.   (Hanna IV)
He is 'the one who builds,'   (Joseph V)
who 'plans the new Home and then builds It.'
He is the Head
and we are the limbs,
always ready to serve.
He descends to you and speaks to you.
You seek Him ... and He finds you.

Beneath His Heel: death.
He is the Son.

Every bullet pierces His Heart.
He is the Son, God's crucified Son.
He may be known, He may be reached.
He is the Child, the Son who bled for us,
who let Himself be entombed for us.

NOW HE CAN BE BROTHER,
RELATED TO YOU
IN THE HIGHEST KINSHIP OF EARTH.

This is the end and the beginning:
the body becomes WORD.
The *New Name* is the white, mysterious,
ungraspable, downward-pointed cone.
It is the incandescent white *point,*
the promise never more broken.
Fulfillment!
Do not tarry, oh radiant Light!
Do not delay!
The path is nearly ready,

THE WAY OF LIGHT TO EARTH,
WHERE THE HEAVENLY CONE
JOINS THE EARTHLY CONE.

Each of its rays is a wonder:
the smile of the Divine,
the whip of the Divine,
the ray of the Divine White Eye.

The last hour has struck.
Friday becomes Saturday.
Saturday is intermission.
But when the day of the Lord dawns:
Light bursts forth.

All that has long since been, all that is,
and all that will be:
the old body dies and is buried.
But when the day of the Lord dawns,
the body resurrects.

Matter is filled with Light.
The old body, the old teaching, the old thought
receives Light, becomes free, resurrects.
The dawn of the Lord's day
is the triumph of Divine Love.

The Divine Son, the Human Son,
is the Crown of creation:
the seven-pointed crown, wonder.

You see the Son:
but the Being of Light who comes
you cannot see, you cannot feel.

WHAT YOU HAVE RECEIVED THUS FAR
IS BUT THE FOUNDATION, IS BUT PREPARATION.
EARTHLY UNION WITH *HIM*
IS BUT THE BEGINNING,
ONLY HALF OF THE NEW TEACHING.
ONLY AFTERWARDS DOES THE TEACHING
OF LIGHT COME.

Our teaching came in the name of the Seventh Force.
Take it! Eat it! Act it!
The teaching is truly nourishment, truly bread.
To the one who asks for it: *give!*
To the one who does not ask: *give salt,*
give thirst-awakening words,
and the one who was damned will shine.

The day of the Lord dawns.
My beloved ones, in every trial *He* is with you.
He loves you.

October 22, 1944

81. DIALOGUE

The old teaching is pagan:
Life, glowing life.
After it comes death, annihilation, end.

The intermediate teaching: transformation,
resurrection after death,
the redeeming turning point.

The new Teaching is different, completely different.
Neither birth nor death,
but eternal life, glory, song.

This is the secret of Eternal life:
may all your deeds, all your love,
all your faith, all your thoughts,
be of *equal measure,* unwavering.

Each half-heartedness
is fainting, wasting away.
Each sluggish pause
is agony, death.
Each repentance, each new beginning,
is healing, resurrection.

The new is different, completely different:
EVERLASTING LIFE,
EVERLASTING THOUGHT,
EVERLASTING ALL-AWARENESS.

Our workshop building and the sheds in the park are quite isolated. Our only immediate neighbor, the owner of a large industrial firm, fled the country some months ago. His spacious and beautiful house and property have been taken over by the German SS, the very thought of which sends chills up our spines. My 'headquarters-hut' stands alone in the middle of the garden, and I have grown accustomed to the silence of the night. This tranquility comes to an abrupt end one night when we hear shouting and wild shooting in the street from the youthful Nyilas – Hungarian Nazis – who are intoxicated with their new feelings of power. Again and again, I make the rounds to establish whether any of our entrances have been broken in or damaged.

October 25, 1944

82. DIALOGUE – Morning

A hard word:
WAR IS GOOD.

Take care!
Falsely used force becomes destructive,
becomes devastating;

It would never come to a halt
without the weak – the victim – who absorbs it.
That belongs to the past.
It had to be that way.
Past wrongs cannot be righted.
But the victim absorbs and extinguishes the horrors.
If the persecutor finds the persecuted,
death is satiated.
The weak shall be glorified
and no more lambs shall be slaughtered
upon the altar.
War was unavoidable.
Now the bitter chalice is filled.
Fear not! As full as it is of bitterness,
it is equally full of Divine Drink,
of Eternal Serenity.

> *Hanna suffers bitterly from the misery of the world,
> and at the same time, she is aware of the infinite Joy
> of the coming new World.*

Your way is not improvement, not mending.
Your way is that which has not yet been:
creation through Divine Force.
Force coming from the Divine
and returning to the Divine
in ecstatic joy: Divine Circulation.

> *Silence.*

> *I have not understood the teaching of the 'unavoid-
> ability' and 'good' of war, so the angel returns to
> this topic.*

412

I teach you:
When matter devours *too much* matter,
the body is provoked to send corroding acids,
which destroy the 'excess' food:
The danger decreases
but the blind acid remains,
and when there is no more *'excess,'*
it attacks the organic wall.
Thus the entire body is threatened.
The solution is the *lye.*
The lye is the annihilated victim,
but it extinguishes the fire of the acid:
the lye brings the body relief.

> *Late in the afternoon, Hanna again hears the words*
> *of the angels. Taken by surprise, I am able to*
> *record only a small fragment.*

The one who believes to possess *'own force'* errs.
The force of the weak is the Divine.
The weak is a living, sacrificial offering.
Destructive force is damnation.
But the weak will be glorified,
for within dwells the Force of the Divine.
The weak is weak only in the eyes of the world.
Judged by the Divine, the weak is strong.
The weak takes up no weapon,
does not flee and does not resist.
But the 'winner' receives a brand upon the forehead.

> *These words about the task of the weak raise many*
> *questions in me. Why did Joseph go to the work*
> *camp without putting up the least resistance? Why*

413

have none of my friends tried to save themselves with false papers? Is it their fate to be victims? Suddenly I remember a strange dream that Hanna had told me a long time before. As she and Joseph rode to the Dürer Festival in Nuremberg in their student days, they both dreamed the same dream during the night: In Medieval Nuremberg, Hanna chased in desperation after a cart to which Joseph was bound as he was being led to his execution. Joseph dreamed the same dream of being bound to the cart and seeing Hanna chasing behind in desperation.

I ask myself if both of them have taken on the role of the victim, of the 'weak,' long long ago (?). I refrain from asking Hanna this question, however: she has more than enough to bear already.

Late in the evening, the angels are again with us and I am able to record this encounter in its entirety.

When the lover comes,
the beloved yields:
the two become ONE.
No more bond is needed,
for there is no more separation.
Eternal penetration, eternal ecstasy.

This is the mystery of the Holy Trinity:
Lover ... love ... beloved.
The three are one and yet distinct.
Eternally active is the Word: the YES.
The only truth: Ő IS.

October 29, 1944

83. DIALOGUE

The inheritance which Ő has left you
is eternal life,
the vineyard eternally bearing fruit.
Mysterious, marvelous teaching:
Light-Awareness in truth is love,

ETERNAL IMMACULATE CONCEPTION.

Three steps to time:
the past is purification,
the present is giving of oneself,
the future is the wedding.
Lover and loved originate from the Divine,
who gives birth eternally.

In place of *bodiless light*
and *lightless body*,
the new: the two lovers united.

THE WORD BECOMES MATTER
AND MATTER BECOMES LIGHT.

Seven steps lead to eternal being,
seven steps that you can take.
The first birth is pagan: matter.
The second is purification: plant.
The third is harmony: giving of oneself.
The fourth is the adorned bridal chamber.

Down the three upper steps
descends the bridegroom, the LIGHT.
When bride and bridegroom unite,
death dies forever.

Immaculate conception is Eternal love,
no longer followed by Bethlehem,
nor by the tomb, nor by resurrection.
The new Christ,
with eye of fire and hair of flame,
is clothed in LIGHT.
Then there is no more birth and no more death.
Birth pains and death pains,
for they are still wounds,
still separation.

Felicity, union.
The new House is *the fourth,*
built since the beginning of time,
adorned for the bridegroom.
The old house is a cracked and decaying frame:
abandon it while you can!
The bridegroom cannot enter there:
the eternal lover, the LIGHT,
the only fulfillment of desire.

You are the vine, Ő is the germinating force.
Thus the miracle of the vine
that eternally gives fruit is born.
The mud, primal matter, remains below;
the vine absorbs it and rises up.

THUS MUD ASCENDS TO LIGHT
AND LIGHT IS CLOTHED IN MATTER.

　　Silence.

Light descends from Heaven: Wisdom.
Wise matter is the fruit, tangible Light:
The creation bears fruit:

LIGHT OF MATTER,
MATTER RADIATING LIGHT.

Rejoice!
Water kills – fire quickens.
The Virgin gives birth, is in labor.
The last birth is *the fourth:*
The Child is carried to Heaven,
HEAVEN DESCENDS TO EARTH:
FOR EVER AND EVER.

> *I am amazed to again and again see new perspec-*
> *tives opening in the dialogues. The image of the*
> *woman 'dressed in the sun' appeared two thousand*
> *years ago in the Apocalypse of St. John. She and*
> *her Child ascended to heaven and thus disappeared*
> *from our field of consciousness. But* now *the Child*
> *reappears and descends to earth with* all of Heaven,
> *along with the feminine part of the Divine:* Wisdom.
> *This* Wise Light *transforms matter and redeems it.*
> The fourth *dimension is shown to us by means of*
> *ever varying symbolic events.*

Friday, October 31, 1944

84. DIALOGUE

SUFFERING TEACHES NOTHING AND
SUFFERING DOES NOT REDEEM.
THERE IS NO NEED FOR SUFFERING.

Expect no good, no fruit, from suffering!
It fills the wound.
The wound is sin,
and suffering is its answer.
The wound is emptiness,

417

filled by healing.
This is not the fruit, this is not the *more:*
it only appears to be.
Suffering is but a temporal fragment.

If suffering were the whole,
and not just a part,
then deliverance which puts an end to suffering
would be nothing but betrayal.

Blows and punishment need not be:
Suffering need not be!
Giving of oneself, sacrifice,
extinguishes it.
This is the most sacred Grace.

Adam strays aimlessly, without a goal.
Although he was given the eye of light,
he does not see the Way, the Truth and Life.
Sin has closed his eye.
Adam, conceived in joy,
led astray by the serpent,
is now blind and dead.
But Christ gave Himself: the lamb was sacrificed
and behold: Adam revives.
He is life.
With Him, through Him, in Him,
everything is given new Life.

After the sin comes purification.
After purification,
the giving of oneself, the wedding.
After giving oneself,
the immaculate conception,
the new Dwelling.
Death remains outside,

suffering remains outside.
The abyss is filled, and suffering ends forever.
Resplendent matter: LIGHT-MATTER.

Adam is eternally the Child of God.
Adam, the outcast, enters the new Dwelling:
the return of the prodigal son.
In place of futile joys,
he finds the true Home: Eternal Life.

Later the same night, the angels return:

… take care of 'the small one,'
that she might bear her burden!
The seven daggers carve wounds.
The little servant offered her heart,
and the offering is carried by our hand
to the feet of the Divine.
Take heed!
Do not be afraid!
Take care of 'the small one'!
Ő will protect her through you.

These words weigh heavily on me. I feel that the 'little servant' referred to is Hanna. Do the angels see a means of protecting her that I have not perceived? The general situation looks worse by the day and I am extremely worried. Our workshop is more and more becoming a dangerous target rather than the haven of refuge it was meant to be. Things have gotten so bad that I advise the women to leave immediately if they have any other possible means of hiding. I assure them that I would not reveal their disappearance to the military authorities.

One of the jolly jokers sharing the tool shed with Hanna and Lili, a very discreet woman, asks us, to our great amazement, if she might spend the evening with us. Years later, she explains to me: "I had no idea of the significance of your gatherings, but when I saw Hanna's transformed, radiating face as she returned to the workshop in the evenings on several occasions, I became convinced that I, too, should participate. My usual modesty and shyness were so absent that I would have broken down the door if I had been denied entry." The fourth occupant of the tool shed, who is very attached to Lili, also wishes to attend.

Friday, November 3, 1944

85. DIALOGUE

Lili lights a candle.

The flame rises up and light flows everywhere.
Matter is purified by burning.
Air corresponds to the spirit,
the flame to individuality, the 'I' that has become One.
Air is invisible,
matter is heavy, dense and blind.
The flame connects them.
Without air, matter cannot burn.
Without matter,

420

there is no redeeming individuality.
I will teach you how to light it:
In the beginning: the wax is cold, the air is cold.
What ignites the flame?
The wax? No. The air? No.
Only the already burning flame ignites.
The fourth flame unites, warms, transmits fire.
In the fourth flame, Heaven and earth can unite,
but only above water, above wavering feeling.
Nothing is more simple! Always transmit the fire!

Each degree of life is flame, is fire.
They are united by their essences.
The name of each fire,
its light and its intensity,
is different from the others.
To the Human, a Fire is given which unites the Seven:
The Heart of Light joins every light and Fire,
be it *earthly flame* or heavenly Fire,
earthly love or heavenly Love.

THE VIRGIN BODY IS NOT REQUIRED
WHEN THE FLAME IS PURE
AND THE PASSION HOLY.

The new Light can come only
if you light the Seven Flames one after the other.
Every Flame, every Light is already in you.

*From the war front nearby, we hear the thunder of
cannons and explosions.*

Destruction all about you –
but in you, there is eternal renewal,
purification, giving of oneself, wedding.
Have no fear!

Everything might be destroyed,
even Heaven and earth,
but all that means nothing
if the new Fire burns in you.
Love Life! Love the Seven!
BURN!
If the Seven are united,
if Heaven and earth are united,
then comes: GIVING.
Seven Divine Souls, Seven Flames, Seven Levels:
Burn!
Every individuality is wholeness: be whole!
Join the Seven together!

In the Plan of the eternal Creator,
everyone has a guide:
Seven Flames of Spirit guide you.
Ó gives the *Name.*
Name is not mere adornment.
Name is not coincidental.
The *Name* is eternal part of the Divine.

I belong to the Seven;
above me a guide also shines.

    Addressed to me:

This message is for you,
for your heart has asked.
Every organism consists of Seven Flames.
Above each of the Seven there is a peak: the guide.
Alone, this guide would be of little value:
but it is part of a new circle of Seven
with a new crown.
Thus each Flame knows both serving and guiding.

85. DIALOGUE

Hanna draws a sketch, subsequently lost, which I later attempted to reproduce. I believe this drawing captures the essence of the original.

('Ad infinitum...': See next page)

Without a wick, the candle could not burn.
Without a body, there would be no Individuality.

The Heart of Light beats high above.
If your gift of self reaches it,
heavenly Grace flames up.

THUS:
ONLY THROUGH THE HUMAN BEING
CAN GRACE DESCEND.

The Seventh – the highest GUIDE – teaches you.
The strength of the Seventh descends upon you.
Thus from infinity comes space
and from space comes infinity,
from eternity is born the temporal
and from the temporal: eternity.

The thundering from the nearby front increases in volume:

May the Strength of the Seven Forces be with you!
Burn!

Lili's friend, present for the first time, listens with intense concentration. After the dialogue, she says to Hanna: "Right from the beginning, I also heard all of the words you pronounced inside of myself. Your words corresponded exactly to those that I heard, with one exception." She named the word, and Hanna replied, "You are right; here I made a mistake." Having corrected it in my notes at the time, I have since forgotten what this word was.

ad infinitum ...

85. DIALOGUE

November 5, 1944

'Father' Kun, the former priest now commanding the Nyilas, *appears to have discovered the secret reason for the existence of our war factory. His followers take to shooting their guns every night in front of our garden, which is anything but a good sign.*

On Sunday afternoon, hordes of Hungarian Nazis break down our front gate and storm into the garden. A woman who sees them coming just manages to send off a desperate SOS to the nunciature.

The great hunt begins: The cellar, the work rooms and the attic are searched, and all of the women are herded into the main work room.

The notorious Nazi commander, 'Pater' Kun himself, appears in a black priest's robes with a wide red belt stuffed full of daggers and revolvers.

He demands to see the 'commander.' I step forward. He then proceeds to deliver a lengthy sermon to his followers, explaining to them that I, as a Christian who has lowered herself to aid Jews, am more sinful than the Jews themselves. He will arrange for me to have 'special treatment.'

When Hanna and Lili hear these words, their illusion of my being out of danger as an 'Aryan' is destroyed. I am ordered to state the exact number of workers in our operation. If my answer should prove to be false, I would be shot immediately. I do not have the slightest idea how many women might have been able to escape through the secret openings in our garden fence. Unable to give an answer, I remain silent.

Suddenly, I hear myself saying: "Seventy-two." The counting begins. Seventy-one persons are found to be

*present. There is a heavy silence. Suddenly the door
bursts open and a Nazi shoves a young girl, who had
been hiding in the bathroom, into the room.*

*'Father' Kun stares at me without a word and then
turns his back. Before leaving the room, he orders his
soldiers to lead me away under special guard. Three
Nazis, armed to the teeth, push me to the floor, kick
me repeatedly and spit on me.*

*The 72 women are lined up in rows. It grows dark and
a gentle rain begins to fall. We are marched off through
the streets, destination unknown.*

*The well-placed kicks into my abdomen have their
effect, and I am forced to stop behind a tree. The 3
soldiers never let me out of their sight: they surround
me and stare at me as if I were a log. Strangely, only in
this moment do I really notice that I have lost my
freedom.*

*After a march of about half an hour, our group is
overtaken by an automobile from the War Ministry.
The nunciature had relayed our SOS to them, and the
officer who embarks from the auto holds a 'renewed'
war production certification of protection in his hand.*

*The Nazis are furious, but they are forced to release us,
and we return to the cloister. I walk silently beside
Hanna and Lili and ask myself in the darkness:*
" ... how much longer?"

November 10, 1944

86. DIALOGUE

The fourth flame, the fourth element,
is Light-Awareness.
Behind this WORD, a secret shines.

Ó speaks and the soul trembles,
but it does not comprehend the Word,
for the third flame, the third element,
feeling, dominates your soul
with vibrations irregular and vague,
and the fruits are in accordance.
The third flame, the third element is *feeling*.

Raise up your feelings
and the vibration will intensify.
What raises feelings?
Longing? No.
Faith? It is only a possibility.
The force which raises feelings
is the offering of yourself,
the giving of yourself.
Only thus can the new Dwelling be attained
– the fourth floor –
which is meant to be your eternal Home.

Ó speaks and the soul burns
to discover the Heart of the Seven,
the fourth degree of life,
the middle of the Seven
where the foot no longer walks,
where it stands still,
where the soul no longer requests,

but always receives.

Silence.

I teach you:
THOUGHT IS STILL MATTER,
staggering and blind, pulling you down;
it is a serpent biting its own tail.
Therefore its sign is the wheel,
the wheel revolving about itself,
ruled neither by cart nor machine.

Earthly smoke smolders and
the soul stumbles, faints,
errs about, revolves about itself,
just revolves.

In the hand of the *Black Fisherman,* a hook.
Attached to the hook, the bait:
the human thought.
Fish! Do not snap it!
Your throat would be torn!
The fish dies
and the *Black Fisherman* smiles.
The fisherman's creel fills,
the catch packed tightly,
the heart constricted in anguish.
The soul is cast in gloom.
The wheel revolves.

Adam, the outcast,
exchanged Divine Childhood
for knowledge – for thought.
Thoughtless, carefree joy was taken away.
Light-Awareness was unable to come
over such feelings, such thoughts.

Paradise was taken from Adam:
no more sinless act,
no more innocence.
But the lamb is the way
that leads back.
And what is no longer possible on earth
is possible in God.

The message speaks of the new Flame:
it shines, it glows high above.
Oh, human being! Now you can reach it!
He is the *Way* which leads to it.
He is the *Truth,* whereon the new House is built.
He is the *Life,* the eternal Life.
May the fourth vibration penetrate you!

Burn, but do not destroy through burning!
Burn, burn Divine Fire!
If Heaven burns in you,
even the incombustible enflames.
Take care! Listen well!
Always listen to the WORD:
the eternal, true and only WORD.

LET THOUGHT BE BOUND TO THE *ETERNAL WORD!*
MAY THE WHEEL CEASE
TO REVOLVE AROUND ITSELF.
THE WHEEL IS ONLY FREE
IF IT IS A PART THAT IS SERVING THE WHOLE,
THE ONE.
MAY ALL-AWARENESS PENETRATE THE THOUGHT!

In the daughter of unfaithful Adam,
who revolved around himself, unredeemed,
in the womb of the daughter of Adam,
Christ was conceived.

Rejoice! Eternal Light shines forth.
Now you are free – no longer slaves.
Your eye shall *see*.
Your hand shall *act the Divine Will*.
We rejoice with you.
Your act and *our* song are touching one another.
White Light blazes,
White Light in which all colors blend together,
join for eternity.

*Work in the clothing factory resumes in an atmosphere
of oppressive fear, which increases in intensity when a
German SS-officer takes up residence in the villa next
door.*

*One day, a German soldier rings at the door. Panic
breaks out. I hurry to the door and see, to my great
relief, that it is not an SS-soldier, but one from the
defensive forces, the Wehrmacht. It turns out that he
was a student friend of Hanna in Munich, and is
currently working as an illustrator for the military
forces newspaper. As I am talking with this decent and
upright man, I suddenly have a fantastic idea:*

*I must try to have our women protected by the SS-
soldiers!*

*The Hungarian Nazis are in command here. The only
authority they recognize is the German SS. I thus
devise the following plan together with Hanna's soldier
friend: I will prepare some illustrations for a cultural
article about Hungarian folklore in exchange for an
employee's identification card with a highly visible
swastika stamp from the German military newspaper.*

*This identity card is to serve as my means of intro-
duction to the neighboring SS-establishment. I have*

observed that the SS-officer returns home only late at night and that his soldiers are alone the entire day.

And so, a few days later, I approach the neighboring garden and address the SS soldiers. As the daughter of an Austrian, I speak fluent German and I immediately adopt the local dialect of the corporal, upon which they all see me as a fellow citizen in a foreign land.

I tell them that I have given up my artistic profession so as to dedicate myself to supporting the war effort and that I am now the directress of the war factory next door. 'Coincidentally' my German identity card, received immediately upon delivery of the illustrations, is in my handbag, and it succeeds in lending credence to my story.

As a loyal compatriot and neighbor, I invite the soldiers to visit my plant. To spare them the long way around through the street, I have an opening made in the fence separating our adjoining gardens.The soldiers are war weary and are delighted to come over for a glass of fine old Hungarian wine and homemade pastries.

During one of their visits, I complain about the 'undisciplined hordes' of Hungarian troops disturbing the noble efforts of our war sewing plant.

Thanks to the trust inspired by my card and perhaps also in anticipation of a rapidly approaching and fatal end of the war, the soldiers promise to protect me and my workers. The 'non-Aryan' origins of the women are left unmentioned.

All of the women are informed of the situation. Never before had the shop operated with such discipline and obvious eagerness as during the visits which the SS-corporal paid to me – but which he paid mainly to the source of wine!

In the case of future attack by the Hungarian Nazis, the secret opening in the fence between our gardens would serve the purpose of enabling the women and children to flee through the garden of the SS officer to the great Janoshégy Forest.

Friday, November 17, 1944

87. DIALOGUE

The Seven speaks.
The Six acts.
The Five sings.
The Four is all-aware: IT LIVES.
Enlightening Light, the Truth,
penetrates the Heart.

Heaven and earth glorify the One Who unifies.
Without beginning, without end,
we sing a Song of Glory.

To Lili:

Your song is: heal the wound!

To Hanna:

Your song is: offer your heart!
Maintain the Balance, the Four!

To Joseph, no longer present:

Your song is: breath of Heaven
that the earth has lost.

Peace that is not merely a pause
between two wars,
but silence, eternal peace,
given a home on earth through you.

To me:

Your song is: bring down the Six,
the Light that is given to you!
Strength and Light,
the coming Light of the Divine.
Not Law, not Grace, but Light: pure Light,
uplifting Force,
yet also capable of searing to cinder.

To us all:

Awaken! Jesus lived, He was and He shall be.
The new is nigh.
Jesus appears always and calls His disciples.
He assumes a body that you can bear.
For behold: *every* body is part of Him.
He is the Son.
The Father has given Him all:
The One, the Two, the Three,
the Four, the Five, the Six,
that all may serve under His feet.

We again hear explosions from the nearby front.

The devil thunders,
with the whirling globe in hand:
the poisoned apple, the devil's only realm.
Say softly: "We do not need it!" –
and that will suffice.
If the Light of the Seven burns in you,
then darkness cannot harm you.

Raise your heart high above,
and then the Light can come.

Burn! Live!
Be filled with Light!
Awake, Arise!
Your Light is needed.
Your being glows.

The end is near:
the Seven nears.
May no more doubt dwell in you,
may there be no offense in you!
Be perfect, as the Creator conceived you perfect!
Ő gave you the Name: the eternal Name.
When you not only think you live,
but LIVE, LIVE Life,
then everything becomes possible.
Ask only from Heaven; to the earth, *give!*
Act, and your faith will move mountains!
The mountain is matter, the mountain is weight.
With your little finger,
you can unbalance the mountain.

Everything takes on new Meaning.
Proclaim new Laws!
The impossible becomes possible!
Old values crumble;
yesterday is gone,
and all that was sinks into nothingness.

   Silence.

But the immaculate, virgin matter remains: MARY.
Upon her head, the crown of stars,
at her feet, the moon;

her dress, the rays of the sun.
MARY – the smile of creation,
miracle hovering above the waters.
In matter: virginity.
In Light: matter.

LIGHT-MATTER, RESPLENDENT, DWELLS IN YOU.

The Son of Light, the Seven, is born of MARY.
Her Name is Thirst, her Name is eternal Love.
The new Name of MARY is: Light-Awareness.
She is the eternally fruit-bearing tree,
there above and here below.
In place of the poisoned apple,
this tree bears the Apple of Light.

Proclaim it: deliverance is near!
The Seven spoke. The Six acted.
The Five sang the 'Good News'
which is now reality:
LIGHT.

Friday, November 24, 1944

88. DIALOGUE

*In the silence before the dialogue, I feel an utterly
intense presence and suddenly I know that this will
be our last, farewell encounter.*

In the beginning was Silence.
In the Silence within,
Sound was born.

435

Sound is love.
Sound is the Son of the Divine.
The Divine is Silence.

In the womb of Silence
reposed Sound.
Sound became body and was born.
Love is the first radiated image.

THE BODY IS LOVE
WHICH HAS BECOME MATTER.

The Divine sets in motion.
Sound is impulse.
Creation is radiated image:

DIVINE LOVE EMBODIED.

Thus Life originated:
From One Sound: Seven.
From One: the two halves of Life,
opposition: attraction and repulsion.

From One Sound: Seven;
and from Seven: all forms of Life.
Miracle – wonder!
Endless stream of Sound.
Creation sings, resounds:
Divine Symphony.
Endless stream of Sound,
yet always the Seven.

The two halves of life
and the seven souls are the key.
The two halves of life
concentrate and disperse,
attract and repulse.

Now concentration.
The line of the Holy Plan is: concentration.

The Divine is: Silence
The Divine is: Sound
The Divine is: Harmony
The Divine is: Love

*The Hungarian Nazi hordes make their nightly
rounds with wild yelling and shooting.*

Uproar, noise, confusion,
destructive force which injures the Law.
Noise is emptiness,
and this Ő does not tolerate.
Lips gone silent
are not yet Silence.
Sing, my loved ones, sing here below!
Soon the noise will end.
In noise you cannot sing,
but prepare yourselves: listen!
Above we sing. Listen well!
Learn! Prepare yourselves!
Be one with us!
Immeasurable, everlasting Love,
the Divine Heart is ours.

Cracked pitchers, defective and empty pots and vessels
are smashed and cast away.
That is the noise
your ears now hear.
Be new Vessels!
Golden Chalices!
Chalices of transparent gold,
ready to receive Divine Love!
Chalices in which eternal Life can breathe.

Yet even the flawless Chalice
is but radiated image.

The Creator is Silence.
The Son is audible Silence: Sound.

The eye says: Light.
The ear says: Sound.
The hand says: Act.
The heart says: Love.
Understand: all of these are radiated images.
The key to the hidden secret is
ALL-AWARENESS.
With the coming of the LIGHT,
all can SEE through it.
Light-Awareness of the two halves of life,
Light-Awareness of the Seven Souls;
Light-Awareness joins all together.

The Four of the Seven is the Heart,
which attracts, concentrates and calls
all the Divine blood,
all the Divine force,
to Itself.
Thus the Seven becomes SONG.
Thus the two halves become ONE.
Thus the wall crumbles
and the lack is filled.

THE DIVINE
is Number, Law, Salt.   (I)
THE DIVINE
is Love: growing, streaming Love.   (II)
THE DIVINE
is Rhythm, Vibration, Movement.   (III)

THE DIVINE
is Song: free song. (V)
THE DIVINE
is the Light: radiating, acting Light. (VI)
THE DIVINE
is the Highest. (VII)

There, where the two halves are wed,
there the WORD is born:
THE WORD – THE FOCAL POINT –
ALL-AWARENESS.
Thus the millions become ONE. (IV)

From an infinity of salts
comes the all-powerful Word. (I + VII)

From streaming Love
comes acting Power. (II + VI)

Rhythm and Vibration
carry the Song. (III + V)

May the Song resound!
The dividing wall has crumbled.
The wall was emptiness.
Victory over death!

In jubilation the Four Who Sing
the glory of the Seven.

THE TWO HALVES OF LIFE
HAVE BECOME ONE.

Believe:
Eternal Life is already yours.

The Red Army is slowly but surely descending upon Hungary: we hear daily reports of their advances in our direction. Everything in the city begins to disintegrate and a sense of the inevitable end is in the air.

On December 2, the young girl who has been keeping watch suddenly crashes into the workroom and breathlessly informs us that a company of Hungarian Nazis has broken down the front gate and is approaching the house.

I race madly out the back door and through the secret opening in the fence to our German SS neighbors to call them to help us. These are the darkest moments of my life. I know that every instant is of the essence and I run with all the strength I can muster, yet I have a feeling of being nailed to the earth with an enormous weight. I sense impending catastrophe in every cell of my body.

At last, I arrive at the SS quarters. The German soldiers immediately grab their hand grenades and run with me to the clothing factory! At the sight of the approaching SS, the Hungarians retreat in confusion.
My calmness returns and I gain a clear presence of mind. While the Hungarian commander hesitates, I discreetly signal to one of the women that all of the others should immediately take flight through the garden of the SS.
As we stand in front of the house (see sketch), an incredible development unfolds in the backyard: the German Nazis stand guard for the Jewish women and children so that they can escape from the Hungarian Nazis. Two German soldiers take position on either side of the escape hole through our common fence and

The great forest "JÁNOSHEGY"

The escape route of Jewish women and children

House of the German SS officer and his soldiers

Secret opening → between the 2 gardens
German soldiers with hand grenades for our protection

The Workshop

Gitta and the German Nazi corporae

Hungarian Nazi company

Gitta's "hut of command"

Tool shed, where Hanna and Lili slept

openings in the fence for a possibee escape to the side street

Road to Budakeszi

hedge, ready with their hand grenades to defend against any intervention by the Hungarians. With powerful gestures, they encourage the women: "Quickly! Run fast!"   At the same time, the German corporal, the Hungarian officer and I are engaged in an animated discussion in front of the house. Then Father Klinda rushes up completely out of breath and he attempts with religious arguments to convince the Hungarian officer to retreat. However, the officer only turns his back and displays the deportation orders.

Father Klinda sadly whispers to me that the nunciature has no further means of influence, at which point I realize that I have only one possibility left: to try and gain as much time as possible.

With this in mind, I deliberately translate the statements of the German to the Hungarian so badly that he becomes thoroughly confused. I am not risking anything by doing this, because neither of them understands a word of the other's language. So as to bewilder the Hungarian officer all the more, I wave my German identity card under his nose and declare that the sewing factory is under German protection.

He is obviously impressed by the swastika on my card, for he immediately becomes more polite. Now it is my turn to be threatening: I haughtily declare that there will be extremely unpleasant consequences for his military career if he should attempt to harm even a single person from our group. At that, he becomes even more uncertain, and he requests time to think things over. Unfortunately, the man is quite intelligent. After several minutes, he declares himself ready to pull back his soldiers, but solely on the condition that the German commander – if only by telephone – confirms that the workshop is truly under German protection. Now the decisive moment is approaching: time is running out. Once again, my only chance is to try and gain a few more precious minutes.

A woman whispers to me that most of the women and children have fled through the secret opening to the forest – only a handful remain who were unable to decide to flee. I angrily reply that everyone must *leave the house immediately. Then the German corporal, the Hungarian officer and I move inside to the office, where our telephone is located. The corporal makes contact with his superior and, as I had suspected, the German commander has not had the slightest inkling of the friendly relationship between his soldiers and their next-door neighbors, and he reprimands, then sternly instructs his corporal to "not interfere in this affair."*

With that, my delaying tactics come to an end and the SS soldiers retreat. Together with the Hungarian Nazis, I leave the office and he is horrified to see that no more workers are present: the house is empty!

I look out into the garden, and now it is my turn to be horrified: a group of 13 women, guarded by Hungarian soldiers, stands lined at attention and ready to march. It is those who are too old to flee, or too weak, and those who have made the decision not to flee: Hanna and Lili.

I know how much both of them love life and how foreign the idea of voluntary martyrdom is. They are not submitting to deportation without reason. On the one hand, they fear that I will be shot on the spot if the Nazis find no one to deport and it is obvious that I have been deceiving them. I suspect an additional reason: Hanna has often said to me that, of the four of us, it is

*I who must stay alive to save the message of the angels
and give it on.
The 13 women are immediately deported to Ravens-
brück.*

*Only one of the 13 women survived. She later told me
that Lili was such a radiant, loving force in the death
camp that her fellow prisoners would volunteer to
work with the hard-labor detachtments, or* Komman-
dos, *as they were called, where Lili could always be
found, so as to be in her consoling, strength-giving
presence.
I am unable to remember much of what she told me
about Hanna, because I was too upset to concentrate.
But there is one incident that I have not forgotten. As
the SS guards shaved the heads of the prisoners, one
of them called out to Hanna: "Hey, what are you doing
here, with your blue eyes, your straight nose and your
long, blond hair? Are you an Aryan?" Hanna replied: "I
am a Jew."
It was certainly not a desire to be a victim that caused
Hanna to answer in this way. She had conveyed the
word of truth for 17 months and must have become
incapable of uttering even the smallest lie.
The woman added: "Had it not been for Lili and
Hanna, I would not have survived. When Hanna said
to us: 'We are not the ones who have been beaten. All
of this does not touch us ...' – of course I still felt the
effect of the blows on my body, but the human
degradation lost its power over me. I didn't feel it
anymore."
As the Allied forces approached, the women were
again herded away, naked and shorn, and packed
standing tightly together into cattle cars. Ravaged by*

epidemics and soiled with their own excrement, most of the women died of hunger. Lili died one hour after Hanna.
The SS commander had the survivors sign a statement attesting that the others had died 'a natural death.'
Joseph died at about the same time in a Hungarian camp.

All of the women and children who fled through the garden of the SS survived.

Talking with Angels in other languages:

Edition Aubier 13, Quai de Conti, F-75006 Paris – Tel: 43 27 77 51
Dialogues avec l'Ange, 1976
Les dialogues tels que je les ai vécus, 1984
Les dialogues ou l'enfant né sans parents, 1986
Les dialogues ou le saut dans l'inconnu, 1988-89

Edium, Edizioni Scuola Vita, 15, Via G. Vasari, I-20135 Milano
Tel: 25 45 56 41
Dialoghi con l'Angelo, 1979

Daimon Verlag, Am Klosterplatz, CH-8840 Einsiedeln, Switzerland
Tel: (0041 55) 53 22 66
Die Antwort der Engel, 1981
Die Engel erlebt, 1983
Weltenmorgen, 1987
Sprung ins Unbekannte, 1988-89

Lemniscaat, Vijverlaan 48, NL-3062 HL, Rotterdam
Gesprek met de Engelen, 1986
Terugkeer van de Engelen, 1987

Typofot, 15/a Vas utca, Budapest VIII
Az Angyal vàlaszol (in preparation)

In Madrid: *Dialogos con el Angel*, 1988-89 (in preparation)

DAIMON PUBLICATIONS - English Language Titles
Talking with Angels, 1988
Distribution:

All territories
Daimon Verlag
Am Klosterplatz
CH-8840 Einsiedeln,
Switzerland
Tel: (0041 55) 53 22 66

Great Britain
Element Books Ltd.
Longmead Shaftesbury
Dorset SP7 8PL, England
(0747) 51339

Central USA
Bookslinger
213 East Fourth St.
St. Paul, Minn. 55101
(612) 221 0429

West Coast
The Great Tradition
750 Adrian Way
Suite 111
San Rafael, Calif. 94903
(415) 492 9382